The Global President

The Global President

International Media and the US Government

Stephen J. Farnsworth,
S. Robert Lichter, and Roland Schatz

ROWMAN & LITTLEFIELD
Lanham • Boulder • New York • Toronto • Plymouth, UK

Published by Rowman & Littlefield
4501 Forbes Boulevard, Suite 200, Lanham, Maryland 20706
www.rowman.com

10 Thornbury Road, Plymouth PL6 7PP, United Kingdom

British Library Cataloguing in Publication Information Available

Library of Congress Cataloging-in-Publication Data

Farnsworth, Stephen J., 1961–
  The global president : international media and the US government / Stephen J. Farnsworth, S. Robert Lichter, and Roland Schatz.
    pages cm
  Includes bibliographical references and index.
  ISBN 978-0-7425-6042-0 (cloth : alk. paper) — ISBN 978-0-7425-6043-7 (pbk. : alk. paper) — ISBN 978-1-4422-2572-5 (electronic) 1. Communication in politics—United States. 2. Communication, International. 3. Presidents—United States—Public opinion. 4. Presidents—Press coverage—United States. 5. Mass media—Political aspects—United States—Public opinion. 6. United States—Politics and government—21st century. 7. United States—Foreign public opinion. I. Lichter, S. Robert. II. Schatz, Roland. III. Title.
  JA85.2.U6F37 2013
  327.73001'4—dc23   2013017309

∞™ The paper used in this publication meets the minimum requirements of American National Standard for Information Sciences—Permanence of Paper for Printed Library Materials, ANSI/NISO Z39.48-1992.

Printed in the United States of America

Contents

List of Tables

Acknowledgments

Above all, we would like to thank Christian Kolmer of Media Tenor International for his vital research assistance throughout this project. Without his expert ability to coordinate the data and his extraordinary patience in generating new data runs, this project would not have been possible.

We also benefitted greatly from the sage advice of professional colleagues along the way. Emile Lester and Ben Hermerding read the entire manuscript and offered their consistently valuable insights and close copyediting skills above and beyond the call of duty. Special thanks are also due to Diana Owen and Stuart Soroka, who provided very valuable insights on this manuscript as it took shape. Reviewers and commentators of conference papers that previewed some of this book's findings also have our appreciation, including Matthew Baum, Bryan Gervais, Christina Holtz-Bacha, David Paletz, Jesper Stromback, and Travis Ridout.

We also thank Jungmi Jun Wu and Judy Goss, former students who have now embarked on their own academic careers, for valuable research assistance during the course of this project. We thank Markus Rettich for research assistance during this book's early phases. In addition, our colleagues and students at the University of Mary Washington, McGill University, and George Mason University have helped shape our discussion of international mass media.

Our appreciation also extends to Jon Sisk, Benjamin Verdi, Patricia Stevenson, and the rest of the Rowman & Littlefield team, who endured with grace the many delays inherent in a project that repeatedly grew beyond its authors' original plan.

Family members have been supportive and patient at just the right times. Thanks to Tanya DeKona for her support of this project.

We give thanks as well to *Electronic Media and Politics* for permission to reprint some of our tables and arguments here.

Thanks are likewise due to the University of Mary Washington, UMW's Center for Leadership and Media Studies, George Mason University, GMU's Center for Media and Public Affairs, the Council for Excellence in Government, the Canada-US Fulbright Program, and the McGill Institute for the Study of Canada for the support—financial and otherwise—necessary to develop and then to proceed with this project. We also thank the Pew Research Center for access to the US and international public opinion surveys used here.

Finally, we thank the many, many coders who have been involved in this multiyear project at Media Tenor.

All errors and omissions, of course, are our responsibility.

CHAPTER 1

Global Communication and the US Government

When the US government speaks, the world listens, regardless of whether people like what they hear. News reporters and citizens around the world pay considerable attention to the statements of US presidents and the actions of the US government. Whether journalists are located in nations that are close allies, wary potential adversaries, or somewhere in between, reporters from around the world draw considerable public attention to the latest developments from Washington.

Over the past dozen years, the global media attention fixed on the nation's capital has found plenty to report upon: the terrorist attacks of 2001 and America's homeland security response, the US-led military operations in Afghanistan and Iraq and the aftermath of both, the Middle East prisoner-abuse scandal, concerns regarding allegedly lagging US responses to global warming, a nomination contest between the first viable female and African American presidential candidates, an international financial collapse, the election and reelection of the first African American president (and one who promised a major expansion of international collaboration), and the passage of a major US health reform bill, to name a few of the bigger events in Washington (so far) during the presidencies of George W. Bush and Barack Obama.

These two presidents have sought to shape international news content relating to the United States in a less critical if not more favorable direction. As hostility to US policies grew in many places during the George W. Bush years, government officials engaged in a number of programs designed to improve international attitudes regarding America. A particular area of concern for US policymakers was the negative coverage of the Bush administration in the Middle East, and the administration tried repeatedly to encourage more positive coverage from the region's media outlets. But how successful was the Bush team in changing the international conversation and improving America's image?

1

Barack Obama, of course, hoped that international perceptions of the United States would improve once the Bush presidency ended and as the new administration's more globally oriented, collaborative approach to foreign policy took root. Even in the summer before his election in 2008, candidate Obama sought to win the hearts and minds of Europeans during highly publicized visits to Germany, France, and the United Kingdom. Candidate Obama also sought to establish his international bona fides with less prominent trips to Afghanistan, Iraq, and Israel (Gall and Zeleny 2008). Once in office, the Obama team continued its international charm offensive, with trips to Turkey and Egypt early on, and with regular appearances by Obama and administration officials on Arabic-language and other international media. How successful, though, was the Obama team in changing international news reports in ways more favorable to the United States?

This study of international news content can help answer questions of how America's two most recent presidents have been able to shape the international conversation (or not) in ways that advance American interests. Our consideration of the modern international media environment brings us back to where US presidency studies once began, with the old admonition from Richard Neustadt (1990) that the key challenge chief executives face concerns their ability to persuade. While the presidential range of concern Neustadt first wrote about more than fifty years ago focused almost entirely on presidential efforts to convince Congress and other Washington elites to support administration initiatives, today's persuader-in-chief speaks to a global audience. In recent years in particular, that global audience has grown skeptical of White House motives as a result of media reports that often condemn US leaders and policies.

This study of international news coverage of the United States covers a period of unusual ferment in international relations. While some foreign policy experts have noted that America's global standing has become somewhat weaker in recent years—a potential longer-term trend that may transcend the ability of any one president's attempts to revive international public opinion regarding the United States—the country remains highly influential in the global political environment. Even so, the nation's international influence seems more likely to be reduced than increased in the coming years regardless of what any president says or does (Sanger 2010a, 2010b, 2012; Zakaria 2008). Rising powers, above all, seem unlikely to defer to the traditional global domination of the United States and the advanced Western democracies that serve as America's closest allies (Kupchan 2012; Schatz 2009). The global outlook for US interests may not be entirely bleak, however. In the increasingly fluid international environment, persuasion may become at least as effective as military force in the years ahead, particularly given the hugely expensive and at best modestly successful military occupations of Iraq and Afghanistan.

Our findings reveal important trends in the nature of international news coverage of the United States. To summarize, we find that news about America has become a smaller share of the news media diet in many countries in recent years. This suggests declining influence for the United States in the media-led international discourse, even beyond the Bush years. Barack Obama may be well received internationally and his coverage may be more positive than that of George W. Bush on many international newscasts, but the first term of Obama's presidency has done little to reverse the reduced amount of attention the United States has received from these international news outlets in recent years. Indeed, when one looks at the most recent years of this study, one might argue that international news outlets could do more to help the world understand the complexities of the United States and how its policies relate to their own nations. These are some of the issues that we discuss at greater length in the chapters that follow.

Examining International Television News

This study provides an expansive international examination of news coverage of US political communication, using what we believe is the largest database of international television news content ever created. (Indeed, the US government itself has relied on Media Tenor reports for some of its own analysis of international news content. Our interpretations and analysis, however, are our own.) This study pays particular attention to international television reports on the United States during the presidencies of George W. Bush and Barack Obama. These two administrations were widely celebrated (or condemned, depending on the political orientation of the evaluator) for highly aggressive public communication operations in both the domestic and the international environments.

Despite extensive marketing efforts, the United States nevertheless suffered from severe international criticism problems during parts of their presidencies— times when the US government endured negative media treatment in many countries as Bush's war plans for Iraq failed to generate substantial international support (and the US-led occupation of that Persian Gulf nation descended in a guerrilla-fueled quagmire) and during Obama's expansion of US military involvement in Afghanistan, the new administration's growing use of aerial drone attacks, and its decision to keep open the Guantanamo prison. While such actions by Obama may represent reasonable White House assessments of US security needs, these early steps by Obama nevertheless generated hostility from people in the United States and abroad who had expected a greater departure from the hawkish Bush years (Sanger 2010a, 2010b, 2012). But even though international public opinion toward the United States during the Obama years cooled somewhat, as we discuss in greater detail below, global views toward the United States remained well above the levels recorded during the Bush years.

As a candidate and during his early months as president, Barack Obama tried to demonstrate that the nation was leaving the Bush years behind. Above all, the new president sought to reduce international tensions generally as well as international skepticism of the United States. From the hundreds of thousands of adoring Europeans who greeted the presidential candidate in Germany in 2008 to the new president's 2009 speeches in Istanbul and Cairo (notable for their attempts to connect with Muslim publics), Obama sought to separate himself from the highly negative views of his predecessor in both Europe and the Middle East (Alter 2010; Shear and Sullivan 2009; Zeleny and Cowell 2009; Zeleny and Kulish 2008).

Of course, even an enthusiastic international welcome for an Obama presidency, which may have been more an expression of relief over the end of the Bush years than anything else, did not mean the end of criticism of America abroad (Hatlapa and Markovits 2010). The differences may be a matter of international power disparities, differing national psychologies, or both. America simply may be too large, too rich, and too globally influential ever to be all that loved abroad (cf. Niebuhr 2008). If so, those systemic realities greatly constrain any US president, even one who is highly popular and is trying hard to build relationships in the international arena.

To be sure, the president's media management efforts are primarily concerned with shaping public opinion in the United States. But international media outlets cover these same events and report on the same ongoing developments for their own populations. What is reported can be quite different when one is producing news for US audiences or for consumption by news consumers beyond America's borders. Just how different these streams of reporting are is a major theme of this book.

Data derived from the analysis of hundreds of thousands of news stories from North America, Europe, the Middle East, Africa, and Asia are used in this international news project. The arguments presented here are based on content analysis conducted by Media Tenor, an international media research organization with offices around the world. Media Tenor uses native-language speakers to code news reports on the US government on a sentence-by-sentence basis, providing the most thorough dataset on international television news coverage of the United States of which we know.

To identify differences in global coverage of the United States, we often compare these international news reports to analyses of US news coverage of the US government—particularly the reports aired on the evening newscasts of ABC, CBS, NBC, and Fox News. That is not to say that US coverage of the United States is better than reports produced elsewhere—as we will see, domestic news reporting has severe flaws of its own. Rather, we believe that a more comprehensive understanding of how international media treat the United States and its most recent presidents requires frequent domestic and international comparisons of news content.

The list of television news outlets examined here is extensive, using the leading media outlets from a variety of key countries around the world. Altogether, this study looks at the content of news relating to the United States over an eight-and-a-half-year period from thirty-nine different international television broadcasters, coupled with four US television news outlets. That period includes much of the George W. Bush presidency as well as the first eighteen months of Obama's time in the White House.

The list of media outlets considered here is extensive, though not all outlets are used in all parts of the project. Starting with Europe, we focus primarily on the evening television newscasts found in Germany (ARD Tagesthemen, ZDF heute journal, RTL Aktuell, ARD Tagesschau, ZDF Heute, SAT.1 News, and ProSieben Newstime) and the United Kingdom (BBC1 10 O'clock News, ITV News at Ten, BBC2 Newsnight, ITN Early Evening News, BBC1 6 O'clock News, and BBC World). We also use four television news programs in traditionally neutral Switzerland (SF DRS Tagesschau, SF Rundschau, SF Eco, and SF Börse). We also use one channel each for France (TF1), Italy (RAI Uno), and Spain (TVE1), other important nations in Europe and important shapers of international public opinion in their own right.

In order to examine closely the news content of leading Arabic-language media, our native-speaker coders analyzed the content of a variety of broadcasters based in the Middle East: Al-Arabiyah, based in Saudi Arabia; Al-Jazeera, based in Qatar; Nile News, based in Egypt; the Lebanese Broadcasting Corporation (LBC) and Al-Manar, also based in Lebanon; and Dubai TV, based in the United Arab Emirates.

We also examine the content of Turkish television news reports (TRT) and those of China (CCTV) for parts of our analysis.

In order to make sure that we have a distinct perspective away from the world's most powerful nations and away from the volatile world of the Middle East, we also use an extensive content analysis of a variety of television news programs in South Africa—and in a variety of languages in that very linguistically diverse nation (SABC 2 Afrikaans News, SABC 3 English News, E-TV News, SABC Zulu/Xhosa News, SABC Sotho News, SABC 3 News @ One, SABC 3 News @ Ten, SABC 3 Africa News Update, SABC SiSwati/Ndebele News, SABC Venda/Tsonga News, and Summit TV).

In order to provide further perspective on the international news coverage of the United States, we examine the content of the US evening newscasts of ABC, CBS, NBC, and the Fox News Channel (hereafter referred to as Fox News), which were analyzed via the same methodology. There are sometimes striking differences between the way a news story from the United States is covered in domestic and international media, and there are often striking similarities as well.

All told, this book relies on content analysis of more than 770,000 television news stories between January 1, 2002, and June 30, 2010. In a world of more than 190 nations, we do not pretend to offer a global news summary in this study—our sample is clearly biased in the direction of the relatively small number of nations whose media we examined. We have no analysis here of news produced in Russia or in the nations of Latin America, for example. But our results do offer a variety of news media perspectives over several years from some of the world's influential nations and its most volatile regions. As demonstrated in the discussion of other research below, the amount of news analyzed here and the range of media outlets considered in this project compare very favorably with many other studies of international media impact.

For some parts of this book, we use story-level coding. At other times, we drilled down more deeply for a sentence-by-sentence analysis of news content. For this more focused perspective, we examined more than 206,000 individual statements on international and US newscasts relating to the United States and to the Bush and Obama presidencies between January 1, 2005, and June 30, 2010. In addition, we analyzed more than eighteen thousand individual statements relating to the leading 2008 candidates for president during the primary and general election phases of the 2008 presidential election.

With these more closely analyzed statement-level data, we can offer an exceptionally comprehensive examination of how the United States, its government, and its political leadership were presented in a variety of nations during one of the nation's most politically challenging periods. We discuss how America's news content about its government and about US involvement in the world contrasts with what many other nations saw regarding the United States and its two most recent presidents.

Comparative research offers two basic comparison approaches: the most similar systems design and the most different systems design (Wirth and Kolb 2004). Our research focuses on the latter approach in most of these comparisons, as the United States has very distinct presidential and media systems when compared to the other nations in this study. Even among the other advanced Western democracies in the study, the separation of powers system in the United States is quite different from a parliamentary system like that commonly found in Europe (Stromback and Dimitrova 2006).

America's heavy reliance on private companies to provide the news (a natural outgrowth of a long-standing suspicion of concentrated central governments and its cultural fondness for the free market) is quite distinct from the design of many international media environments, which generally include powerful public broadcasters supported by and sometimes influenced by government pressure. Even in the mixed-media systems where private and public broadcasters compete for market share, the public media voice generally is a far larger part of the media discourse than in the United States, where state-supported broadcasters such as PBS or NPR have very small audiences when compared to for-profit US media (Project for Excellence in Journalism 2012). Comparisons within a national or regional media group may involve more similar outlets than comparisons that pit a US broadcaster against an international one.

STUDYING TELEVISION NEWS
SCIENTIFICALLY WITH CONTENT ANALYSIS

The study of television news coverage is a very controversial area, as people tend to have strong opinions about the media's performance. These emotional reactions can make it difficult to evaluate the news media objectively. For example, readers and viewers often remember particular stories that resonate with them personally, including those that make them angry or irritated or provide information that they consider consistent with their existing opinions (Paletz 2002). These isolated impressions (and sometimes mis-impressions) on the part of individual viewers may produce unrepresentative opinions about a particular news outlet or the news media as a whole (Graber 1988). For these reasons, it is very important to study the media as scientifically as possible.

This is why we rely on content analysis, in which a news story or each segment of a news story is carefully coded into categories that describe whether the story or segment was positive, negative, or neutral toward each nation or president. Each story is also coded into categories that describe which topics were addressed (e.g., policy issues, personality traits, leadership skills, campaign strategy, etc.). We then break down policy issues into individual topics, such as economic and environmental policies, as well as a variety of foreign policy topics, including America's standing in the world, US policies relating to Afghanistan and Iraq, as well as US involvement in the Middle East. Because presenting news about America involves more than governments, wars, and politicians, we also study media conversations about the United States in the world of sports, business, crime, and culture. In other words, each news story is analyzed along several different dimensions that allow for studies of media content relating to the United States from many different perspectives. (A far more detailed discussion of the content analysis methods used here can be found at mediatenor.com.)

Because this project examines a variety of international television outlets that provide news reports in different languages, no one person could watch and understand all the newscasts. So Media Tenor International has thoroughly trained a small army of content analysis researchers who study newscasts airing in their native language. (These researchers, to whom we owe an immense debt of gratitude, all use a standard numerical coding system so that we can compare these newscasts across languages and national boundaries.) By insisting that native speakers of the language used in the newscast do the analysis, we maximize the chances that our coding will be as valid as possible. Nuances of language can escape even well-trained foreign ears. Sarcasm, for example, is far more likely to be coded as the person speaking intends if the person doing the coding is a native speaker of the language being used. We double-checked the reliability of the coding by having a sample of stories in each language coded by more than one coder to make sure the results matched.

These data, as reliable as we can make them, allow for a quantitative study of how international television news coverage has changed from year to year over the past decade, as well as how it differs across national boundaries (and even within linguistic groups). We see whether the huge public opinion boost regarding the United States that the election of President Obama triggered in many nations created an international media honeymoon for the new president, and if so, how long it lasted. In addition, we will discuss how what international audiences see in their news reports on the United States differ from what Americans see in US network news reports on the same events, political figures, and policy issues.

Examining mass communication and the public relations strategies of recent presidencies is an essential part of understanding how the modern American presidency operates. As each new president stands behind one made-for-television backdrop after another, we see support for the adage that "image is everything" (cf. Waterman et al. 1999). White House staffers have sought to manipulate media coverage for decades, recognizing that a presidency that looks good on television and in the newspapers is likely to be a successful presidency, and one that may be rewarded with a second term by the nation's voters. Internationally, positive media portrayals of the United States and its presidents may help secure greater acquiescence, if not support, from international leaders and publics considering US international policies.

To that end, White House news events are presented in ways designed to maximize media coverage of good news and minimize coverage of bad news for all reporters, regardless of nationality. Political figures engage in this process of marketing by trying to substitute their perspectives for the "framing" often done by the reporters and producers—and by White House critics on Capitol Hill or elites in the nation where the news is being aired (Hollihan 2001; Paletz 2002; Patterson 1994). Indeed, even busy lawmakers domestically and internationally rely on mass media reports from the White House to learn of the president's priorities (as well as examining the news coverage to get some sense of whether lawmakers can safely oppose or at least ignore a presidential priority). Allies and potential adversaries scour international news reports from Washington closely, trying not only to understand America but also to figure out how to react to it.

While the massive White House public relations operation is used mostly for domestic political purposes, it also serves the needs of international reporters writing about Washington (cf. Aday et al. 2005; Bennett et al. 2007; Cohen 2008; Entman 2004; Farnsworth, Soroka, and Young 2010; Han 2001; Mueller 2006). After all, international news reporters are comparatively limited in their access to authoritative sources in Washington and therefore may be more reliant on the extensive White House media relations operation than US television news (cf. Hamilton and Jenner 2003; Hannerz 2004; Hess 2005). This pattern of differential access to Washington sources may lead to more positive coverage of a president in international media, particularly once the intense early days of US military involvement—a time when critical domestic and international voices tend to keep their own counsel—have passed (cf. Auletta 2004; Bennett et al. 2007; Entman 2004).

This chapter next considers international news coverage dynamics relating to the United States. In order to understand presidential communication efforts, the chapter then turns to a discussion of those efforts aimed at the White House's key audience: the domestic citizen. But these internally oriented communication efforts can also have great impacts beyond national borders, as these same public appearances, news conferences, and other governmental activities that aim to secure positive US media coverage can help create favorable international news reports as well. We conclude with an overview of the remaining chapters in the book.

The Dynamics of International News Coverage

Given the language challenges inherent in studies involving a range of countries, many international comparisons of news coverage have concentrated on relatively small numbers of nations, often grouped by language or region. General classifications of media systems that transcend these common groupings are difficult to develop, even though they can be of great value in international media comparisons.

Jesper Stromback (2007, 2008 with Kaid) developed one leading classification scheme for different media systems. His four-stage level of media influence argues that the first phase is reached when the mass media become the key links between the governors and the governed. This is a key aspect of political development that nearly all modern nations have reached, regardless of the political system in operation. The second stage arrives when the mass media are largely independent from governments and other political actors. In the third stage, the media have become so influential that political actors adapt their behavior to media-oriented visions of newsworthiness in order to maximize their influence in the ongoing political debate. The fourth stage takes this trend a step further, as political actors internalize these values and allow media-oriented visions of newsworthiness to become the dominant ways government officials and citizens evaluate policies and politicians. Adherents of this perspective stress that the progression from one status to another is not necessarily linear or unidirectional. Advanced democratic nations, for example, may temporarily work under the fourth stage during campaigning but perhaps govern under the third stage (Stromback 2007, 2008 with Kaid).

Another widely recognized classification system for analyzing media systems in advanced Western democracies involves three categories: a Liberal model, a Democratic Corporatist model, and a Polarized Pluralism model (Hallin and Mancini 2004a). The first category is marked by a relative dominance of market mechanisms and commercial media, as found in the United States and to a lesser degree in the United Kingdom and Canada. While the Democratic Corporatist model also contains commercial media, those media tend to be tied to organized social and political groups, as found in Sweden, the Netherlands, and Germany. The Polarized Pluralist model is marked by a strong centralized state and a relatively weak development of commercial media. This model is found in Italy and other nations of southern Europe, and to a lesser extent in France. Although this model was designed to compare North American and European media, scholars have sought to use this perspective far more widely in subsequent studies of global media (cf. Hadland 2012; Hallin and Mancini 2012; Kraidy 2012; Voltmer 2012).

For our purposes, the Hallin and Mancini (2004a) perspective suggests that news coverage in Liberal nations such as the United States and the United Kingdom will be greatly influenced by commercial preferences—that is, by responses to audience tastes. News in Democratic Corporatist nations, such as Germany, may reflect elite political preferences. In Polarized Pluralist media systems, such as Italy and France, news coverage may be closely tied to policy preferences of government officials or quasi-governmental authorities controlling a given news outlet. (This third category also is the closest approximation of the groups to the Arab media examined here.)

In addition, this three-part model underscores the importance of considering different journalistic norms around the globe. Interpretative journalism is particularly common in the Polarized Pluralism cultures, where reporters traditionally take a more supportive position toward politicians. This approach is far less common in Liberal media cultures, where journalistic norms encourage reporters to take more critical or adversarial positions vis-à-vis authority figures (Stromback and Kaid 2008).

By and large, scholars engaging in comparative research have found key differences between market-based news, like that in the United States, which is oriented toward consumer preferences to maximize market share and profit, and news produced by more public-interest-oriented state media outlets, which tend to provide reports that are purportedly more useful for the democratic needs of a society (cf. Kolmer and Semetko 2010; Pfetsch 2004). But those distinctions may be eroding (Hallin and Mancini 2004b). Some researchers suggest the existence of transnational reporting styles vary less among broadcasters, particularly among those catering to US and European audiences, than one might expect given profound differences of perspective (cf. Donsbach and Patterson 2004; Esser 2008). But there are limits to the acceptance of those transnational media norms, particularly in times of international division. A study that focused on US and Arab media during the George W. Bush years, for example, found that Arab media were generally too quick to offer "the Arab view" on political events as opposed to a larger range of perspectives that could help create a more informed viewing audience (Seib 2004).

Foreign news reports and international impressions about the United States are based only partly on the reality of the US experience—the characteristics of the beholder audience are of great relevance to international reporters (Brooks 2006). For example, a study that compared African and US news coverage of the 1998 US embassy bombings in Kenya and Tanzania found that US news focused on American deaths, even though far more Africans were killed in both terrorist attacks. Non-US media outlets, in contrast, offered news content more balanced between in-country and international concerns (Schaefer 2003).

Language differences can have a powerful impact on international news content relating to the United States as well. English-language broadcasters, for example, may provide more extensive US news than broadcasters producing news content in other languages. When a president speaks in English—as they do almost exclusively—longer sound bites and greater attention would likely be paid by English-language media as compared to foreign-language media, whereas every English sentence would have to be subtitled or translated for the non-English-speaking audiences. With this foreign-language barrier for many international news audiences, a White House might have greater luck framing the discourse in international English-language media than in non-English media. In the latter case, news reporters would likely move quickly beyond English speakers to rely more on speakers in the language of that broadcast.

AN "INTERNATIONAL TWO-STEP FLOW"?

Studies that compared news in the United States and Canada have found some evidence of an "international two-step flow" in English-language coverage of

US-oriented news north of the border (Farnsworth, Soroka, and Young 2010). A "two-step flow" in political communication, following from work by Lazarsfeld et al. (1944), typically refers to a process whereby information is first received and interpreted by opinion leaders, who then pass that information—along with their own interpretations—to others. The majority of citizens thus receive information through this two-step flow, and opinion leaders can have particularly powerful effects on the course of public opinion. An "international two-step flow" can refer to a cross-border dynamic that may exist between any domestic and foreign media, at least where domestic coverage is concerned. In short, just as opinion leaders may get information first, so, too, do domestic media. And domestic media, like opinion leaders, may have an opportunity to filter and/or interpret this information before other media outlets pick it up.

This international two-step flow is likely not a matter of attentiveness, but rather of access and resources. Previous studies of foreign news correspondents found that they generally have a more difficult time than domestic correspondents getting access to authoritative local political actors, including leading politicians and the most influential interest group actors (Hess 2005). In contrast, international reporters have no trouble obtaining news footage of White House briefings, which may give the administration an even greater coverage advantage over its critics in international news reports from Washington.

Key US political actors have limited time for media correspondents, and in most cases they are interested in finding a domestic rather than an international audience when they agree to be interviewed. A US politician looking for support for a given bill is not going to benefit much from BBC coverage, after all. US journalists, therefore, will be more likely to get access to US politicians—particularly the harder-to-reach critics of administration policy—than will international journalists, who may be forced to rely more on the administration's news briefings available to all reporters (Fraser 2007; Goldbloom 2007). As a result of differential access to policymakers and critics away from public media spectacles like presidential appearances, international news may be more positive than domestic reporting, particularly in their first reports relating to new policy developments. But there is a limit to the presidential advantages of spin in global media, as international reporters closely watch domestic news content for clues about how to shape their own stories. In other words, the US media's interpretation of US events may set the tone for subsequent international reporting on US affairs.

In addition, the number of full-time, highly specialized international correspondents has been in decline in recent years, with many experienced international reporters being replaced—if at all—by less trained freelance writers and part-time journalists (Hamilton and Jenner 2003; Hess 2005). A declining number of specialists who can fully immerse themselves in the country where they are posted also makes it more difficult for a foreign bureau to compete with domestic news production in any country (Hamilton and Jenner 2003; Hannerz 2004; Hess 2005). This pattern suggests additional incentives for the more resource-limited international news outlets and their reporters to follow the path created by domestic news organizations.

Of course, theories based on studies of the United States and Canada may have little relevance for other cross-national studies that involve countries separated by greater distances. Overlaps in the news agendas of the United States and Canada, a frequently used international news comparison, often emphasize the geographic and cultural proximity of the two nations (Farnsworth, Soroka, and Young 2010; Mazur 2009; Soderlund et al. 1994; Soroka 2002a, 2002b; Soroka et al. 2012, 2013; Wittebols 1992, 1996). In addition, past research has found great similarities in reporter norms and media outlet approaches used on both sides of the border (Hallin and Mancini 2004a).

Despite these similarities, there are often important differences as well. The cross-national variation in media between Canada and the United States that does exist, particularly in foreign affairs coverage in the two nations, has been attributed partly to Canada's less "hawkish" public opinion on military policy (Adams 2003; Brooks 2006; Haglund 2006; Pew 2009b). Similarly, coverage of climate change and other environmental news in Canada tends to be more extensive than in the United States, perhaps as a result of greater elite and public acceptance of the reality of global warming among those north of the border (Soroka et al. 2012, 2013). Whether the "international two-step flow" found in US-Canadian media studies will be replicated in comparisons of US/UK, US/German, and US/Arabic-language news is another area of inquiry in this book.

FOREIGN POLICY COVERAGE DIFFERENCES

Even if there are some similarities in how a given topic is covered by domestic and international reporters, we still expect important differences in US and international news coverage, particularly in areas distant from domestic concerns. Given relatively limited interest in international news matters on the part of many Americans, brevity and simplicity often define US news reports about foreign affairs, particularly those distant from US military action (Brown 2003; Entman 2004; Farnsworth and Lichter 2006a; Iyengar 1991; Norris et al. 2003; Seib 2004).

When US news is compared to less market-oriented media systems, like those found in much of Europe, the international news outlets east of the Atlantic give greater prominence to global news, encouraging higher levels of news consumption and public awareness of ongoing events around the world (Curran et al. 2009). Geographic proximity and national interests are key measures for predicting how much coverage of a foreign country will appear in a given nation's television news programming (Kolmer and Semetko 2010).

Researchers have found that, for a variety of military conflicts, the US mass media tend to be notably pro-US government in the tone of the coverage, particularly during and leading up to the early stages of military activity (Boaz 2005; Dickson 1992; Dimitrova 2001; Entman 2004; Farnsworth and Lichter 2006a; Gutierrez-Villalobos et al. 1994; Hallin 1986). A comparative study of news coverage of the Abu Ghraib prison scandal found that US media were far less likely to use the term *torture* than were their counterparts working for news organizations in Britain, Canada, Italy, and Spain (Jones 2006). Instead, the US media relied on more innocuous terms such as *abuse* or *mistreatment* (Jones 2006).

Despite varying methodological approaches and bases for comparison, many studies of the news coverage of the Iraq War found consistent pro-US government results in US media. In addition to the examples cited above, researchers have found that US media outlets were too quick to accept the George W. Bush administration's views of matters in Iraq and were not questioning enough (Kull 2004). A comparative study of coverage of the 2003 Gulf War on CNN and Al-Jazeera found that both media outlets disseminated propaganda messages consistent with the norms of their home regions (Youssef 2009). A study that compared US news reports on the three networks and Fox with that of Al-Jazeera found the international broadcaster to be more critical of US policies than all three US television networks, all of whom were roughly even-handed; Fox stood out as extremely supportive of the US military operation (Aday et al. 2005).

Along these same lines, another study found a spectrum of opinion on the network evening news shows, with Fox the most supportive and ABC the most critical of the war (Media Monitor 2003). Yet another comparison confirmed the now well-supported point: that US news was disproportionately pro-allied. US news was more positive than television reports in the United Kingdom, Germany, the Czech Republic, and South Africa, and the US media were also more critical of the Iraqi side than those other media outlets (Kolmer and Semetko 2009).

THE CNN EFFECT?

For more than a decade, academics have debated an alleged "CNN effect" that links media content to political action. Under this theory, the growing pervasiveness of news forces politicians to become increasingly sensitive to the content of televised news reports being beamed around the world (cf. Robinson 2002). The international media presence in nearly all corners of the world allegedly makes it more difficult for individual actors—even presidents—to shape media coverage of international matters to their liking, particularly during armed conflicts (Brown 2003; Hall 2001).

> The new media environment is marked by a vast increase in the flow of information from and to war zones via news organizations, NGOs and individuals. . . . As information flows out of the battle space more quickly, it becomes more feasible for external groups to exert influence through their political response to events. These external groups may be the American public, governments sympathetic or opposed to the cause, allied publics and the Arab street. Reports are events in their own right. (Brown 2003:47)

The effects of this new media environment are not limited to military matters. Once images of humanitarian crises, whether of widespread starvation in Ethiopia, concentration camps in Serbia, or flooding in Bangladesh, are aired worldwide on television, government officials in Western democracies may come under pressure to respond to public outrage (Entman 2000). While Western nations sometimes intervene (as in Kosovo), they often take insufficient measures (as in the genocides in Rwanda in 1994 and in Sudan a decade later). Thus, political leaders do not always face a domestic public outcry associated with the "CNN effect" theory (Kristof 2004; Power 2002).

In addition, some research suggests that the pattern of influence is actually opposite from what was hypothesized by this perspective. Government officials may use the media to build up public pressure for intervention, rather than responding to the "bottom-up" pressure proposed by the CNN effects theory. In the case of the widespread violence in Somalia in 1992, for example, government officials in the administration of George H. W. Bush sought to draw media and public attention to the civil unrest before the television networks had turned their attention to the troubled country (Mermin 1997). The second President Bush, of course, used a wide range of arguments to get the US public and other nations to support an invasion of Iraq (Farnsworth 2009). Other research findings suggest that this "reverse direction" CNN effect is most pronounced when policymakers are divided over a course of action and the debate among elites spurs greater news coverage (Robinson 2002). Still other findings suggest that the CNN effects in either direction are most prominent where reporters are absent—that is, that lack of media coverage of a particular crisis area contributes to a lack of policymaking in that area (Hawkins 2002).

EMPHASIZING MIDDLE EAST NEWS

Scholars studying international media in recent years have increasingly turned their attention to Al-Jazeera, a Qatar-based satellite news broadcaster that became highly visible internationally following 9/11. The network was the only media outlet that had reporters inside Taliban Afghanistan at the time of the terrorist attacks, and its coverage of the subsequent war offered a street-level perspective that focused on the events of late 2001 during a US-led invasion and occupation that drove the Taliban from power (Jasperson and El-Kikhia 2003). Al-Jazeera's reporters provided much less coverage of the military aspects of the war—which were covered in great depth by many Western media outlets—and instead focused on the human costs. The sufferings of Afghan civilians, the collateral damage of Western bombing campaigns, and other humanistic portrayals of the costs of war were standard fare (Jasperson and El-Kikhia 2003). In addition, the network became the preferred place for Osama bin Laden to communicate with the world.

While Al-Jazeera viewed itself as a prime example of democratic debate in a region where such discussions are in short supply, the channel faced much criticism in the West for allegedly becoming "the bin Laden network" (Bessaiso 2005; Seib 2005). Quantitative analysis of the network's coverage found that evaluations of its objectivity seem to depend, at least in part, on cultural variables. News content that looks like objective coverage of the Iraq War in one culture may seem harsh or unfair in another (cf. Aday et al. 2005). Another study found that Al-Jazeera's coverage of the war did not differ greatly from that of German and UK television during the first two weeks of the Iraq War (Kolmer and Semetko 2009).

The importance of Al-Jazeera as an access point for international news conversations in the Arab world has long been apparent to US policymakers. In the months following the Afghanistan War of 2001, the US government focused much of its public diplomacy efforts on Al-Jazeera, offering experts for interview programs to help promote the US government's views regarding the Middle East (Zaharna 2005). President Obama has likewise made it a priority to try to build connections with political leaders, the mass media, and the public in Muslim nations (cf. Alter 2010; Shear and Sullivan 2009; Wilson 2010; Zeleny and Cowell 2009; Zeleny and Kulish 2008).

INTERNATIONAL VIEWS OF THE UNITED STATES AND ITS LEADERS

One consistent finding of previous research into television networks—be they state-owned enterprises or in the hands of private investors—is the importance of the domestic market in shaping news content. Both public and private broadcasters seek audiences, and the best way to increase media penetration is to give viewers what they want to know. A second journalistic mission, giving viewers what they need to know, is also an important calculation for reporters and editors, of course. But the health of the media enterprise—and one's own reporting job—depends at least as much on the first issue as on the second one.

With that in mind, we look at a spring 2012 survey conducted by the Pew Global Attitudes Project (Pew Global 2012). Table 1.1 illustrates public opinion in a variety of nations regarding the United States during 2008, the last full

Table 1.1.   International Views of the United States, 2008–2012

Question: "Please tell me if you have a very favorable, somewhat favorable, somewhat unfavorable, or very unfavorable opinion of the United States."

(The percentages below combine *very* and *somewhat favorable* responses.)

	2008	2009	2012	Change 2008 versus 2012
United States	84	88	80	–04
Italy	53*	–	74	21
Japan	50	59	72	22
France	42	75	69	27
Poland	68	67	69	01
Brazil	–	–	61	–
Britain	53	69	60	07
Spain	33	58	58	25
Mexico	47	69	56	09
Czech Republic	45*	–	54	09
Germany	31	64	52	21
Russia	46	44	52	06
Lebanon	51	55	48	–03
Tunisia	–	–	45	–
China	41	47	43	02
India	–	–	41	–
Greece	–	–	35	–
Egypt	22	27	19	–03
Jordan	19	25	12	–07
Turkey	12	14	15	03
Pakistan	19	16	12	–07

* Results from 2007 survey.
Dashes signify that the question was not asked by Pew in that country in that year.
Source: Pew Global (2012).

year of the George W. Bush presidency, and during the spring of 2009, shortly after Obama's inauguration. We then compare those results with those from the spring of 2012, when the visions of what Obama would do were replaced by assessments of what the new president had done.

The first, and most obvious, point is that Americans consistently have a more positive view of themselves than any other nation's peoples surveyed about the United States. That should come as no surprise, as Americans often express high levels of patriotism and pride over their nation's values and its place in the world (Brooks 2006; Farnsworth 2003). Nor should one be surprised by the dramatic increase in positive feelings about the United States in all areas of the world once Barack Obama replaced the internationally unpopular George W. Bush as president (Holsti 2008).

After the United States itself, the most positively disposed nations regarding the United States in the survey are our closest allies: Japan and fellow NATO members such as Italy, France, Poland, Britain, Spain, the Czech Republic, and Germany. Hemispheric allies such as Brazil and Mexico also have high levels of public regard for the United States. Muslim nations, including Pakistan, Turkey, Jordan, and Egypt, are particularly critical. Greece, in the middle of its deepest economic crisis in decades, is more or less mad at everyone right now, including the United States. People living in potential global economic rivals such as India and China are slightly more negatively than positively oriented toward the United States in 2012.

The four-year change in evaluations of the United States from 2008 to 2012 was quite positive for nearly all the nations surveyed. Not counting the United States, three of the four most positively disposed nations on this measure (Japan, Italy, and France) all increased their ratings of the United States by more than twenty percentage points. Poland was largely flat, as public opinion in that nation generally is marked by considerable enthusiasm for the United States regardless of who is minding the store.

Only four nations contained in the study were more negatively disposed in 2012 than they were in 2008: Lebanon, Egypt, Jordan, and Pakistan. By 2012, all four nations were either convulsed by political turmoil or had reason to fear that they or their volatile neighbors would be the next to face the crowds in the Arab Spring movement. Most notably, US-Pakistan relations have been on a strong downward trajectory in recent years. Many Pakistanis resent the US decision not to provide their government with advance warning of the US raid to kill Osama bin Laden deep in Pakistan. Many Pakistanis also object to extensive use of aerial drone strikes to kill Al-Qaeda figures in Pakistan and in other parts of the Middle East (Gall and Schmitt 2011; Walsh 2012).

In table 1.2, we see international responses when publics are asked whether the US president can be trusted "to do the right thing regarding world affairs."

Table 1.2. International Views of George W. Bush and Barack Obama, 2008–2012

Question: "For each, tell me how much confidence you have in each leader to do the right thing regarding world affairs: a lot of confidence, some confidence, not too much confidence, or no confidence at all [George W. Bush/Barack Obama]."

(The percentages below combine the first two categories.)

	Bush 2008	Obama 2009	Obama 2012	Change 2008 versus 2012
United States	37	74	61	24
Germany	14	93	87	73
France	13	91	86	73
Britain	16	86	80	64
Czech Republic	36*	–	77	41
Japan	25	85	74	49
Italy	43*	–	73	30
Brazil	17	–	68	51
Spain	08	72	61	53
Poland	41	62	50	09
Mexico	16	55	42	26
India	55	–	41	–
Lebanon	33	46	39	06
China	30	62	38	08
Russia	22	37	36	14
Egypt	11	42	31	20
Greece	–	–	30	–
Tunisia	–	–	28	–
Turkey	02	33	24	22
Jordan	07	31	22	15
Pakistan	07	13	07	0

*Results from 2007 survey.
Dashes signify that the question was not asked by Pew in that country in that year.
Source: Pew Global (2012).

Once again, we have Pew numbers from 2008, the final year of the Bush presidency, from 2009, Obama's first year in office, and from 2012, the spring of the year Obama sought reelection. Once again, one sees America's closest allies at the top of the list: Germany, France, and Britain take the top three spots, with at least four out of every five respondents believing in 2012 that Obama would do the right thing internationally. These three nations all recorded massive gains in public support for that US president, as the difference between responses in 2008 and 2012 were more than sixty percentage points. (The one-year gains between 2008 and 2009 were even higher—rising seventy points or more in all three nations.)

Two-thirds of the populations of four other nations surveyed—the Czech Republic, Japan, Italy, and Brazil—also felt positively about Obama's international performance. The gains were not as dramatic for these nations as for the three dominant nations of Europe, but these four all registered four-year gains of thirty percentage points or more between 2008 and 2012. Spain also registered a huge increase, with a fifty-three-point gain in approval of the US president over those for years. (For all of those countries, the increases would have been even larger if the comparison had been between 2009 and 2008, Obama's first year as president and Bush's last year in office.)

For Americans, the election of the new president also triggered a greater sense that the new president would do the right thing in world affairs. In 2008, only 37 percent thought Bush would do the right thing in world affairs, as compared to the 74 percent approval Obama enjoyed on that question a year later and the 61 percent support level Obama enjoyed from Americans looking at his foreign policy approach in 2012. These approval numbers are considerably higher than Obama's overall public approval ratings, which were in the upper forties during much of 2012, a presidential election year (Balz and Cohen 2012). Poland, the one nation with only modest gains here, may have remained less than thrilled with Obama's decision to cancel the construction of antimissile defense installations in the nation early in his presidency (Baker 2009).

Once again, the most critical publics are found in the nations of the Middle East. The problematic US-Pakistani relationship once again is in evidence in these data, with only 7 percent of Pakistanis saying that they would expect Obama to do the right thing in world affairs. That is exactly the same level of disapproval Pakistanis gave Bush four years earlier, marking it as the only nation in the survey as critical of Obama as of Bush. (Obama did have a bit of a honeymoon with Pakistanis in 2009, when a grand total of 13 percent of the nation's residents—about one out of every eight—thought he might do the right thing in world affairs. But even this tepid acceptance cooled quickly.) Other highly critical nations include many from the Middle East region—Jordan, Turkey, Tunisia, and Egypt—as well as Greece, arguably the Eurozone's most troubled economy.

Taken together, these two surveys show that the peoples of many nations were much more positively disposed toward the United States once Barack Obama became president. He enjoyed extraordinary levels of popularity when he was first elected, and in many of the nations surveyed by Pew, his very highly favorable assessments remain largely intact into his fourth year in office. Approval levels relating to the US government generally track those presidential patterns, albeit at a somewhat lower level. Nearly everywhere Pew surveyed, the world remains happier with Obama as president, not Bush. The greatest doubts about Obama are found in the Muslim-majority nations of the Middle East, which also had the greatest doubts concerning Bush.

Presidential Media Strategies: Examining Bush and Obama

Modern mass media have given the American public the opportunity to gain a sense of who the president is as a person and what the president intends to do by way of public policy. Despite the far greater amount of information now available in these two areas of interest, both sets of impressions can be flawed. Presidents—and presidential candidates before that—aggressively seek to manage all aspects of how they are presented to the public. Successful campaigns and effective modern presidencies use massive public relations operations to ensure the president is presented as likable and working diligently to supply the public with popular policy outcomes. These media management efforts frequently involve selective revelations and nondisclosures.

This portion of the chapter examines the interrelationship of public opinion and presidential marketing strategies in the American context. We will focus most extensively on the efforts of Barack Obama and George W. Bush to build and retain their personal popularity as well as promote their policy agendas to domestic audiences. Throughout this portion of the chapter, we will draw upon US public opinion surveys and pay particular attention to two key policy challenges: the war in Iraq for Bush and subpar economic performance during Obama's first two years. But this discussion is about character definition as well as selling policy outcomes. Because few citizens pay close attention to the legislative particulars, much presidential marketing shapes the public views of the president, who could be thought of as the "spinner in chief" of the modern media environment (Farnsworth 2009). While the main audience for these efforts is domestic, international reporters are covering the same events and may be at least as susceptible to executive branch framing as US reporters. Indeed, these days an American president may be the closest thing the world has to a global "spinner in chief."

PRESIDENTIAL SPINNING IN AN ERA OF "SOUND BITE" POLITICS

In today's short-attention-span politics, politicians do not have much time to explain themselves. Forty years ago, for example, the average length of time a presidential candidate was given on the US evening news to explain himself was over forty seconds (Adatto 1990). In 2004, the length of time of unmediated candidate commentary—called a sound bite—has shrunk to ten seconds (Farnsworth and Lichter 2011a). Needless to say, a short news clip does not give a politician much time to explain how he or she will fix Social Security or Medicare or deal with economic troubles. There really isn't time to express a complicated thought, and even the simplest thoughts may take more time than the average network news sound bite. Pepsi, after all, spends thirty seconds to convey an extremely simple, basic suggestion: "you want to buy this soda."

Politicians trying to reach voters through the news have to play the cards they are dealt, and US television's extremely brief sound bites shortchange serious discussion of issues. Because politicians want to be heard on the evening news, they have to tailor what they say to the extremely brief format. Government officials who refuse to speak simply—that is, who refuse to abide by the one- or two-sentence conventions of television sound bites—are giving up free airtime they desperately need to promote their policies and themselves. Elected officials generally have mastered this technique; otherwise they probably would have lost to a more media-savvy rival. Elected officials who have not mastered the sound bite will not be able to compete effectively in the struggle between partisans to set the public agenda and to frame ongoing events. Shorter sound bites also encourage international reporters to use the clip in their own newscasts, particularly if translation out of English is required for their own audiences.

George W. Bush was generally good at sound-bite politics. In his 2002 State of the Union speech, he relied on the term *axis of evil* as shorthand for the three countries Bush said were aligned against the United States (Frum 2003). Indeed, perhaps the best media moment of his presidency was when he stood atop a wrecked fire truck at Ground Zero in the days after 9/11 and vowed revenge: "The people who knocked these buildings down will hear all of US soon!" (Frum 2003:140).

Obama generally has not been very good at engaging in sound-bite politics in the White House. Although his 2008 campaign masterfully focused on the poetry of "change" and "hope," the administration's rhetoric of governing has been quite prosaic throughout most of his first term. For example, Obama's decision to leave many of the details of the health care bill to Congress may have been smart politics, particularly considering that Clinton tried and failed to pass a health care bill in 1994 that his administration had designed. While Obama's lower-wattage media strategy did not enhance his leadership credentials, it likely improved his win-loss record on major legislation.

This understated style made it difficult for Obama to trumpet the health care bill's positive aspects, which did not help the Democratic Party's candidates in 2010. In addition, the uncertain pace of economic recovery has not given the administration much to talk about along those lines either. "It could have been worse" is not a message that generates much media attention, not to mention much voter enthusiasm. (Unfortunately for his own political prospects, Republican rival Mitt Romney's emphasis on economic matters during the 2012 campaign was undermined by the Obama team's efforts to portray the former Massachusetts governor as an out-of-touch plutocrat.) Of course, a president's communication challenges are even greater in the international arena, where there is less focus on the US government and its activities than in domestic media. Language barriers may also be a hurdle for presidents trying to secure greater international understanding of the US government and its policies.

DOMINATING THE DOMESTIC DISCOURSE WITH PERSONALITY NEWS

In the modern media environment, chief executives have become dominant voices in national political conversations. Members of Congress may be able to spend a lot of time in their districts during work periods, and they may be quoted frequently in the local news media, but in Washington the legislative branch struggles to compete before the cameras. Indeed, modern presidents have a huge advantage: they can get on national television news just about any time they want to (Cook 1989, 2005; Farnsworth and Lichter 2006a). Likewise, running for president has become a years-long affair, once again crowding out media attention that could spend more time on the legislative branch. Campaign news, of course, is often an intensely personal affair, as candidates sell themselves in the media first on the basis of who they are and then, if they become viable, on the basis of their issue positions.

All this public visibility comes with problems for modern presidents, though, as increasing public expectations of the chief executive often trigger eventual citizen disappointment with a president who can only do so much in a cumbersome political system of separate institutions and overlapping powers (Jones 1994, 1995; Lowi 1985). For Obama, whose election in November 2008 was heralded as a transformative event like few presidencies of the past half century, the expectations were extraordinarily high, and the dashed public hopes started to emerge rapidly (Campbell 2009; Ceaser et al. 2009; Conley 2009; Harris and Martin 2009; Pew 2008). The 2010 midterm elections, when the Republicans gained more than sixty seats in the US House as well as six Senate seats, revealed the extent to which America's most engaged citizens turned against Obama and his Democratic allies on Capitol Hill (cf. Murray and Bacon 2010). Obama's reelection in November 2012, coupled with voter retention of a Republican majority in the US House of Representatives, demonstrated that enthusiasm for Obama may not be what it once was, but that the president enjoyed more favorable public views than in 2010.

In the highly partisan modern media environment, White House public relations teams frequently attempt to use the media to enlist public support in order to give the president leverage in convincing Congress to back the White House. This strategy involves two steps: presidents sell themselves and their policies to the public; then the citizens who receive these media messages in turn encourage lawmakers to support the president's policy agenda (Kernell 2007). Although results of this "going public" strategy are mixed at best, presidents devote enormous energy to selling themselves and their policy preferences to the public (Edwards 2003, 2004, 2006).

Perhaps each president is optimistic that he possesses marketing skills that previous chief executives lacked. Regardless, one can only make so much progress trying to sell the public on policy specifics, which are only marginally interesting to many citizens and therefore of little concern to reporters trying to satisfy public demand for news. So presidents try to manage the news and shape policy by controlling how they themselves are portrayed before the public. Presidents might prefer to focus on policy issues, as they are in office only for a short time, but reporters rarely find such matters all that compelling (Farnsworth and Lichter 2006a, 2011a). Policy issues may be even tougher to sell to international reporters, unless the topic in question is highly salient to that foreign reporter's own national audience.

To be sure, defining character is a difficult business. US politicians, particularly presidential candidates, need to be likable to win an election (Barber 1992; Brooks 2006). Americans have a fondness for presidents who are like them—that is, who have (or at least appear to have) the common touch (Brooks 2006). In US presidential elections, character routinely trumps experience. People want to like their president, perhaps because television and Internet news makes the chief executive a regular fixture in the nation's living rooms. Reporters, particularly those working in television, find it easier and more interesting to write about character than issues.

Consequently, many candidates have lost to more personable opponents. Jimmy Carter, elected primarily on a smile and an honest demeanor in 1976, was beaten four years later by Ronald Reagan, a former movie actor and governor of California who was solid gold when the cameras were on (Barber 1992). Bill Clinton connected with the public in 1992 in a way that George H. W. Bush could only dream about (Ceaser and Busch 1993). In 2008 voters dismissed the lengthy resume of US Senator John McCain (R-Ariz.) in favor of an eloquent Democratic wunderkind who had been in the US Senate for less than four years on the night he was elected president (Ceaser et al. 2009).

BARACK OBAMA: "CHANGE WE CAN BELIEVE IN"

Barack Obama was a little-known state senator running for a US Senate seat in Illinois when he gave an electrifying speech at the 2004 Democratic National Convention. Four years later Obama was his party's nominee, and his convention speech had to be held at an outdoor arena to accommodate his enthusiastic mass following. Even before he was elected president, Obama was the political equivalent of a rock star. A July 2008 public rally in Berlin drew hundreds of thousands of adoring Europeans (Zeleny and Kulish 2008), and a Paris press conference featured French president Sarkozy gushing over the Democratic candidate to a degree that bordered on the unseemly for a successor of de Gaulle (Zeleny and Erlanger 2008). Obama filled stadiums and arenas across the country that fall, and his inauguration brought one of the largest crowds ever to the Washington Mall. Obama's media strategies also suggested he was a new kind of politician. From the start the Obama team appreciated the importance of new media, connecting with younger voters, and their parents, via Facebook and YouTube (Goldfarb 2007; Owen 2009).

Obama's campaign call for "change" resonated with a nation reeling from the continuing wars in Iraq and Afghanistan and rendered breathless by the sudden and catastrophic financial collapse of September 2008. The brilliance of the "change" mantra is that it allowed people to fill in the blank: whatever change an individual desired could be grafted on to the slogan (Ceaser et al. 2009).

OBAMA'S WEAKNESS: HE DOESN'T UNDERSTAND US

The new president may have been born in extremely modest circumstances—his immigrant father was largely absent and broke, his mother struggled to pay the bills, and his grandparents ended up playing a key role in raising the future president—but Barack Obama has regularly been pilloried as an elitist. His hard childhood and lean years of community organizing have been trumped, in the minds of many voters, by the degrees from Columbia and from Harvard Law School. From the start of his 2008 presidential campaign, Obama consistently faced suspicions, fueled by conservative media and conservative activists, that he was not really born in America as he claims, and that he is a Muslim, not a Christian (cf. Kurtz 2007a, 2007b). Generally left unsaid in polite company—but not without its consequences for identity politics—was the fact that Obama would be (and eventually became) the nation's first African American president.

During the nomination campaign of 2008, Obama briefly refused to wear a pin featuring a US flag. Although he said it was a matter of principle, Obama quickly learned it was also a matter of politics. In the end, his advisors convinced him that the controversy over not wearing the pin, routinely found on the lapels of so many other politicians, distracted the public from his policy messages. He relented, but the controversy left some with a sense that he might not be all that patriotic. For those who expect a president to wear his patriotism on his sleeve, here was a man who would not even wear it on his lapel. After a stunningly poor performance in a bowling alley (the future president bowled 37 in a game with a total possible score of 300), such critics had further evidence that he was not a "real" American (Van Natta 2008).

The most damaging evidence in this regard came from the secretly recorded comments candidate Obama made at a private California fund-raiser early in 2008. He remarked that some Americans were bitter and were "clinging to guns and religion" during these hard times (Owen 2009). These comments were widely portrayed by reporters and by the Hillary Clinton campaign as dismissive and elitist. Taken together, such incidents fed suspicions among some white, working-class voters that Obama does not have enough in common with the people he serves as president—and he may not respect ordinary Americans all that much either!

When policies disappoint, as the half-hearted economic recovery did for many voters in 2010, skepticism about a president's character makes it very hard for an administration to shape the public discourse to its liking. That is why character is so important for a president—a likable president can get the benefit of the doubt in tough times. Of course, if you do not define yourself, your critics will be glad to undertake that task for you (Keller 2011). Interestingly, Obama's relatively diffident, low-key approach as president may be more appealing to some international audiences—who had tired of the perceived arrogance of American presidents over the years—than to domestic audiences.

GEORGE W. BUSH: CONVEYING FRONTIER TOUGHNESS

Americans like frontier figures, one of the most heroic types celebrated in a century of Hollywood filmmaking (Scott 2000). Presidents who present themselves as tough outdoorsmen tend to be viewed positively by many citizens. Whenever he wanted to emphasize his toughness during the 1980s, Ronald Reagan could be seen cutting brush on his California ranch. George W. Bush also liked to be seen cutting brush on his Texas ranch.

Bush's image of personal toughness presaged his muscular approach to foreign policy. When crises arrived, Bush consistently favored the aggressive response. Indeed, his promise of quick military action in Afghanistan following the terrorist attacks of 9/11 captured the public desire for revenge. When Bush decided to invade Iraq, he justified it on the basis of that country's alleged weapons of mass destruction (WMD) program as well as links between Saddam Hussein and Osama bin Laden. A majority of the US public supported his decision to go to war, at least at first (Edwards 2003). Bush's direct public speaking style fits the mold of the straight-talking, uncomplicated western sheriff or even a Texas Ranger, another popular role in the American cultural imagination (Scott 2000). Although he was born and educated largely in New England, even his accent was more Texan than Ivy League.

Toughness may be appealing to the public, but that quality is not always an asset in a president. Bush proudly declared that he was a "decider," and that he would not second guess or otherwise agonize over tough decisions (Stolberg 2006). When Bush made a decision, he stuck to it—not apologizing for mistakes, nor even admitting that he made any (Kinsley 2003). When voter sentiment turned strongly against the Iraq War in 2006—in part because of increasingly critical media reports—Bush ignored the political setbacks and vowed to escalate the war. Ever confident, at least before the cameras, the increasingly beleaguered president said his unpopular approach would be justified by future historians.

BUSH'S WEAKNESS: QUESTIONS OF COMPETENCE

From the time George W. Bush first burst on the national stage, reporters and some citizens wondered whether the Texas governor was up to the job of being president. Bush was not a strong student in college, and during his years of public life he sometimes found it challenging to speak in coherent English sentences. Before entering politics, Bush had failed in the oil business in Texas, only to be rescued by his father's friends (Minutaglio 1999).

Concerns over whether Bush was capable of being president did not entirely evaporate after 9/11. Paul O'Neill, Bush's first treasury secretary, said many of the Bush team's problems stemmed from the president's own lack of intellectual curiosity (Suskind 2004). Richard Clarke, a former top National Security Council official, criticized the Bush team for its unwillingness to take the Al-Qaeda threat seriously until after 9/11 (Clarke 2004). As the level of violence in occupied Iraq increased in subsequent years, Bush's war management seemed increasingly questionable as well (Woodward 2006).

The view of Bush as less than effective came ashore in New Orleans with gale-force winds in 2005. As a result of the administration's preliminary misjudgments, the US Federal Emergency Management Agency (FEMA) fumbled its response to the devastation wrought by Hurricane Katrina. Pictures of bodies floating in bogs, angry crowds standing on freeway overpasses, and the horrific conditions inside the Superdome created a major public health crisis and a public relations nightmare for the Bush administration (Nagourney 2006; Shane and Lipton 2005). To make matters worse for Bush, his appointed head of the FEMA had no professional experience in emergency management. Michael ("Brownie") Brown had been a horse-show association official and a Republican loyalist before Bush appointed him to run the nation's chief disaster response agency (Dowd 2005; Krugman 2006). Bush then compounded the problem by telling "Brownie" before the television cameras that he was doing "a heckuva job" (Dowd 2005).

In terms of character, the records of these two presidents suggest that what may be appealing in the US context represents a liability on the international stage. Many international audiences were less sanguine than US voters about Bush's "decider" role. And Obama found that what works well for a US president in Paris or Berlin can fail to impress in Paris, Texas, or Berlin, Wisconsin.

Consequences of Media Strategies: US Public Assessments of Presidents

Table 1.3 demonstrates how effective presidents can be in selling themselves to the US public, particularly in the early going. Following Obama's January 2009 inauguration, more than two-thirds of the country approved of Obama's job performance, according to *Washington Post*–ABC News surveys. Even after more than a year of high unemployment, sluggish growth, and pummeling from congressional Republicans regarding Obama's economic stimulus package, his health care reform bill, and the bailouts of the banking and auto industries, roughly half the country approved of his job performance.

Things also started out reasonably well for George W. Bush eight years earlier. Even though his presidential selection was marred by extraordinary controversy and a contentious 5–4 Supreme Court opinion, Bush emerged with relatively favorable job approval numbers. Within one hundred days of his inauguration, 63 percent of the country said they approved of the job Bush was doing. The number skyrocketed as the nation reeled from the 9/11 attacks later that year. The percentage of the nation approving of Bush's job performance shot up from 55 percent to 86 percent in less than a week and remained high for a year. His approval numbers revived at the time of the US-led invasion of Iraq in March 2003. But as questions of competence arose for Bush, his approval numbers fell. As the occupation of Iraq became more problematic, Bush's numbers fell. Katrina pushed Bush's sinking numbers even further under water.

National public opinion surveys conducted for the *Washington Post* during Obama's first year showed high approval of the president's character, as did

Table 1.3. Public Opinion and Presidential Approval, 2001–2012

Question: "Do you approve or disapprove of the way [Barack Obama/
George W. Bush] is handling his job as president?"

	Approve	Disapprove	No opinion
Obama			
07/08/12	47	49	4
01/15/12	48	48	4
01/16/11	54	43	3
01/15/10	53	44	2
02/22/09	68	25	7
Bush			
02/01/08	33	65	2
01/19/07	33	65	2
01/08/06	46	52	2
01/31/05	50	45	5
01/18/04	58	40	2
01/20/03	59	38	2
07/15/02	72	25	2
03/10/02	82	16	2
10/09/01	92	6	1
09/27/01	90	6	4
09/13/01	86	12	2
09/09/01	55	41	3
04/22/01	63	32	5

Source: Balz and Cohen (2012).
This *Washington Post*-ABC News poll was conducted by Abt SRBI of New York, by telephone July
  5–8, 2012, among a random national sample of 1,003 adults, including users of both landline
  and cellular phones. The results from the full survey have a margin of sampling error of plus
  or minus 3.5 percentage points.

surveys of Bush during 2001. As shown in table 1.4, evaluations of Obama as a person were consistently high during his months as president-elect and as a new president. (Unfortunately, pollsters do not frequently ask this question, so we do not have comparable numbers across Obama's first term.)

At the roughly one-hundred-day mark of his new presidency, roughly three-quarters of Americans agreed that Obama is "honest and trustworthy" and that "he is a strong leader." Similar percentages said that Obama "understands the problems of people like you" and that "he can be trusted in a crisis." But the highest score of all was reserved for agreement with the following statement: "He is willing to listen to different points of view." Fully 90 percent of those surveyed viewed Obama as being open-minded, a powerful example of how his early vows to try to govern in a less partisan manner shaped public opinion.

Table 1.4.   US Public Opinion on Presidential Character, 2001-2009

Question: "Please tell me whether the following statement applies to [Obama/Bush] or not."

"He is honest and trustworthy."

	Yes	No	No opinion
Obama			
4/24/09	74	22	4
1/16/09	75	19	6
12/14/08	67	22	11
Bush			
1/19/07	40	57	3
5/23/04	53	45	2
7/15/02	71	26	3
7/30/01	63	34	3

Question: "He understands the problems of people like you."

	Yes	No	No opinion
Obama			
4/24/09	73	25	1
1/16/09	72	24	4
Bush			
1/19/07	32	67	2
5/23/04	42	57	1
7/15/02	57	41	2
7/30/01	45	54	2

Question: "He is a strong leader."

	Yes	No	No opinion
Obama			
4/24/09	77	22	2
1/16/09	72	18	10
Bush			
1/19/07	45	54	1
5/23/04	62	37	1
7/15/02	75	24	1
7/30/01	55	43	2

Question: "He can be trusted in a crisis."

	Yes	No	No opinion
Obama			
4/24/09	73	21	6
1/16/09	69	18	13
Bush			
1/19/07	42	56	2
5/23/04	60	39	1
7/30/01	60	37	3

Question: "He is willing to listen to different points of view."

	Yes	No	No opinion
Obama			
4/24/09	90	10	1
1/16/09	89	9	2
Bush			
1/19/07	36	63	1
5/23/04	49	50	1

* = less than 0.5 percent
Source: Cohen and Agiesta (2009).
This *Washington Post*-ABC News Poll was conducted by TNS of Horsham, Pennsylvania, by telephone April 21–24, 2009, among a random national sample of 1,072 adults using both landline and cellular phones. The results from the full survey have a margin of sampling error of plus or minus three percentage points.

(First impressions, though, are not permanent. Other surveys discussed below and the results of the 2010 midterm election suggest a significant public cooling regarding Obama took place over the course of his first term.)

Assessments of Bush as a person trended downward during his second term, as shown in table 1.4. By January 2007, only 40 percent of those surveyed said they would describe Bush as "honest and trustworthy," far below the 70 percent who would use those words to describe him in a December 2002 survey. Even as late as May 2004, 53 percent said they would apply those terms to Bush.

Republican efforts to present President Bush as someone with a common touch were less successful post-Katrina. In a January 2007 survey, only 32 percent agreed with the statement that Bush "understands the problems of people like you" (Balz and Cohen 2007). More than six out of ten citizens saw Bush as understanding their problems in a January 2002 survey—a few months after 9/11—but an August 2005 survey marked the last time that at least four people in ten would apply that statement to Bush. Only 42 percent of those surveyed in January 2007 thought Bush could "be trusted in a crisis," as compared to 60 percent who said he was trustworthy in a July 2001 survey. Americans also increasingly saw Bush as stubborn: only 36 percent said in January 2007 that they thought the president was "willing to listen to different points of view" as compared to 49 percent who thought that was true in May 2004.

The Bush figures, as well as those for Obama, demonstrated that early impressions do not last forever. Despite continuing White House efforts to enhance the president's image, media marketing can take an administration only so far. The longer someone is president, the more actual events color public assessments. Putting a shine on a candidate's character during the "getting to know you" phase of a presidential campaign or a first year in office is one thing; retaining the president's reputation as the years go by is quite another.

Domestic Media Strategies and International Impacts

Presidents who seek to win domestic public approval for policies must first win the hearts of the public. From a candidate's first public emergence, extreme care is paid to the public presentation of his or her personality. Nowhere does the matter of character have more impact than in the White House, where the president—or at least the president's transmitted image—is effectively a frequent guest in Americans' living rooms. A winning personality, which includes a friendly and open demeanor, is a prerequisite for obtaining the office and for successful governing.

Modern White Houses are engaged in permanent marketing campaigns to build and retain public affection for the president and win over some of the less committed moderates who can be persuaded to view the president in a largely positive light. Although today's hyperpartisan politics mean that every president has a core of die-hard supporters who will support nearly everything and a core of die-hard opponents who will reject nearly everything (each group is about one-third of the electorate), there are still significant numbers of voters who could be coaxed into supporting any president at least some of the time.

Presidents and presidential candidates spend so much time discussing their characters because they believe that winning and keeping public approval is essential for presidents trying to govern. Congress may not be easily won over by presidential efforts to market policy alternatives, particularly regarding domestic matters. But presidents who "go public" imagine they have a trump card—that the public backs the president. Legislators, this theory suggests, fear presidents with strong public support and worry that opposing a popular president will hurt their own reelection prospects. Although little evidence suggests that going public is an effective political strategy, we see that presidents nevertheless cultivate their public image and the public's response with an intensity that borders on obsession.

Although Bush and Obama won their elections at least in part because they possessed effective media management teams, their strategies sometimes diverged in response to different events. Even though he was elected on a wave of exceptional enthusiasm, during his first term in office Barack Obama never had the public opinion highs Bush attained after 9/11, nor did he have a Congress or public so willing to support his actions in a bipartisan fashion as Bush did then. Indeed, the 2001 terrorist attacks pushed foreign policies to the forefront: precisely the area where the presidential advantage in shaping public opinion is strongest.

In addition to being the national father in times of crisis, wartime presidents can also make far greater use of an administration's inherent advantages in releasing—and withholding—information relating to national security questions that are then dominating public and media attention. Given that domestic issues are far more prominent so far during his presidency, Obama has yet to be able to focus consistently on foreign policy. Nor could he control the information flow as effectively as Bush could in the period between 9/11 and the quagmire that emerged in postwar Iraq.

The media management operations of Obama's presidency during his first four years have been more defensive in nature. Legislatively, Obama achieved extraordinary success in his first two years—securing passage of a major health care reform, a major stimulus package, and a regulatory package designed to prevent future fiscal meltdowns. But neither he nor most Democrats trumpeted these measures as they faced voters angry at the government both for not doing enough to fix the economy and for increasing the debt.

Overpromising, that staple of presidential spinning, seems like a particularly high-risk strategy. Although it may work to secure some short-term policy goals, the approach can hurt a president's standing later on. Presidents who sell themselves and their policies through less-than-honest marketing often face an eventual day of reckoning. Bush's credibility was lost shortly after the start of his second term as the Iraq operation turned out to be the opposite of what Bush and his team predicted. Obama's credibility was undermined, at least temporarily, because the administration underestimated the severity of the economic crisis and the persistently high levels of unemployment that would emerge despite the stimulus package. Because people were led to believe in 2009 that a robust recovery was just around the corner, they punished the Democrats in 2010 because things did not get better as quickly as administration officials had promised.

Changes in the media since the 1980s have expanded greatly the channels presidents and presidential candidates use to communicate with citizens. But they also give the president's critics new venues to reach the public. The now wide-open media landscape also gives citizens greater opportunity to join in the political debate, via emails, blogging, or even posting videos online. This greater democratization of the modern media system, as both Obama and Bush have learned, does not always help in the process of disseminating the president's spin to the nation and to the world.

What Comes Next?

In chapter 1, we have outlined the content analysis procedures and materials we will be using in this study and examined past comparative studies involving US and international news coverage of American government and politics. We have also given a general outline of the international perspectives relating to the two most recent presidents, how they sought to create appealing media images for themselves in domestic media, and the extent to which those efforts at news spinning also affected international news reports on the United States.

In chapter 2, we turn to news coverage of US government policies, as seen through both international and domestic television news. We focus on how the United States is seen generally, including both political and cultural perspectives as gleaned from international television news. We examine the role the United States plays in international news discourse in recent years and in different regions of the world. This chapter discusses US public diplomacy efforts undertaken by George W. Bush and Barack Obama and their foreign policy teams.

In chapter 3, we turn our focus to Barack Obama's presidency. We examine first his efforts to turn the page on his controversial predecessor in the foreign policy arena, paying particular note to his efforts to woo international audiences as a new president (and indeed as a presidential candidate). By a detailed examination of his coverage month-by-month during his first eighteen months in office, we ask whether the "presidential honeymoon" chief executives sometimes enjoy with US media during the opening act of a new presidency can also be detected in international media. We examine international media outlets closely to see how coverage differs in Germany, the United Kingdom, and Arabic-language television. In particular, we address the Obama administration's extensive outreach efforts to the Muslim world and consider the effectiveness of those efforts, at least in terms of news content. In this chapter, we pay particular attention to how the new president is seen in terms of his personality as well as his perceived ability to govern.

In chapter 4, we examine some of the same issues as they relate to the second term of George W. Bush. We examine how his coverage differed over time, and in different national media. We likewise examine international coverage of Bush as it related to reports on his personality and his perceived ability to govern. In addition, the Bush administration treated various international media outlets differently, particularly in the Arab world. Access to administration policymakers can also affect coverage, and we evaluate the well-publicized Bush administration efforts to be more visible on Al-Jazeera.

A more direct comparison of these two chief executives is the focus of chapter 5, the book's main policy chapter. By focusing on two eighteen-month periods of these presidencies, we examine closely news coverage of America's standing in the world and media reports on Bush's and Obama's policies regarding Afghanistan, Iraq, and the Israeli-Palestinian crisis, as well as US policies on terrorism and the state of the environment.

In chapter 6, we focus on how the 2008 US presidential elections were covered by international television news. Given that elections are a key component of democracy—and a key part of the democratic practices the United States is hoping to strengthen around the world—international coverage of US elections can be influential in establishing or undermining US credibility. Our extensive dataset allows the United States to examine both the nomination and the general election campaign coverage, focusing our study on four leading Republican candidates for the GOP presidential nomination as well as three leading Democrats hoping to represent their party in 2008. We look at the amount and tone of coverage overall and on leading topics and policy issues.

In chapter 7, we conclude by discussing the consequences of media coverage. We consider the effectiveness of presidential persuasion efforts on international audiences as well as evaluating the various public outreach efforts undertaken by the US government over the dozen years. This chapter also looks at various media strategies that the US government may use in the future to improve its coverage in some of the outlets examined here. With the global rise of social media, we also consider how new media can affect international understanding and evaluations of the United States.

CHAPTER 2

The World Is Watching, Don't Look Back: News about US Politicians, People, and Policies

In terms of international public opinion, Obama and the United States benefitted from the change many people envisioned would take place in the wake of the 2008 presidential election. As the international public opinion evidence in the previous chapter showed, Obama largely succeeded in making the world view him and the country he leads more positively. Though the enthusiasm for the new president has cooled slightly over time for most nations surveyed, it remains far higher than it was during the Bush years (Pew Global 2010b). In fact, Obama's decline in public support over his first term in office has been far greater within the United States than abroad. The reason for this disparity, above all, is that American citizens and people outside the nation's borders are not looking at the same things.

The difference is not primarily the result of the fact that American journalists emphasize different international matters than foreign reporters do. Rather, it is that Americans rarely think much about international matters at all. Throughout Obama's presidency (and even during much of the Bush years), US citizens have remained deeply focused on domestic matters, even during periods of international tumult. Pew Research Center survey data (Pew 2010a) reveal the extent to which Americans worry more about domestic matters than international ones.

In 2010, for example, 83 percent of Americans said that "strengthening the nation's economy" should be a top priority and 81 percent identified "improving the job situation" as a top concern. Defending the United States against terrorism was identified as a top priority by 81 percent, ranking third. That issue is the only one of the top eight most important problems for Americans that had even a partial international component. The other leading concerns were as follows: securing Social Security (the fourth highest priority, cited by 66 percent), improving the educational system (a top concern of 65 percent), securing Medicare (63 percent), reducing the deficit (60 percent), and reducing health care costs (57 percent). Few of these topics would generate much of an audience beyond the US borders. Other internationally oriented concerns, such as dealing with global trade issues or global warming, bring up the rear in this survey, being listed as a top priority by only 32 percent and 28 percent respectively. Unfortunately for Obama's domestic standing, the US public regarded his foreign policies as more effective and less important than his domestic ones.

A lack of attention to some of these issues may explain part of the reason why Americans do not rate some topics as more significant (cf. Farnsworth and Lichter 2006a, 2011a). Climate change in particular generates relatively little sustained attention in US media (Soroka et al. 2012, 2013). But whatever the cause, any White House administration has to take these feelings seriously. A president, in other words, who wants to be a success must cater to the electorate's highly domestically focused views. These relatively homeward-oriented US public views represent a sharp contrast from the decades-long efforts to create a pan-national European Union and the far greater international concern over climate change expressed on the opposite side of the Atlantic.

Pew surveys from previous years show similar patterns: few international matters have been important to US citizens over the past decade, and the international issues that matter most to Americans involve homeland security and/or military concerns. While defending the United States against terrorism ranked third behind the twin economic concerns of growth and jobs in 2010, the threat of terrorism was seen as the most important problem identified by the US public in 2002 and 2006, closer in time to 9/11 and its aftermath (Bennett et al. 2007; Farnsworth 2009).

US News Regarding the World and International Conflict

Much like Pearl Harbor sixty years earlier, the 2001 Al-Qaeda attacks on the World Trade Center and the Pentagon triggered disbelief among Americans, not only over the massive loss of life but also over the magnitude of change that would be required in the American public's global frame of reference. No longer could the United States stand on the sidelines as other parts of the world raged with extremist violence. The "Pax Americana" thought to have descended on US shores after the collapse of the Soviet Union had proved fleeting. When US military involvement in the world increases or when US national security is seen as being imperiled, the volume of international news increases (Farnsworth and Lichter 2006a).

For the broadcast network news departments, the terrorist attacks signaled the need for greater attention to international matters, particularly as the US military presence in the Muslim world increased. According to a content analysis study of US evening newscasts on ABC, CBS, and NBC conducted by the Center for Media and Public Affairs (CMPA), foreign news coverage during 2001 before September 11 accounted for only 21 percent of total news coverage. After the terrorist attacks, it rose to 36 percent for the rest of the year.

But the increase in international news triggered by the terrorist attacks and the subsequent war in Afghanistan was only temporary. In 2002—a year when President George W. Bush pressured Congress to authorize an invasion of Iraq, the US government frequently issued warnings of impending terrorist attacks, and Osama bin Laden remained at large—foreign news dropped to 27 percent of all coverage, comparable to the amount of foreign news coverage that the networks aired during the early 1990s, according to the CMPA study.

A year later, increased military action led to additional news coverage of the world beyond the nation's borders. The US-led invasion of Iraq in 2003 triggered a huge increase in the amount of international news on network television. Iraq alone was the subject of one-quarter of all news stories that aired on the broadcast network evening news shows that year. But the focus on international news was quite concentrated: all the other nations of the world (except the United States and Iraq) accounted for only 19 percent of the network newscasts. The war and subsequent occupation of Iraq generated over ten times as much news in 2003, as did Israel, the foreign country that ranked second, and more than twenty times the coverage of North Korea and Afghanistan, which ranked third and fourth. And all four of these nations are involved in significant international conflicts, or potential conflicts, where the United States plays a major role.

Content analyses of other time periods likewise have found evidence of deep domestic focus in US media coverage, with international news declining along with US military involvements abroad. The end of the Cold War, as well as network news budget cuts, had already led to substantial declines in the number of expensive foreign news bureaus operated by the networks—and hence the share of their broadcasts devoted to foreign news—well before the 2001 terrorist attacks (Shanor 2003). Coverage of international news topics had fallen by more than a third during the Bill Clinton presidency, from the 34 percent of nightly news reports that focused of foreign topics in 1991 to as low as 20 percent of the newscasts in 1996 and 1997 (cf. Farnsworth and Lichter 2006a).

Cultural factors also help explain the decline in international coverage during the relatively peaceful years of Bill Clinton's presidency. Apart from the Cold War, America's long history of isolationism encourages little interest from either the media or the public in international matters. Americans engage in less international travel and less second-language training than residents of many other affluent nations (Brooks 2006; Curran et al. 2009; Stacks 2003/2004). When Americans do think about the world beyond their shores, they frequently dislike what they see. A recent study found that Americans are mistrustful of the international order and inclined to see the international arena as a "dog eats dog" environment and one best avoided if possible (Brewer et al. 2003). Given these factors, it should come as no surprise that US broadcasters closed expensive foreign bureaus and reduced international news in response to a demonstrable lack of public interest in the years leading up to 9/11 (Stacks 2003/2004).

The growing financial difficulties faced by US broadcast networks, coupled with the increased ability of news organizations to monitor online traffic, also helped convince US news executives to reduce their international news content, particularly if the story in question involves a nation with little direct US military involvement (Curran et al. 2009; Shanor 2003).

Thus, public preferences push US news content in two key directions: (1) toward domestic rather than international news; and (2) toward coverage of wars, particularly those involving US troops, rather than other international news topics. Neither adjustment in US news content is likely to promote greater international understanding or to reduce global conflict in the years ahead.

Indeed, US media portray a world of greater violence than do media from other nations—including nations directly experiencing international tumult. (Of course, US domestic news content also focuses greatly on crime news and other violence, giving Americans a sense that the United States is a far more dangerous place than it actually is [Gilliam and Iyengar 2011; Pew 2011].)

In sum, it is only when US military tensions mount (such as during the Cold War, after 9/11, or during the invasion and occupation of Iraq) that international news makes up even one-third of US news reports. That international coverage—particularly at its high-water mark—is heavily focused on military matters, and US military matters at that. For US television news consumers, the international coverage they receive is laden with domestic impact, as national security and the actions of the US military dominate international news topics.

When a president tries to promote greater peace and understanding through efforts to burnish the US image abroad, it matters far more to an international audience than to broadcasters and audiences in his own nation. And generally speaking, the attention he does get from US media regarding those international outreach efforts is more negative than on comparable news outlets in Europe or the Middle East.

Given these media and public opinion factors, presidents who try to reduce international tensions do not receive many short-term benefits in their own countries for doing so. Even Obama's selection as a Nobel Peace Prize winner did not trigger improved coverage of the new president in US media (Farnsworth, Lichter, and Schatz 2010). Even as he earns international acclaim, many citizens routinely fault the president for not paying closer attention to domestic matters, particularly the economy (Alter 2010).

In light of the episodic nature of much international news content on television, and the heavy reliance on US military news in the international news arena, it is not surprising that US citizens view the rest of the world largely unfavorably. To TV news viewers in the United States, the world is filled with thwarted US ambitions, violence in foreign lands, and unfamiliar peoples whose views often seem inexplicable or worse. As conditions abroad consistently prove to be more complicated—and bloodier—than politicians and the media have led the US public to believe at first, many Americans prefer to leave the rest of the world to its own devices. (Note, for example, the considerable US public hesitation to assist Greece and other European nations during their financial crises, and the deep hesitation to get involved in the civil war raging in Syria at the time of this writing.)

From time to time, Americans (and American journalists) feel they do have to concentrate on international matters, usually in the wake of a military crisis. At these times, news coverage and public concern intensifies, at least temporarily. But coverage soon turns downward in volume and tone, as the news from abroad turns more negative and many Americans wish once again to focus on problems at home.

Media Tenor content analyses reveal the considerable extent to which US media content follows the preferences of US news consumers. News coverage of Obama on NBC, the top-rated US evening newscast, between January 1, 2009, and June 30, 2010, reveals how much the US news coverage of this internationally focused president turns on domestic matters. The most frequently covered topics related to Obama on NBC during this period—a period when he engaged in a number of high-profile international trips and was awarded the Nobel Peace Prize—involve his public appearances, followed by health policy, economic policy, and personality matters, which include reports on a president's personal character. International terrorism ranks fifth, with international politics seventh, warfare eighth, and stories involving America's position in the world ninth.

On Fox News Channel's *Special Report*, a popular source of news for conservative Americans (cf. Pew 2008), international news also took a back seat to Obama's public appearances and the debate over his plans to reform health care in the United States. On Fox, international terrorism ranks a bit higher, third in the amount of coverage during Obama's first year and a half as president. But the most heavily covered issues on Fox also demonstrate the extent to which US media discourse about the new president remains domestically focused: only one other international category, international politics/foreign affairs, cracks the top-ten coverage areas for Obama on Fox.

The result of this limited international news reporting is that Americans may find themselves less prepared for understanding, much less dealing with, the world. We see a US public that, generally speaking, possesses little tolerance for the complexity that marks many international issues, particularly the problematic matters involving war and peace. Minimal recognition of the barriers to effective international coordination in many areas leads to a US public that expects too much at first and later is frustrated with presidents who find it difficult to keep their foreign policy promises or get bogged down in international matters (Brooks 2006).

Whether it was President George W. Bush vowing after 9/11 that he would catch Osama bin Laden "dead or alive," or President Barack Obama promising rapid progress on the long-running US-led war in Afghanistan, American voters wonder why international matters take so long to resolve and why the outcomes are not more positive. Citizens take their frustration out on US presidents for focusing on international matters rather than the US economy and other domestic concerns (cf. Page with Bouton 2006). Even when a president secured a major foreign policy success—such as the killing of Osama bin Laden or the US support that led to the overthrow of Libyan strongman Muammar al-Qaddafi—US public opinion registered relatively minor and short-lived effects (Baker 2012; Calmes 2011b).

To make matters worse, the limited volume of international coverage presented to Americans is not very informative. When network television decides to cover multifaceted international policy issues, news reports tend to be brief and inadequate, focused on US military activities and described in ways that often lack sufficient context and appropriate complexity (Baum and Groeling 2010; Entman 2004; Farnsworth and Lichter 2006a, 2011a; Norris et al. 2003). Studies show that Americans receive far less international news than their international counterparts: foreign coverage on the main news channels in Britain (BBC1 and ITV), for example, was 50 percent higher in volume than that on network television in the United States (ABC and NBC) during four weeks during the winter of 2007 (Curran et al. 2009).

The World and America: A One-Way Mirror?

While the US media may focus inwardly, the United States gets a good deal of attention from international media, as shown in table 2.1. Our examination of 94,877 international news stories aired on the evening newscasts of television broadcasters in Germany, the United Kingdom, and South Africa during 2005 and 2010 found that the United States ranked first in the amount of international coverage in 2010 and second in 2005, behind Iraq, where the US-led occupation was encountering severe difficulties. (Many news stories coded as being primarily about Iraq nevertheless have a significant US component.) Our international

Table 2.1. International and US News Coverage of International News of Selected Nations, 2005–2010

	Intl. 2005 %	US 2005 %	Intl. 2010 %	US 2010 %
United States	11.57	*	9.50	*
Afghanistan	1.03	2.17	6.57	15.57
Australia	1.55	0.19	1.63	0.39
Brazil	0.28	0.12	0.58	0.38
Canada	0.62	0.81	0.75	1.09
Chile	0.12	0.08	1.90	3.6
China	2.11	1.66	3.55	3.0
Egypt	0.79	0.92	0.62	0.36
Euro area	0.26	0.0	0.86	0.08
Europe in general	1.22	0.77	1.69	1.77
EU/Europe institutions	1.85	0.26	1.74	0.05
France	3.49	1.63	2.81	1.06
Germany	0.94	0.7	1.18	0.67
Greece	0.33	0.13	1.81	0.81
Haiti	0.04	0.06	4.11	11.09
Hungary	0.13	0.01	0.58	0.28
India	0.78	0.25	1.67	0.78
Indonesia	1.73	1.96	0.48	0.52
Iran	1.58	2.49	1.63	5.44
Iraq	13.68	36.3	2.04	6.25
Ireland	0.55	0.08	0.83	0.41
Israel	1.58	1.79	1.04	1.77
Italy	1.97	1.27	1.09	0.71
Japan	1.13	0.67	1.07	0.73
Kenya	0.63	0.05	0.64	0.08
Mexico	0.33	0.61	0.83	1.99
Middle East region	1.24	1.79	0.65	0.16
Netherlands	0.46	0.21	0.71	0.47
New Zealand	0.36	0.05	0.58	0.25
North Korea	0.46	1.4	0.59	2.2
Pakistan	1.39	1.83	2.94	4.46
Poland	0.55	0.41	0.91	0.47
Russia	1.53	1.12	1.85	1.97
Republic of South Africa	0.35	0.08	2.45	1.41
South Korea	0.26	0.33	0.62	1.36
Sweden	0.14	0.06	0.51	0.36
Switzerland	0.51	0.07	0.59	0.19
Thailand	0.75	0.63	0.70	0.39
Turkey	0.84	0.14	0.65	0.13
UK	5.33	6.71	5.51	9.32
Vatican City	2.59	4.18	1.83	1.41
Yemen	0.13	0.02	0.58	1.91
Total	100	100	100	100
N	52,326	10,608	42,551	6,396

Notes: N refers to number of stories relating primarily to each nation. Only the most-covered nations are reported here.

Percentages are determined as a share of the nondomestic news. (BBC coverage, for example, excludes UK coverage.) Stories that focus on two or more nations will be coded for the dominant nation in the story, excluding the nation of origin of the news outlet.

* US international media coverage calculations exclude US domestic news.

(All sources are used in both study years unless otherwise noted.)

US: NBC Nightly News, ABC World News Tonight, CBS Evening News, Fox News

Germany: ARD Tagesthemen, ZDF heute journal, RTL Aktuell, ARD Tagesschau, ZDF heute

UK: BBC1 10 O'clock News, ITN Early Evening News, ITV News at Ten, BBC2 Newsnight, BBC1 6 O'clock News (2005 only)

South Africa: SABC 3 News @ One, SABC 3 News @ 10, SABC 2 Afrikaans News, SABC 3 English News, SABC 3 Africa News Update, E-TV News, SABC Zulu/Xhosa News, SABC Sotho News, Summit TV, SABC SiSwati/Ndebele News (2010 only), SABC Venda/Tsonga News (2010 only)

sample found the United States received 11.57 percent of the international coverage on these outlets in 2005, behind the 13.68 percent recorded that related to Iraq. The United Kingdom, which was also part of the Iraq occupation, ranked third in our sample, with 5.33 percent of the international news content recorded within our international media group. (This table excludes domestic stories from each international media outlet: in other words, the UK story count includes no stories from UK outlets, and so on.) France ranked fourth with 3.49 percent of the coverage from the international news group, and China ranked fifth with 2.11 percent of the coverage. Russia, the final permanent member of the UN Security Council, was further back in the pack, with 1.53 percent of the coverage. It failed to make the top ten in 2005, lagging behind the Vatican, Indonesia, Italy, Israel, Iran, Australia, and a more general category covering the European Union and other transnational European institutions.

Although the total percentage of news focusing on the United States was lower in 2010 than in 2005, falling from 11.57 to 9.5 percent, the United States was the most talked-about nation that year in our international media sample. With Iraq fading as a major international hotspot, Afghanistan captured second place in 2010, with 6.57 percent of the coverage. The United Kingdom slipped to third place, with 5.51 percent of the international coverage, with Haiti, the site of one of the world's most devastating earthquakes, ranked fourth in the amount of international news with 4.11 percent of the coverage. China was next, with 3.55 percent of the coverage, followed by Pakistan, a troubled, divided nation unsure how to respond to the Taliban. Rounding out the top ten were France, South Africa, Iraq, and Russia.

Using the same techniques to examine the international news content of the four US television outlets (ABC, CBS, NBC, and Fox News), we see that US international coverage is focused on wherever the United States is or may soon be at war (and to a lesser extent our allies in those endeavors). Our analysis of the 17,004 news stories about international matters on the evening news programs in 2005 and 2010 found that the top nation for US international coverage in 2005 was Iraq, with 36.3 percent of the news reports focusing on that hapless nation. As shown in table 2.1, the United Kingdom ranked a distant second with 6.71 percent of the international news reports, and the Vatican third with 4.18 percent.

Afghanistan ranked first in US international news coverage in 2010 with 15.57 percent of the coverage. Haiti, with its natural disaster, was second with 11.09 percent, the United Kingdom was third with 9.32 percent of international coverage, and Iraq and Iran rounded out the top five (with 6.25 percent and 5.44 percent respectively). Further back in the pack we find Pakistan in sixth place with 4.46 percent of the coverage. Chile, the site of long-running stories of miners trapped deep underground (and eventually rescued in heroic fashion), was in seventh place with 3.6 percent of the coverage. Rising power China, with 3.0 percent of the coverage, ranked eighth, and the pariah state of North Korea emerged in ninth place.

Our study of US international news offers us several opportunities to discuss what Sherlock Holmes called "the dog that didn't bark." European media may look relatively closely at the United States, but with the exception of the United Kingdom, American media did not return the favor. Germany, Western Europe's largest economy, received less than 1 percent of US coverage in both years, and France, another linchpin state of the EU, was only barely above 1 percent. Russia, for so long the superpower rival of the United States, was not the subject of even one in fifty international news reports in either year.

America's closest neighbors, geographically speaking, also did not receive much attention on the evening news in the United States. Mexico received 1.99 percent of the US coverage in 2010, much of it focused on the negative issues that relate primarily to the instability of the US-Mexico border region: illegal immigration, deadly violence, and drug cartel activity. Canada, the top trading partner of the United States, received only 1.09 percent of US coverage that year. The percentages for both nations were even smaller for 2005.

As a whole, this table tells us that America remains important to many international media outlets, but America's international attention is focused almost exclusively on nations where the United States has an occupation army, runs ongoing military operations, or may become militarily engaged someday: Iraq, Afghanistan, Pakistan, Iran, and North Korea all get lots of US media attention, comparatively speaking.

News reports relating to the United Kingdom, perhaps America's closest military ally, and to the Vatican, which speaks with a voice of great importance to America's many Catholics, seem to be more longer-term exceptions to the pattern of US military activity, drawing the bulk of US international news attention. Then there are a few one-time matters that generate temporary redirection of coverage. Natural disasters such as Haiti's or stories of high drama such as the trapped Chilean miners bring focus temporarily to less covered locales. The selection of a new pope focuses attention in the United States (and elsewhere) on the Holy See. The emphasis here is on the temporary nature of this media attention. When the crisis or at least the uncertainty is resolved, or when a new crisis emerges to take its place, the media's gaze shifts elsewhere.

The preponderance of domestic news on US newscasts has been a frequent target of criticism of the US mass media. But wouldn't most television broadcasters focus on matters closest to home? To answer that question, table 2.2 examines the pattern of self-reporting: domestic news coverage for United States and in-country coverage by our sample of international media outlets. Here we look at the amount and tone of news reports relating to the United States for

**Table 2.2.   Domestic News Share on US and
International News, 2002–2009**

Nation/Region	2002 %	2007 %	2009 %
United States	68.2	73.7	64.9
Germany	54.5	55.5	55.7
France	*	67.5	68.1
United Kingdom	63.5	64.1	44.7
Italy	*	69.4	70.0
Switzerland	*	53.6	53.6
Spain	*	62.1	64.4
Arabic TV	*	10.8	05.3
Turkey	*	61.2	77.0
China	*	*	71.1
South Africa	71.0	68.7	67.8
Total N	**131,086**	**278,947**	**251,333**

* News media from that nation were not analyzed during that year of the study.
Notes: *N* refers to number of stories from each nation's examined media outlets. (Because differ-
   ent outlets are coded in different years, the Ns are not comparable.) Amounts are expressed
   as a percentage of the news reports from that nation's media that is devoted to a domestic
   (within-nation) topic.
(All sources are used in all study years unless otherwise noted.)
US: NBC Nightly News, ABC World News Tonight, CBS Evening News, Fox News
Germany: ARD Tagesthemen, ZDF heute journal, RTL Aktuell, ARD Tagesschau, ZDF heute, SAT.1
   News (2002, 2007 only), ProSieben Newstime (2002 only)
UK: BBC1 10 O'clock News, ITV News at Ten, BBC2 Newsnight (2007, 2009 only), ITN Early Evening
   News (2002 only), BBC1 6 O'clock News (2002 only), BBC World (2009 only)
South Africa: SABC 2 Afrikaans News, SABC 3 English News, E-TV News, SABC Zulu/Xhosa News,
   SABC Sotho News, SABC 3 News @ One (2007, 2009 only), SABC 3 News @ Ten (2007, 2009
   only), SABC 3 Africa News Update (2007, 2009 only), SABC SiSwati/Ndebele News (2009 only),
   SABC Venda/Tsonga News (2009 only), Summit TV (2009 only)
France: TF 1 (2007, 2009 only)
Italy: RAI Uno (2007, 2009 only)
Switzerland: SF DRS Tagesschau (2007, 2009 only), SF Rundschau (2009 only), SF Eco (2009
   only), SF Börse (2009 only)
Spain: TVE1 (2007, 2009 only)
Arabic: Al-Arabiyah, Al-Jazeera (2007, 2009 only), Nile News (2009 only), LBC (2009 only), Al-
   Manar (2009 only), Dubai TV (2009 only)
Turkey: TRT (2009 only)
China: CCTV (2009 only)

three years: 2002, the "transition year" that followed the 9/11 terrorist attacks
and preceded the Iraq War; 2007, the year the Bush administration began the
"surge" of additional troops into Iraq to quell the long-running instability there;
and 2009, the first year of the Obama presidency.

   The US television networks, in fact, generally are more domestic in their
news focus than the news of most other nations whose media we examined in
this study. In 2002, for example, domestic news content represented 68 percent
of US news, while news about the United Kingdom represented 63.5 percent of
the news budget for UK media. For Germany, the domestic share was smaller

still: domestic news in Europe's largest economy represented 54.5 percent of total news aired by the German broadcasters we examined. News coverage in South Africa that year was even more domestically focused, though, coming in at 71 percent of all news coverage.

In 2007, US coverage of itself increased to nearly three stories out of every four: 73.7 percent of news reports on ABC, CBS, NBC, and Fox News, ranking first among the ten national or linguistic media groups examined here. Italy ranked second in its self-attention, with domestic news comprising 69.4 percent of all the news aired on RAI Uno, the only Italian broadcaster examined here. The lowest of the ten national samples was the Arabic-language group, where coverage of the originating nation of those broadcasts reached only 10.8 percent of total news. The unusually low amount of domestic news may be the result of a deliberate strategy not to offend domestic rulers by drawing critical attention to nations other than one's home base (cf. Bessaiso 2005; Jasperson and El-Kikhia 2003; Zaharna 2005).

While US news coverage of the United States remained high (at 64.9 percent) in 2009, the last year of the three examined in table 2.2, a variety of other nations provided more internally oriented news coverage than did the United States. Indeed, three nations—Turkey (77 percent), China (71.1 percent), and Italy (70 percent)—all focused on domestic matters more than international concerns in at least seven stories out of ten. On the other hand, key European allies such as the United Kingdom and Germany spent less time in 2009 reporting on themselves than Americans did.

Nadia Bilbassy, a Washington-based reporter with MBC TV, said in an interview that the lack of attention to international news can lead to major misunderstandings on a variety of issues important to US-Arab relations, such as the proposal to build a Muslim worship center in Lower Manhattan, plans by a preacher to burn the Koran, and the Middle East peace process.

> There was no genuine understanding of both the west and the Muslim world. It's glossed over by superficial media reports that are often biased and negative when it comes to Muslims. Therefore, when a controversial story comes to the surface, like building an Islamic Center in New York, all hell breaks loose and we go back to a zero sum game. (Bilbassy 2010:43)

Of course, one might note that for all its flaws, US treatment of Muslims is not clearly worse than that of other Western nations. Adoption of something akin to the French "headscarf" ban seems inconceivable in the United States, given public opinion support for religious freedom. Conditions are troubling enough to provoke rioting in Muslim neighborhoods outside Paris, a clear distinction from the American experience.

DIFFERENCES IN AMOUNT AND TONE OF INTERNATIONAL NEWS COVERAGE OF THE UNITED STATES

Of course, the amount of collective international news coverage we have discussed so far answers only part of the question regarding how the United States is treated in international news media. How do the tone and volume of coverage differ among our different national groups? This portion of the analysis involves a total of 28,003 international news stories that focus on the United States across these three years of 2002, 2007, and 2009.

Because we examine different media outlets in different years, according to the availability of data, the most important figures reported here are expressed as percentages. These include percentages of the amount of total international news coverage devoted to the United States as well as the tone of that coverage. We calculated tone as the percentage of stories coded as mainly positive minus the percentage of stories coded as mainly negative. Stories coded as neutral, the vast majority of the stories in most categories, do not affect the calculation of net tone. In other words, a collection of twenty stories where two (10 percent) were positive in tone and four (20 percent) were negative in tone—with the rest neutral—would have a 10 percent net negative tone.

Among the three media outlets examined in 2002, we see in table 2.3 that the United Kingdom's television networks devoted the largest amount of their international coverage, 16.1 percent, to the United States. But Germany is not far behind, with 15.6 percent of its coverage focused on the United States. South Africa, not a NATO ally, spent a bit less time on the United States: 11.8 percent of its international coverage. (All three of those figures are far higher than the amount of US news coverage devoted to those nations in either 2005 or 2010, as we saw in table 2.1.)

The United Kingdom also ranked first in the highest percentage of international news devoted to the United States in 2007, with 14.8 percent of the coverage. The United Kingdom was followed closely by Italy and then South Africa and Germany. In 2009, the United Kingdom was again first, this time with 17.6 percent of the coverage. Switzerland was second that year in terms of US news volume, followed by Italy, France, South Africa, China, and Germany. The Arabic-language group had the least amount of international news devoted to the United States in both years, only 6.2 percent of the reports that excluded the country of origin for each news outlet. (In both 2007 and 2009, the percentage each nation devoted to the United States was far higher than the percentage of US international news coverage devoted to that nation in 2005 or 2010.)

The amount of coverage of the United States has varied a good deal over time in some nations. The amount of US coverage in German news represented

Table 2.3.   Amount and Tone of Coverage of the United States on International News, 2002-2009

Nation/Region	2002 % Amount	2002 % Net Tone	2007 % Amount	2007 % Net Tone	2009 % Amount	2009 % Net Tone
Germany	15.6	−2.4	11.3	−25.8	12.4	−15.5
France	*	*	9.6	−19.7	14.3	−19.6
United Kingdom	16.1	−17.0	14.8	−21.5	17.6	−14.9
Italy	*	*	14.3	−10.8	14.6	−16.6
Switzerland	*	*	9.2	−16.0	15.7	−4.2
Spain	*	*	6.5	−19.7	11.9	−2.6
Arabic TV	*	*	6.2	8.9	6.2	−3.7
Turkey	*	*	*	*	12.0	−10.1
China	*	*	*	*	13.4	0.4
South Africa	11.8	9.9	12.5	−0.1	13.6	0.0
Average Percentage	14.9	−3.2	9.6	−11.8	9.9	−7.4
Total N	6,997		7,608		13,398	

* News media from that nation were not analyzed during that year of the study.
Notes: *N* refers to number of stories relating primarily to the United States from each nation's examined media outlets. (Because different outlets are coded in different years, the *N*s are not comparable.)
Amounts are expressed as a percentage of the international news from that nation's media that is devoted to a US topic.
Net tone is calculated as the percentage of positive tone stories minus the percentage of negative tone stories.
(All sources are used in all study years unless otherwise noted.)
Germany: ARD Tagesthemen, ZDF heute journal, RTL Aktuell, ARD Tagesschau, ZDF heute, SAT.1 News (2002, 2007 only), ProSieben Newstime (2002 only)
UK: BBC1 10 O'clock News, ITV News at Ten, BBC2 Newsnight (2007, 2009 only), ITN Early Evening News (2002 only), BBC1 6 O'clock News (2002 only), BBC World (2009 only)
South Africa: SABC 2 Afrikaans News, SABC 3 English News, E-TV News, SABC Zulu/Xhosa News, SABC Sotho News, SABC 3 News @ One (2007, 2009 only), SABC 3 News @ Ten (2007, 2009 only), SABC 3 Africa News Update (2007, 2009 only), SABC SiSwati/Ndebele News (2009 only), SABC Venda/Tsonga News (2009 only), Summit TV (2009 only)
France: TF 1 (2007, 2009 only)
Italy: RAI Uno (2007, 2009 only)
Switzerland: SF DRS Tagesschau (2007, 2009 only), SF Rundschau (2009 only), SF Eco (2009 only), SF Börse (2009 only)
Spain: TVE1 (2007, 2009 only)
Arabic: Al-Arabiyah, Al-Jazeera (2007, 2009 only), Nile News (2009 only), LBC (2009 only), Al-Manar (2009 only), Dubai TV (2009 only)
Turkey: TRT (2009 only)
China: CCTV (2009 only)

15.6 percent of international reports in 2002 and only 12.4 percent seven years later. But an increase in attention paid to the United States in 2009 was more common. France, for example, registered a 4.7 percentage point increase in the amount of coverage devoted to the United States from 2007 to 2009 (up to a level of 14.3 percent of international news). Spain and Switzerland likewise paid significantly more attention to the United States in 2009 than two years earlier.

Other nations reported little change. United Kingdom coverage of the United States rose slightly, up 1.5 percentage points from 2002 to 17.6 percent in 2009. South Africa also reported increased attention paid to the United States between 2002 and 2009.

In 2002, the most pro-US coverage was found in the nation that devoted the least attention to the United States: South Africa, with coverage that was 9.9 percent net positive. United Kingdom coverage of the United States during 2002, the year after the 9/11 attacks and at a time when Bush was trying to secure UK involvement in the planned war with Iraq, was 17 percent net negative. Coverage in Germany was much closer to even-handed, with 2.4 percent net negative coverage. (A zero score represents an exact balance between positive and negative stories.)

In 2007, the most pro-US coverage was once again found where the volume of coverage was the lowest, in this case within the Arabic-language media group. Even as the European television networks expressed high levels of outrage at US policies in the Middle East and elsewhere, the media within the region where the conflicts were under way provided news reports on the United States that were 8.9 percent net positive in tone. News from South Africa once again was comparatively favorable, with reports on the United States that were basically neutral (0.1 percent net negative) in tone.

Coverage from the six European nations examined in 2007 was consistently critical, ranging from Italy, which was 10.8 percent net negative in tone, to Germany, which was the most harsh with reports that were 25.8 percent net negative in tone. The United Kingdom, a close ally with US military operations in Afghanistan and Iraq, had the second-most critical coverage of the European nations, with reports that were 21.5 percent net negative in tone. France, a nation whose leaders expressed loud objections to the pending war with Iraq, provided news coverage that was 19.7 percent negative in tone.

Thus, French news reports were slightly less critical of the United States than was the United Kingdom, which actually sent troops to Iraq. Even so, France's objections to an Iraq war raised such ire in Washington that Congress insisted that the "French fries" served in the cafeterias of the US House of Representatives be called "freedom fries" (Kornblut 2006), so lawmakers would not have to utter the name of that disfavored nation at lunchtime. (By 2006, the side dish was known in the House cafeteria as French fries once more—still a misnomer, since they are not part of French cuisine.) And, in a form of poetic justice for la francophonie, Congressman Bob Ney (R-Ohio), the House committee chair who insisted it was his patriotic duty to rename the popular cafeteria offering, a few years later was jailed after pleading guilty to corruption in the Jack Abramoff scandal (Shenon 2007). Clearly, he should have focused his attention elsewhere than his lunch plate!

Considering the international acclaim that greeted his candidacy, one might have anticipated that Barack Obama's election would produce a more favorable picture of the United States in foreign media coverage. However, our study found only a slight uptick in America's coverage abroad. In fact, there was still more negative than positive coverage, as the combined international coverage went from 11.8 percent net negative in 2007 to 7.4 percent net negative in 2009. In other words, the international news reports still remained more critical than not. Among individual countries, the most positive coverage during Obama's first year came from China and South Africa, where the coverage was balanced (i.e., the same number of positive and negative stories).

Among the European allies of the United States, the differences between coverage in 2007 and 2009 were also less than one might suspect. The most negative news was found in France, with 19.6 percent net negative tone for 2009, barely different from the 2007 results. Italy actually was one of the few places where the news became more negative in 2009, with news reports on the United States that were 16.6 percent net negative. Coverage in Germany in 2009 was less critical by ten percentage points when compared to two years earlier, but the resulting 15.5 percent net negative tone was hardly a ringing endorsement of the United States and the new president who so excited global public opinion. The UK news also remained quite critical (14.9 percent net negative in 2009), but less so than in 2007. Turkey's coverage of the United States was a bit less critical than some of the other NATO allies, but the results were not all that pretty for the United States either: coverage from that Muslim-majority nation was 10.1 percent net negative. Overall, the least critical reports in Europe were found in Spain (2.6 percent net negative) and Switzerland (4.2 percent net negative).

The Arabic-language media group (3.7 percent net negative), like Italy, was also more negative in 2009 when compared to two years earlier. The Arabic media results in 2007 were the only positive media group examined here, with news of the United States that was 8.9 percent net positive in tone. But the modestly negative result for 2009 was still far less critical than nearly all the other nations in the study. Even so, a less positive result for 2009 does not seem to suggest that Obama's outreach efforts did much to improve things. (Of course, one could argue that the news reports could have been worse had the new president not made the effort. We will examine Obama's impact more extensively when we consider the content of news outlets as they relate to individual presidents in future chapters.)

Taken together the results of table 2.3 suggest that the media in some of America's closest allies, the advanced Western democracies of Northern Europe, provided the most critical coverage of the United States during the years we examined. The nations less closely aligned with the United States, and further from it both geographically and culturally (China, South Africa, and the Arabic-language media group), were less critical. Likewise, nations with media that pay a great deal of attention to the United States, such as the United Kingdom, Italy, and France, tend to be more critical than nations that pay less attention to the United States, such as the Arabic-language group.

AMOUNT AND TONE OF COVERAGE BY TOPIC

As important as the overall tone of media coverage is, the topical focus of the coverage sets the agenda for public opinion. When international news audiences evaluate the United States, what aspects of American life are they evaluating? To find out, we divided the news reports examined above into key issue areas. The results for all the media combined appear in table 2.4. (We combined media outlets here because some nations produced few examples of coverage in individual issue areas. We provide some national media comparisons of several key topics of coverage later in the chapter.)

Above all, we see that the actions of governments and politicians do not consistently dominate coverage of the United States. In 2002, the top issue area was sports, as that year was marked by the 2002 Winter Olympics in Salt Lake City, Utah. Crime ranked second, and international conflicts/war ranked third. Five years later, business was the most frequently covered topic relating to the United States, with sports second and human interest stories, which includes personal tragedies and accidents, third. (War ranked fourth that year.) In 2009, business was again the most frequently covered issue, not surprising considering the nation's troubles in the banking, real estate, and manufacturing sectors that emerged during the fall of 2008 and continued in the months that followed. International conflicts/war ranked second in importance, a matter of renewed priority for a new president, with the economy and public policy in third place. Human interests/accidents were fourth, and sports ranked fifth. (The table only reports results for the top thirteen issue areas, ones that have at least 150 stories in a given category in each of the three years.)

As table 2.4 shows, the rough trajectory of all issue areas demonstrate that international coverage of the United States was on balance negative in all three years, with the most critical coverage coming in 2007. The tone of coverage of the United States in 2009, Obama's first year, was less critical than in 2007, Bush's sixth year as president. But the 2009 broadcasts were still more critical than the international news about the United States in 2002. Perhaps Bush created a more critical media environment than Obama's election and policies could fully repair. Or perhaps 2002 reflected an unsustainable level of sympathy for the United States in the wake of 9/11. Bush was unpopular abroad, but there are limits to any president's ability to woo international audiences, since a president's chief constituency is domestic.

Table 2.4.   Amount and Tone of Coverage of the United States on International News by Topic, 2002–2009

Topic	2002 Net Tone	2002 N	2007 Net Tone	2007 N	2009 Net Tone	2009 N
Business	-30.6	471	-8.0	1,280	-13.6	2,617
International Conflicts/War	-18.9	1,043	-24.0	695	-8.9	1,593
Economy/Public Policy	-3.1	54	-21.4	346	-17.6	1,485
Human Interests/Accidents	-17.8	813	-47.0	1,150	-29.3	1,200
Sports	49.1	1,631	44.0	1,215	46.3	1,154
Social Affairs	6.3	268	-11.8	372	-20.5	888
Party Politics	11.2	116	1.5	339	17.1	883
Crime	-71.5	1,056	-73.1	659	-62.4	848
Energy/Traffic/Science	4.1	222	-5.9	425	8.0	525
Culture	42.6	380	33.8	311	38.3	480
Foreign Affairs	6.1	214	0.6	169	2.4	422
Terrorism/Domestic Security	-42.4	288	-46.9	175	-35.8	324
Domestic Policy	-11.0	154	-34.6	208	-8.3	217
Average Net Tone	-3.2		-11.8		-7.4	
Total N		6,997		7,608		13,398

Notes: N refers to number of stories relating primarily to the United States within each of the categories listed. Not all stories could be classified, and only the major categories are reported here. (Because different outlets are coded in different years, the Ns are not comparable across years.)
Net tone is calculated as the percentage of positive tone stories minus the percentage of negative tone stories.
(All sources are used in all study years unless otherwise noted.)
Germany: ARD Tagesthemen, ZDF heute journal, RTL Aktuell, ARD Tagesschau, ZDF heute, SAT.1 News (2002, 2007 only), ProSieben Newstime (2002 only).
UK: BBC1 10 O'clock News, ITV News at Ten, BBC2 Newsnight (2007, 2009 only), ITN Early Evening News (2002 only), BBC1 6 O'clock News (2002 only), BBC World (2009 only)
South Africa: SABC 2 Afrikaans News, SABC 3 English News, E-TV News, SABC Zulu/Xhosa News, SABC Sotho News, SABC 3 News @ One (2007, 2009 only), SABC 3 News @ Ten (2007, 2009 only), SABC 3 Africa News Update (2007, 2009 only), SABC SiSwati/Ndebele News (2009 only), SABC Venda/Tsonga News (2009 only), Summit TV (2009 only)
France: TF 1 (2007, 2009 only)
Italy: RAI Uno (2007, 2009 only)
Switzerland: SF DRS Tagesschau (2007, 2009 only), SF Rundschau (2009 only), SF Eco (2009 only), SF Börse (2009 only)
Spain: TVE1 (2007, 2009 only)
Arabic: Al-Arabiyah, Al-Jazeera (2007, 2009 only), Nile News (2009 only), LBC (2009 only), Al-Manar (2009 only), Dubai TV (2009 only)
Turkey: TRT (2009 only)
China: CCTV (2009 only)

The extensive coverage of nonpolitical matters in reports on the United States generates both advantages and disadvantages for America's image abroad. Coverage of sports, for example, a key area of media emphasis in all three years we examined, consistently provides highly positive coverage. The tone of coverage relating to sports was remarkably consistent over time, ranging from 44 percent to 49.1 percent net positive during these three years. Although culture was not among the top five issue areas, cultural matters relating to the United States were also generally quite positive, with reports ranging from 33.8 percent net positive to 42.6 percent net positive during these three years.

Then there is the critical coverage. Crime, a top five media target in all three years, ranged from 62.4 percent net negative to 73.1 percent net negative. Of course, crime news is intrinsically negative; the point is that this is a negative aspect of American life that colors the perspectives of international publics. Although not in the top five, stories on terrorism/domestic security matters in the United States were consistently highly critical as well, with reports ranging from 35.8 percent net negative to 46.9 percent net negative over these three years.

Coverage of more explicitly political matters, such as international conflicts/war, tends to be critical as well, if less so than some other areas. Critical reviews of US military policies were most numerous in 2007, when the coverage was 24 percent net negative in tone. But the coverage of this category was also critical in 2002, when it was 18.9 percent net negative, and 2009, when it was 8.9 percent net negative. Foreign affairs (apart from military actions) was not a major issue area in terms of the amount of coverage, but the coverage (even during the Bush years) was relatively positive, ranging from 0.6 percent net positive in 2007 to 6.1 percent net positive in 2002. The median tonal score for foreign policy news relating to the United States was recorded in 2009, the year Obama engaged in such aggressive international outreach efforts.

Business, the most important US topic for international media in both 2007 and 2009, also tends to generate mostly critical reports. The tone of coverage on this issue ranged from 8 percent net negative in 2007 to 30.6 percent net negative in 2002. Coverage of economic and public policy matters also generate critical reviews, with stories ranging from 3.1 percent net negative in 2002 to 21.4 percent net negative in 2007.

Thus, much of the international news coverage was not about politics, even broadly construed. Coverage of many of these issue areas, including crime and sports reporting, did not vary much over time.

Areas where one might have expected heavily negative coverage—say, political topics such as international conflicts/war, or a Bush foreign policy approach derided by European elites as too unilateral—did not end up all that negatively reported by these international media outlets. (Of course, news stories of terrorism/domestic security matters in the United States were reviewed about as negatively as one might expect.)

Table 2.5. Tone of International Coverage of the United States by Key International Topics, 2002–2009

	Topic	2002 Net Tone	2007 Net Tone	2009 Net Tone
Germany	International Conflicts/War	–4.7	–25.6	–2.5
	Foreign Affairs	–4.4	–11.6	27.6
	Terrorism/Domestic Security	–34.1	–53.9	–73.6
France	International Conflicts/War	*	–28.6	–2.5
	Foreign Affairs	*	* *	* *
	Terrorism/Domestic Security	*	–50.0	–26.3
UK	International Conflicts/War	–10.9	–31.9	–8.4
	Foreign Affairs	0.0	–16.7	4.4
	Terrorism/Domestic Security	–5.0	–40.7	–37.2
Italy	International Conflicts/War	*	–19.3	0.9
	Foreign Affairs	*	* *	–8.3
	Terrorism/Domestic Security	*	–38.1	* *
Switzerland	International Conflicts/War	*	–10.9	15.0
	Foreign Affairs	*	* *	15.8
	Terrorism/Domestic Security	*	–46.2	–13.9
Spain	International Conflicts/War	*	–35.7	–10.8
	Foreign Affairs	*	* *	7.5
	Terrorism/Domestic Security	*	0	–15.4
Arabic TV	International Conflicts/War	*	–26.4	–7.0
	Foreign Affairs	*	–22.9	11.0
	Terrorism/Domestic Security	*	–58.6	–41.9
Turkey	International Conflicts/War	*	*	* *
	Foreign Affairs	*	*	* *
	Terrorism/Domestic Security	*	*	* *
China	International Conflicts/War	*	*	0.0
	Foreign Affairs	*	*	* *
	Terrorism/Domestic Security	*	*	* *
South Africa	International Conflicts/War	–51.4	–46.4	14.4
	Foreign Affairs	4.0	9.8	21.4
	Terrorism/Domestic Security	–57.9	–75.0	21.4
Total N	International Conflicts/War	1,043	695	1,593
	Foreign Affairs	214	169	422
	Terrorism/Domestic Security	288	175	324

* Nation's media not analyzed that year.
** Less than ten stories in the category, too few for calculation of tone.
Notes: N refers to number of stories relating primarily to the United States from each nation's listed media outlets for each topic listed. Not all stories could be classified by topic. (Because different outlets are coded in different years, the total N figures are not comparable across years.)
Net tone is calculated as the percentage of positive tone stories minus the percentage of negative tone stories.
(All sources are used in all study years unless otherwise noted.)
Germany: ARD Tagesthemen, ZDF heute journal, RTL Aktuell, ARD Tagesschau, ZDF heute, SAT.1 News (2002, 2007 only), ProSieben Newstime (2002 only)
UK: BBC 1 10 O'clock News, ITV News at Ten, BBC2 Newsnight (2007, 2009 only), ITN Early Evening News (2002 only), BBC1 6 O'clock News (2002 only), BBC World (2009 only)
South Africa: SABC 2 Afrikaans News, SABC 3 English News, E-TV News, SABC Zulu/Xhosa News, SABC Sotho News, SABC 3 News @ One (2007, 2009 only), SABC 3 News @ Ten (2007, 2009 only), SABC 3 Africa News Update (2007, 2009 only), SABC SiSwati/Ndebele News (2009 only), SABC Venda/Tsonga News (2009 only), Summit TV (2009 only)
France: TF 1 (2007, 2009 only)
Italy: RAI Uno (2007, 2009 only)
Switzerland: SF DRS Tagesschau (2007, 2009 only), SF Rundschau (2009 only), SF Eco (2009 only), SF Börse (2009 only)
Spain: TVE1 (2007, 2009 only)
Arabic: Al-Arabiyah, Al-Jazeera (2007, 2009 only), Nile News (2009 only), LBC (2009 only), Al-Manar (2009 only), Dubai TV (2009 only)
Turkey: TRT (2009 only)
China: CCTV (2009 only)

These overall results do not allow us to examine national differences among foreign media. Table 2.5 provides national-level results for coverage of the United States in 2002, 2007, and 2009 relating to three key international topics: international conflicts/war, foreign affairs, and terrorism/domestic security. We see that every nation's coverage of international conflicts/war category became more positive in 2009, in many cases to a substantial degree. The Obama effect seems to be in evidence here. Even so, substantial differences remained in the tone of coverage. For example, much of Europe's media offered substantially less negative news about the United States in this key issue area once Obama became president.

For Germany, the tone of US coverage on relating to the international conflicts/war category moved from 25.6 percent net negative in 2007 to 2.5 percent net negative in 2009. The United Kingdom's change in coverage was of a similar double-digit magnitude, moving from 31.9 percent net negative in 2007 to 8.4 percent net negative in 2009. France had a surge of relatively less critical coverage as well, moving from 28.6 percent net negative in 2007 to 2.5 percent net negative two years later. By contrast, Switzerland's shift in coverage actually produced a net positive portrait of the United States in international conflicts, going from 10.9 percent net negative in 2007 to 15.0 percent net positive in 2009.

But the biggest change was seen not in Europe, but rather in South African media, which moved from 46.4 percent net negative to 14.4 percent net positive in its discussion of international conflicts/war over that same two-year span. The Arabic-language media, based in the region where some of these key military conflicts were taking place, provided more positive news reports relating to the United States and international conflicts/wars than one might expect. Coverage in the region in 2007 was 26.4 percent net negative, rising to 7 percent net negative in 2009. The results from these regional news outlets, in other words, were less critical than the same issue coverage in nations from outside the war-torn region, such as the United Kingdom, France, and Spain in 2007 and the United Kingdom and Spain in 2009.

With respect to foreign affairs coverage, which does not include coverage relating to military conflicts, significant improvements occurred between 2007 (Bush's sixth year as president) and 2009 (Obama's first year). News reports were positive, or at least less negative, in every country that had enough coverage to provide a valid comparison. Unfortunately for the United States' reputation abroad, however, this category received relatively little attention. In all three of the years examined here, coverage of this category lagged behind reports on international conflicts and wars by a margin of more than three to one.

Nevertheless, these reports on US foreign policy were generally positive. Coverage in Germany shifted from 11.6 percent net negative in 2007 to 27.6

percent net positive in tone two years later. Other key allies registered double-digit gains, such as the United Kingdom, which went from 16.7 percent net negative to 4.4 percent net positive. South Africa, home to the most positively disposed television reports relating to US foreign policy in 2007, became even more positive in 2009, with news reports moving from 9.8 percent net positive to 21.4 percent net positive. The Arabic-language media also registered substantial gains, moving from 22.9 percent net negative regarding US foreign policy in 2007 to 11 percent net positive two years later.

The most negative coverage of a key international matter concerns neither foreign policy nor war/conflict, despite widespread international public condemnation of US military policies. Rather, the worst news for the United States in this table relates to how the country has handled terrorism and domestic security matters. The key controversy here concerns the US military prison at Guantanamo, Cuba. The US government was routinely vilified in international discourse over the treatment of inmates at the prison during the Bush years. International voices, and a few voices within the United States, objected to the long-term incarceration of detainees without trial, the lack of due process for assessing the validity of the information being used to detain these inmates, and questions of humane treatment, which all combined to create a public relations disaster for the United States internationally.

Although Obama vowed he would close the Guantanamo prison, he found it politically impossible to convince lawmakers on Capitol Hill to transfer these international prisoners to the US mainland, much less have the hundreds of inmates undergo trials in US-based courts (Finn and Kornblut 2011). So the new president, after making the key promise regarding Guantanamo that international audiences wanted to hear, disappointed them by keeping the prison open throughout his first term. Add to that the difficulties foreigners can face when they try to fly to the United States or obtain a visa since 9/11 and the various high-tech military surveillance and drone attack operations the government engaged in over the past decade, and international news reports are likely to contain few good words about US policy. American presidents who fail to live up to American ideals on civil rights can be treated harshly by reporters, particularly those from European nations with long histories of supporting similar values in their own countries.

Across the board, international coverage of the US policies relating to terrorism and domestic security were extremely negative: coverage of this issue during 2007 in South Africa (a nation whose media were otherwise extraordinarily kind to the United States) was an astonishing 75 percent net negative, even more negative than reports in the Arabic-language media, which were 58.6 percent net negative. Perhaps the long legacy of apartheid in South Africa created a special sensitivity to matters of long-term incarceration of minority groups elsewhere, particularly when those individuals are being held without the due process accorded to American citizens. We would expect Arabic-language media to be highly suspicious of US policies in this area, given the frequency with which concerns about terrorism and/or domestic security had notable impacts on Arab Americans and people from Arab nations trying to visit the United States (Bonner 2002; Kahn 2002; MacFarquhar 2006, 2007; Swarns 2003).

Western European media sources likewise were highly critical regarding US reports on terrorism and domestic security matters during 2007, including Germany (53.9 percent net negative), France (50 percent net negative), and Switzerland (46.2 percent net negative). Television news in the United Kingdom (40.7 percent net negative) and Italy (38.1 percent net negative) were also highly critical, though a bit less than some other European nations. Compared to the media in some of the other NATO nations examined here, TVE1 in Spain was an outlier with its neutral coverage on this topic. Although recent national history with terrorism did not appear to move the needle much in the United Kingdom, perhaps Spain's results reflect the fact that the nation endured the worst terrorist attack in its history a few years before the year being examined here (Sciolino 2004).

Thus, Obama's outreach efforts to generate more positive impressions internationally did not trigger as much change in media coverage as the new administration might have hoped when it came to terrorism and domestic security news. Coverage of this issue area in Germany actually became more negative in 2009—the year of those key presidential appearances in Cairo and Istanbul—than it was two years earlier, rising to 73.6 percent net negative, by far the most critical of any nation's media examined here. As was the case in Germany, coverage of US policies regarding terrorism and domestic security became more critical in 2009 in Spain, falling from neutral to 15.4 percent net negative.

For the Arabic media group, consistently highly critical on this topic, reports on this issue area in 2009 were less critical than two years earlier, though they nevertheless were 41.9 percent net negative. Coverage in the United Kingdom barely budged in terms of tone, with 37.2 percent net negative reports on US policies relating to terrorism and domestic security during 2009, only a few percentage points less critical than two years earlier.

A few places did see a sharply more favorable tone in 2009. The biggest change was found in South Africa, where content analysis reveals a dramatic ninety-six-percentage-point swing in a more positive direction (from 75 percent net negative in 2007 to 21.4 percent net positive two years later). France also saw double-digit improvements, as did the Arabic-language media group. Even so, most media remained highly critical of US policies relating to terrorism and domestic security.

US foreign policy and military policy concerns are quite important to many news consumers around the world, but America's global footprint extends

Table 2.6. Tone of International Coverage of the United States by Key Domestic Topics, 2002–2009

Topic		2002 Net Tone	2007 Net Tone	2009 Net Tone
Germany	Business	−29.2	−12.3	−34.5
	Economy/Public Policy	8.0	−18.0	−24.2
France	Business	*	−70.0	−47.4
	Economy/Public Policy	*	**	−45.0
UK	Business	−64.9	−30.9	−27.6
	Economy/Public Policy	−5.9	−30.0	−20.2
Italy	Business	*	−23.1	−13.6
	Economy/Public Policy	*	−7.1	−4.9
Switzerland	Business	*	−53.3	−15.6
	Economy/Public Policy	*	−28.6	−3.9
Spain	Business	*	−90.0	−30.4
	Economy/Public Policy	*	**	−15.6
Arabic TV	Business	*	−8.1	−1.2
	Economy/Public Policy	*	−14.4	−13.4
Turkey	Business	*	*	**
	Economy/Public Policy	*	*	**
China	Business	*	*	−22.2
	Economy/Public Policy	*	*	0
South Africa	Business	−5.8	−3.8	−8.2
	Economy/Public Policy	0	−20.3	−24.3
Total N	Business	471	1,280	2,617
	Economy/Public Policy	54	346	1,485

* Nation's stories not analyzed that year.

** Less than ten stories in the category, too few for calculation of tone.

Notes: N refers to number of stories relating primarily to the United States from each nation's listed media outlets for each listed topic. (Because different media outlets are analyzed in different years, the total N figures are not comparable across years.) Not all stories could be classified.

Net tone is calculated as the percentage of positive tone stories minus the percentage of negative tone stories.

(All sources are used in all study years unless otherwise noted.)

Germany: ARD Tagesthemen, ZDF heute journal, RTL Aktuell, ARD Tagesschau, ZDF heute, SAT.1 News (2002, 2007 only), ProSieben Newstime (2002 only)

UK: BBC1 10 O'clock News, ITV News at Ten, BBC2 Newsnight (2007, 2009 only), ITN Early Evening News (2002 only), BBC1 6 O'clock News (2002 only), BBC World (2009 only)

South Africa: SABC 2 Afrikaans News, SABC 3 English News, E-TV News, SABC Zulu/Xhosa News, SABC Sotho News, SABC 3 News @ One (2007, 2009 only), SABC 3 News @ Ten (2007, 2009 only), SABC 3 Africa News Update (2007, 2009 only), SABC SiSwati/Ndebele News (2009 only), SABC Venda/Tsonga News (2009 only), Summit TV (2009 only)

France: TF 1 (2007, 2009 only)

Italy: RAI Uno (2007, 2009 only)

Switzerland: SF DRS Tagesschau (2007, 2009 only), SF Rundschau (2009 only), SF Eco (2009 only), SF Börse (2009 only)

Spain: TVE1 (2007, 2009 only)

Arabic: Al-Arabiyah, Al-Jazeera (2007, 2009 only), Nile News (2009 only), LBC (2009 only), Al-Manar (2009 only), Dubai TV (2009 only)

Turkey: TRT (2009 only)

China: CCTV (2009 only)

beyond the international realm. Given America's highly influential role in the international economy, business news has an international audience of considerable size. In table 2.6, we examine international news coverage of two important issue areas that are less explicitly internationally oriented in terms of US policy-making: business and the economy.

The news for America was not good on this front, even before the world was shocked by the financial crisis of 2008. Media based in the comparably advanced economies of Western Europe had little positive to say about business matters in the United States, regardless of the year. Coverage of US business in the United Kingdom, America's closest ally in Europe and a key trading partner, was 64.9 percent net negative in 2002, rising only to a level of 27.6 percent net negative in 2009. Coverage of US business in Germany, Western Europe's largest economy, was 29.2 percent net negative in 2002. In fact, the German reports on US business were most negative in 2009, rising to a level of 34.5 percent net negative that year.

But other nations were even more critical: Spain's coverage of US business matters were 90 percent net negative in 2007, and the French media reports were 70 percent net negative. Switzerland was 53.3 percent net negative in its coverage of US business that year. Europeans may not agree on much, but they do agree on how badly business operates in the United States!

For relatively positive views of US business, one should look far beyond America's top trading partners. South African coverage of US business was only 3.8 percent net negative in 2007 and only 8.2 percent net negative two years later. Likewise, reports on US business in Arabic-language media were 8.1 percent negative in 2007 and almost balanced (1.2 percent net negative) two years later.

Although many German citizens may have been ecstatic when Obama visited Berlin in 2008, that goodwill did affect media coverage of other aspects of American society, particularly business news. The French president may have gushed enthusiastically when candidate Obama stopped by Paris on that same European trip during 2008, but French news reports were the most critical of US business among all the countries we examined. At least the coverage proved less critical in 2009 than it had two years earlier. In contrast, the numbers in the notably less critical United Kingdom barely moved between 2007 and 2009.

For the largest Obama-era swing in the coverage of US business, one needs to look at Spain, where coverage went from 90 percent net negative in 2007 to 30.4 percent net negative two years later, and at Switzerland, where the change was also positive and was deep into the double digits.

International news reports on US economic and public policy matters during the crisis year of 2009 also generated highly critical reviews. The harshest reports in 2009 were in France (45 percent net negative), the non-Eurozone nation of South Africa (24.3 percent net negative), and Germany (24.2 percent net negative). The least critical reports were in China (neutral coverage), Switzerland (3.9 percent net negative), and the Eurozone nation of Italy (4.9 percent net negative).

Of course, supporters of Obama could argue that the international news reports could have been worse. Although coverage of the US economic and public policy matters were less critical in Germany and South Africa in 2007 than two years later, the 2009 coverage was more positive (or less critical) in all the other nations with a sufficient number of news reports in this issue area to compare the two years.

Conclusion

International news coverage of the United States remains highly influential in setting the international news agenda. Our study of international news coverage from several different years during the Bush and Obama presidencies reveals a consistently high level of attention to US actions around the world. In the rare cases where some other country gets more attention from the world's media than the United States does, such as Iraq in 2005, US actions there brought about the spike in international interest. In addition, our findings suggest that the media in most nations care about the United States more than the US media care about those nations.

International news reports directed at the United States often have less to do with controversial wars and unpopular presidents than one might expect. One of the most commonly discussed topics involving the United States is sports, and America's frequent excellence in athletic matters helps convey a more positive image of the nation. Another pleasant surprise for America's reputation is the very positive treatment cultural matters receive. While Europeans sometimes view Americans as unsophisticated in the realms of music, film, and literature, overall coverage of the arts in the United States adds to the positive image of the United States in international news reports.

But, of course, much of the news was not so good for America's national image. The view of America from abroad as a violence-prone society is underscored by the heavy volume of crime news presented by international news outlets. International coverage of US policies regarding terrorism and domestic security was often quite harsh, as were human interest news stories. War news may have been negative, but it was less negative than one might have expected given the volume of international objections to the Bush presidency and above all the US-led war in Iraq.

One reason some of the coverage was more positive than one might expect was the presence in this study of relatively friendly news from unexpected places:

the distant nation of South Africa and the Arabic-language media group, based in one of the world's most volatile regions. Many of the media outlets of its long-term NATO allies, which interacted closely with the United States during the last several decades, soured on the United States during the Bush years. And few European media outlets changed their tune after Obama took office, despite early evidence of his personal popularity in this region.

Thus, while Obama's election in November 2008 may have cheered many citizens in Europe, the tone of media reports on the United States during the new president's first year did not change much. While the coverage of the United States generally improved, it went from very negative to merely somewhat negative. Even the news media of China, a rising power whose government eyes the United States warily, saw more to like in the United States than the media of those nations whose peoples know us best, even when a European-favored candidate sits in the Oval Office. The few nations registering sharp improvements in the news reports on the United States, such as Spain and Switzerland, were never as negative about the United States as were the larger European nations of Germany, France, and the United Kingdom.

Of course, our discussion about international news coverage of the United States has been somewhat broadly drawn. We have analyzed a range of news stories about the United States during some key years of the Bush and Obama presidencies, and we have found somewhat limited changes as the US political system transitions from one president to another. But we have yet to focus on the presidents themselves. In the next several chapters, we do just that. Chapter 3 moves beyond general news coverage of the United States to focus on coverage of Barack Obama himself. In chapter 4, we look at the coverage of George W. Bush during his term in office. In chapter 5, we provide more explicit and extensive comparisons of the two presidents and how they were treated in international media overall. We also compare coverage of these two presidents in several key policy areas, including America's standing in the world, the wars in Iraq and Afghanistan, and US policies in the volatile Middle East. We now shift our own focus toward presidential-focused news.

CHAPTER 3

The Obama Presidency: International Media Perspectives

As a presidential candidate and during his early months as president, Barack Obama sought to build positive feelings, both for the United States and for himself, in the international arena. From the hundreds of thousands of adoring Europeans who greeted the presidential candidate in Germany in 2008 to the new president's 2009 speeches in Istanbul and Cairo (notable for their attempts to connect with Muslim publics and elites), Obama sought to reverse the highly negative views of his predecessor in both Europe and the Middle East (Shear and Sullivan 2009; Zeleny and Cowell 2009; Zeleny and Kulish 2008).

As we saw from the survey results presented in the first chapter, international public opinion polls suggest Obama largely succeeded in making the world view him and the country he leads more positively, though the enthusiasm for the new president has since cooled a bit following the heady days of 2008 and early 2009 (Pew Global 2010a, 2010b, 2012). Since the realities of governing often fall short of the hopes in political campaigns, how could it be otherwise?

But the enthusiasm was extraordinary. In some nations, such as Germany, the percentage of the population believing Obama would do the right thing in international affairs jumped by more than seventy percentage points over Bush. Americans were also quite positive about Obama's handling of international matters, giving him more support on this measure than on his handling of domestic matters (Pew Global 2010a, 2010b, 2012). While the approval ratings for Obama generally dropped somewhat in Muslim-majority nations over the course of his term, they were still far above the comparable numbers for Bush (Pew Global 2010a, 2010b).

While all recent presidents have tried to influence foreign coverage of the United States, few made international outreach the focus that it has been during the Obama and George W. Bush administrations (Alter 2010; Brooks 2006; Entman 2004; Kessler and Wright 2007; Mueller 2006; Pew Global 2006,

2010a; Wilson 2010; Zaharna 2005). Whether the increased US emphasis on the Muslim world during the Bush and Obama years is part of a long-term trend remains to be seen. Such trends will be clearer after America's forty-fifth president takes office.

How effective has Barack Obama been in his international outreach efforts? Did his efforts result in positive media coverage for the United States and for himself? This chapter examines how the new president was treated in a variety of international television evening news programs in the United Kingdom, Germany, and the Middle East during an eighteen-month period from January 1, 2009, to June 30, 2010. The study period is marked by Obama's selection for a Nobel Prize, as well as a decline in Obama's international ratings and a flare-up of Middle East tensions after Israeli commandos killed nine civilians on a Turkish ship near the Gaza strip in late May (Shear 2010).

We examine news coverage of Obama overall as well as specific areas of evaluation, including his personal character and capacity to govern. Throughout this chapter, we compare these international findings with the tone of comparable coverage of Obama on the US broadcast networks and Fox News during that same eighteen-month period. We use the same Media Tenor data set of international media as in previous chapters. But in this chapter we focus on individual statements relating to the themes we examine, drilling down from the more general story-level analysis used in chapter 2.

The White House versus the Media: The Obama Presidency

Two general points about US media coverage of the presidency are particularly relevant to this study. First, every White House deploys a massive public relations operation designed to portray the president and his policies in as positive a light as possible, creating media-friendly venues to shape the coverage to the administration's liking. Those efforts may be more likely to succeed with international news outlets because international reporters have limited access to interviews with competing US newsmakers (cf. Aday et al. 2005; Bennett et al. 2007; Cohen 2008; Entman 2004; Farnsworth, Soroka, and Young 2010; Han 2001; Mueller 2006). Presidential marketing frequently focuses on personal attributes or presidential "character," which are often more within the capacity of presidents to shape than public opinion relating to contentious matters of public policy (cf. Farnsworth 2009; Farnsworth and Lichter 2006a). Character is also less likely to be subject to counterframing than more policy-oriented topics.

The second general issue here concerns the timing of this study. New presidents were long thought to enjoy a "honeymoon" with journalists when they first entered the White House. Traditionally, these media honeymoons were a brief "settling in" period of relative harmony among White House officials and the reporters who cover them, which gave way to more critical coverage as the administration's policymaking began in earnest. Studies looking at a range of Cold War–era presidents found evidence of a honeymoon effect for most newly elected presidents serving during the television age before Clinton, with the clear exception of Jimmy Carter (cf. Hughes 1995). This gentle treatment by reporters should not come as a surprise, as the two sides do have some common interests. White House correspondents seek news and greater visibility within their news organizations, and administration officials want to present their policy preferences to the country. Journalists and administration officials have a mutual interest in obtaining greater publicity for the president (cf. Grossman and Kumar 1981).

However, studies of the contentious first act of the Clinton presidency in 1993 found little evidence of a honeymoon. Nor was there any evidence of one eight years later for George W. Bush, who took office following an unprecedented legal challenge over the legitimacy of the vote count in Florida (cf. Farnsworth and Lichter 2006a).

Barack Obama, who during the 2008 campaign enjoyed the most positive US network news coverage of any presidential candidate over the past twenty years (Farnsworth and Lichter 2011a), entered the Oval Office with a very different status than his two most recent predecessors. In addition to his relatively controversy-free campaign in 2008, Obama won a majority of the vote, something that the scandal-plagued Bill Clinton did not accomplish in 1992 (Ceaser and Busch 1993). In 2000, of course, George W. Bush failed to obtain even a plurality of the votes cast on the way to the Supreme Court decision that landed him in the White House (Ceaser and Busch 2001).

In a break from recent predecessors, the presidential honeymoon returned for Barack Obama, who received significantly more positive news coverage on network television during his first year in office than did Ronald Reagan, Bill Clinton, and George W. Bush (Farnsworth and Lichter 2011b). Obama's early months in the White House involved a wide range of contentious economic and foreign policy issues, as well as the deployment of a massive public relations operation designed to portray the president and his policies in as positive a light as possible (Alter 2010). In fact, Obama's stretch of unusually positive coverage continued into year two in the *New York Times* (Farnsworth and Lichter 2013).

As we have discussed, one of the key ways presidential marketing takes place for Obama, as for his predecessors, is through an emphasis on personal character, which is often more within the capacity of presidents to shape than public opinion relating to contentious policy matters (cf. Farnsworth 2009). In this chapter we examine Obama's first year-and-a-half in office in both US and international media, allowing us to test for evidence of a presidential honeymoon in international news coverage as well as on the US-based television news programs.

Before examining the international media content analysis of presidential influence in the television broadcasts of the United Kingdom, Germany, and the Arabic-language television group, we turn to the evidence of Obama's influence on American media and public opinion. We focus first on the two dominant policy issues of his first term, the nation's economic troubles and his health care reform law, as well as reconsidering the central question of presidential character.

OBAMA AND THE ECONOMY

Since one of the most dangerous public perceptions of a president is that he does not understand the financial problems of ordinary Americans (cf. Ceaser and Busch 1993), administrations often swing into action quickly when trouble strikes. Responses to the economic crisis that hit the United States in the middle of the 2008 presidential election were no exception. Bush, McCain, and Obama all quickly lined up behind an emergency plan to ramp up federal spending to restore confidence to jittery credit markets. Within a month of taking office in January 2009, Obama convinced Congress to pass a major stimulus package designed to accelerate the pace of a hoped-for recovery (Herszenhorn 2009).

In some ways, President Obama was the victim of candidate Obama's extraordinary electoral success (Campbell 2012). The optimism among his White House team and the enthusiasm among many voters that greeted Obama's electoral success triggered highly positive scenarios—some might say unrealistic fantasies—of what the new president could accomplish (Aberbach 2012; Campbell 2009; Conley 2009; Harris and Martin 2009; Pew 2008, 2009c). Scholarly studies of voting behavior in that presidential election subsequently revealed that the election was less transformational than some thought at the time (Denton 2009; Edge 2010; Jacobson 2012; Smith and King 2009; Weatherford 2012), which helps explain why some of those visions of a dramatically different future (so far at least) turned out to be largely a mirage.

Although Obama was elected along with large Democratic majorities in Congress, getting legislation through Capitol Hill proved to be a difficult matter. In these highly partisan times, a Senate majority can still be blocked on most legislative measures if the minority party holds forty-one of one hundred seats. A razor-thin 2008 US Senate race in Minnesota involved months of litigation and recounts and as a result kept the Democrats from obtaining the sixtieth seat that could break a Republican filibuster until comedian and author Al Franken was seated in July 2009 (Davey and Hulse 2009; Sinclair 2012). But that sixtieth

Senate vote for the Democrats did not last for long. Roughly six months later Scott Brown won a special election to replace US Senator Edward M. Kennedy (D-Mass.), who had died of a brain tumor (Cooper 2010). Aggressive Republican use of the filibuster (or, more precisely, the threatened use of the filibuster) meant that key parts of Obama's economic agenda did not come to a vote in the Senate during most of his first term, and those that did pass were often watered down in efforts to secure GOP acquiescence (Edwards 2012; Pear 2011; Sinclair 2012; Weatherford 2012; Weisman 2012).

The first (and largest) piece of Obama's economic recovery plan, a $787 billion stimulus bill, was reduced in scope from the president's original proposal in order to gain the support of three Republican senators who then prevented a GOP filibuster (Herszenhorn 2009). Republicans subsequently complained that the bill, which had been truncated to satisfy a few GOP Senate moderates, failed to generate sufficient improvement in the economy (Stolberg 2010). Republicans continued to make this argument—that the bill they insisted at the time was far too large did not end up doing enough—during the 2012 presidential election (Oppel 2012).

Liberal Democrats, also frustrated by the slow pace of the recovery, faulted Obama for not insisting more strongly that the original bill be larger and more extensive, even though it seemed unlikely that a larger plan could have passed the Senate (Chait 2011). Congressional Democrats further complained that the president did not effectively market his priorities to the public, leaving the economic stimulus measures to be defined largely by the aggressive Republican attacks (Sinclair 2012).

In the first weeks of his presidency, Obama met with Republican House and Senate leaders and offered to dedicate 40 percent of the stimulus bill to tax cuts, a top Republican agenda item, to obtain support from some Republican lawmakers. In response to this olive branch, House Republicans pledged opposition and a lack of interest in compromise. In the end, no GOP House members voted for the compromise bill.

> Republicans concluded that their electoral interests dictated all-out opposition. In a polarized environment, their activists demanded it. And Republicans believed that the voters, already cynical about government, could be persuaded by the attacks on the bill that it represented venal politics as usual. (Sinclair 2012:204)

Three moderate Republicans in the Senate supported the modified $787 billion stimulus bill, which gave the president a way around a filibuster and an early legislative victory. The bill included funding to stimulate the auto industry (including the "cash for clunkers" program to stimulate demand), a massive infrastructure program, a payroll tax cut, and grants to states to minimize the layoffs of teachers, emergency responders, and other public employees. The legislation also extended existing benefits for unemployed workers and provided tax cuts for home energy-saving projects and increased the deficit (Porter 2012).

US television news coverage of economic matters was relatively positive during Obama's first year. A Center for Media and Public Affairs (CMPA) study of evening newscasts on ABC, CBS, and NBC from January 20, 2009, through the end of the year found that coverage on economic matters relating to Obama was 47 percent positive (and 53 percent negative in tone). Coverage of the budget was decidedly negative, with only 26 percent positive, while coverage of the economic stimulus bill was 41 percent positive (Farnsworth and Lichter 2011b). The overall economic news figures were roughly in line with Obama's overall first-year coverage of 47 percent positive and 53 percent negative, and better than the news of economic matters on network television during the first year of Bill Clinton's presidency in 1993 and Ronald Reagan's first year in office in 1981 (Farnsworth and Lichter 2011b). Unfortunately for Obama, and for other presidents presiding over tough economic times, bad economic news generates more media attention than good news does. That focus on bad news also brings down consumer confidence (Farnsworth and Lichter 2006a; Gawthorne 2010; Menz 2010; Schatz 2009). On the bright side, though, media coverage of financial scandals often treats business officials more negatively than the political leaders (Schatz 2010a).

HEALTH CARE REFORM

Although the issue mattered less than the economy to most Americans (and, for that matter, to the international television news viewers whose own economic fortunes would be enhanced by a rapid US economic recovery), Obama focused heavily on reforming health care during his first year in office. In order to avoid the interest group attacks that doomed Bill Clinton's efforts to pass health care legislation in 1994, the new president quickly developed a compromise plan that ensured that two politically powerful organizations in this area—the pharmaceutical industry and American Medical Association—could live with the bill (Abelson 2010; Connolly 2009; Jacobs 2012). Beyond that preemptive compromising, Obama left much of the specific legislative drafting to Capitol Hill.

By putting legislators in the driver's seat, however, the bill was delayed, making health care reform far more controversial as Capitol Hill debates dragged on. Neither legislative chamber passed a bill before the August 2009 recess. The absence of a specific plan for Democrats to defend led to the rise of wild speculation about what would eventually be part of the bill (Sinclair 2012). Some town hall meetings descended into raucous affairs that gave considerable media visibility to the nascent Tea Party movement and helped congressional Republicans argue that the legislation would make health care worse for many Americans than the status quo (Jacobson 2012; Sinclair 2012). Sarah Palin, the 2008 Republican vice presidential nominee who quit her job as governor of Alaska in mid-term to become a pundit on Fox News, spoke of "death panels" that were not part of the bill, but many Americans believed her anyway (Rutenberg and Calmes 2009).

A bill eventually passed Congress with almost no Republican support and was signed by Obama on March 23, 2010. The bill, which fell far short of the government-run single-payer system that liberal Democrats favored, left the private sector in charge of much of the business of US health care. The Obama plan increased the number of people who would be able to obtain health care, reduced health care costs for seniors and young adults, and established a tax for people who refuse to obtain health care (Stolberg and Pear 2010).

Passage of the Affordable Care Act (or "Obamacare") gave Republicans a valuable issue to campaign on during the 2010 midterm elections (Herszenhorn and Pear 2010). Democrats lost more than sixty House seats (and their majority) that year. They retained their majority in the Senate, but the party lost six seats, and it was left with fifty-three of one hundred seats, including the two independents caucusing with the Democrats (Sinclair 2012).

Coverage of the health care debate was relatively positive on US network newscasts. A CMPA analysis of Obama's first year in office found that the health care bill was the number-two topic on the Obama presidency (behind the economic stimulus bill), and coverage of the bill on ABC, CBS, and NBC was 53 percent positive and 47 percent negative. That coverage was far more positive than the stories relating to health care matters during the first presidential years of George W. Bush and Bill Clinton (Farnsworth and Lichter 2011b).

US PUBLIC OPINION FOLLOWING ECONOMIC STIMULUS AND HEALTH CARE REFORM

Having passed a controversial economic stimulus and an even more controversial health care bill, Democrats entered the 2010 midterm elections politically bloodied. Voters may have wanted an activist government, but they wanted that activity focused on reviving the economy. As shown in table 3.1, the American public of 2010 wanted substantial government involvement in a number of policy areas, particularly concerning the nation's financial troubles. The top two categories, as one would expect, involve strengthening the nation's economy and improving the job situation. Each was rated as a top or important priority for government action by more than 95 percent of those surveyed. Also high on the

Table 3.1. US Public Preferences for US Policy, 2010

Question: "I'd like to ask you some questions about priorities for President Obama and Congress this year. As I read from a list, tell me if you think the item that I read should be a top priority, important but lower priority, not too important, or should not be done." (Items were read in random order.)

Issue	Top Priority %	Important %
1. Strengthening the nation's economy	83	14
2. Improving the job situation	81	15
3. Defending the country from future terrorist attacks	80	17
4. Taking steps to make Social Security financially sound	66	28
5. Improving the educational system	65	28
6. Taking steps to make Medicare financially sound	63	30
7. Reducing the budget deficit	60	29
8. Reducing health care costs	57	31
9. Dealing with the problems of poor and needy people	53	38
10. (tie). Reducing crime	49	39
11. (tie). Dealing with the nation's energy problem	49	39
12. Strengthening the US military	49	35
13. Providing health insurance to the uninsured	49	34
14. Stricter regulation of financial institutions	45	36
15. Dealing with the moral breakdown in the country	45	31
16. Protecting the environment	44	42
17. Reducing federal income taxes on the middle class	42	40
18. Dealing with the issue of illegal immigration	40	41
19. Reducing the influence of lobbyists/special interests	36	34
20. Dealing with global trade issues	32	46
21. Dealing with global warming	28	36

Source: Pew (2010a). The results here are from a nationwide telephone survey of 1,504 US adults conducted January 6–10, 2010. The results from the full survey have a margin of sampling error of plus or minus three percentage points.
Note: Percentages do not add to 100 because not all response options are reported here.

public's list were protecting against a terrorist attack, saving Social Security and Medicare, fixing the public schools, and reducing the deficit.

Even as Americans demand aggressive government action in range of policy areas, they also worry about governmental overreach. As the support for the health care bill coalesced, so, too, did its opposition. America remained a deeply divided nation on health care, and US public opinion polls show a roughly even division on many other issues as well (Rockman and Rudalevige 2012). The president's Tea Party critics tapped into a traditional American skepticism of big government that would serve the movement well in the 2010 midterms and beyond (Jacobson 2012).

For Barack Obama, who came to office facing a host of problems inherited from the Bush years, the magnitude of his administration's activities became a major public opinion problem going into the 2010 midterm elections. Even following the near-collapses of the US financial system and the US auto industry, and while the United States remained mired in the worst economic downturn in a generation, Americans' deep skepticism of government's capacity to manage the economy remained robust. In April 2009, just a few months after the government rescued the faltering financial sector, 54 percent of Americans agreed that "government regulation of business does more harm than good," about the same as the 57 percent who agreed with that statement in a 2007 survey conducted more than a year before the crisis hit (Balz and Cohen 2007, 2010).

As shown in table 3.2, the public did not view the Obama presidency or his policy actions all that unfavorably going into the 2010 midterm elections. The president's overall job approval rating stood at 50 percent in October 2010, roughly where presidents usually are at the midpoint of their first terms (cf. Balz and Cohen 2010). In addition, Obama remained far more popular than Congress.

On specific issue areas, the Democrats also fared reasonably well. Voters favored the Democrats over the Republicans on a host of issues, including the key issues of the economy and health care, and particularly on helping the middle class. While the Republicans had slight preferences on policies relating to the federal budget deficit and taxes, the differences were within the margin of sampling error.

Where the GOP really had its advantage was in voter intensity, and differing levels of voter enthusiasm are particularly important factors in midterm elections (Jacobson 2012). While the public was split on the health care bill, the GOP's newly energized congressional leadership announced after the 2010 elections that they planned to try to repeal the new law (Murray and Bacon 2010). Widespread public controversy over the law—and Republican promises to repeal it and drag their feet in funding it—remained in place even after the US Supreme Court declared the measure constitutional in June 2012 (Liptak 2012).

Table 3.2. US Public Opinion: Obama versus the Republicans, October 2010

Question: "Do you approve or disapprove of the way (ITEM) are/is doing their/his job?"

	Approve	Disapprove	No opinion
Barack Obama	50	47	3
Congress	24	73	3
The Democrats in Congress	36	61	3
The Republicans in Congress	30	67	3

Question: "Which political party, the (Democrats) or the (Republicans), do you trust to do a better job handling ___?"

	Democrats	Republicans	Both (vol.)	Neither (vol.)	No opinion
a. The economy	44	37	4	14	2
b. Health care	46	38	1	12	3
c. Immigration issues	37	37	3	17	6
d. The situation in Afghanistan	39	34	4	19	4
e. The federal budget deficit	39	40	2	18	1
f. Taxes	40	43	3	13	2
g. Helping the middle class	50	34	2	11	2

(Half of the sample asked items a–c; the other half asked items d–f, full sample g.)

Question: "Do you think the money the federal government has spent on the economic stimulus has been mostly (well spent) or mostly (wasted)?"

	Well spent	Wasted	No opinion
10/3/10	29	68	4

Question: "Given what you know about them, would you say you support or oppose the changes to the health care system that have been enacted by (Congress) and (the Obama administration)?"

	Support	Oppose	No opinion
10/3/10	47	48	5
3/26/10	46	50	4

Source: Balz and Cohen (2010). This *Washington Post*-ABC News Poll was conducted by TNS of Horsham, Pennsylvania, by telephone September 30–October 3, 2010. It is based on a random national sample of 1,002 adults using both landline and cellular phones. The results from the full survey have a margin of sampling error of plus or minus three percentage points.

OBAMA AND CHARACTER

One key factor that distinguishes the Obama media strategy from those of Bush and Clinton is a greater hesitancy to try to dominate the policy discourse. Despite the powerful advantages a president has in the shaping of domestic news content, Obama tended to be relatively deferential in policy matters, preferring to focus his media team's energies on promoting a positive general image of himself as president rather than agitating aggressively on every policy matter. As noted above, for example, the new administration left many of the health care legislative details to Capitol Hill. Likewise, Obama gave congressional leaders considerable authority to craft both an economic stimulus package and a regulatory reform plan for the banking industry (Sinclair 2012). This may be smart politics, as Congress may be more likely to pass its own creations. But this collaborative approach to lawmaking stands in sharp contrast to Obama's two most recent predecessors, both of whom sought to dominate Washington and the national discourse in a way that Obama has not (Farnsworth 2009).

This same personal diffidence is also sometimes seen in debates over Obama's personality. Nowhere are the consequences of failing to drive the narrative of one's own identity clearer than in the large numbers of Americans who wondered whether their president is a Christian.

Obama's identity as a practicing Christian was made clear during one of the major religious issues of the 2008 campaign, the controversy over the sermons of Obama's outspoken former pastor, Reverend Jeremiah Wright (Denton 2009). But the president's critics still were able to reshape the narrative in a negative way for many Americans. As shown in table 3.3, only 34 percent of Americans were convinced in August 2009 that Obama is a Christian, down fourteen percentage points from a March 2009 survey. While less than one in five Americans believed in 2009 that Obama is a Muslim, a surprising 43 percent said they did not know Obama's religion. The declining percentages of people saying that Obama is a Christian during the first year of his presidency is seen even among supportive groups, as growing numbers of even Democrats and African Americans are saying that they are not sure about Obama's religious preference.

Even after Obama had been president for three-and-a-half years the numbers did not improve by much. In a July 2012 survey, only 49 percent of the US population could correctly identify Obama as a Christian. Some 17 percent mistakenly believed he was a Muslim, and 31 percent said they did not know Obama's religion (Pew Forum 2012). The remaining 2 percent said he was neither a Christian nor a Muslim but rather something else. These results speak to the limited ability of the mass media to shape public understandings of even this basic issue. Although the media often discounted the rumors that Obama was a Muslim, the allegations retained considerable support in a public whose

Table 3.3. US Public Uncertainty Concerning Obama's Religion

	Obama is a Christian		Obama is a Muslim		Don't Know	
	Aug 2010	*Change from Mar '09*	*Aug 2010*	*Change from Mar '09*	*Aug 2010*	*Change from Mar '09*
Total	34	-14	18	+07	43	+09
White	35	-15	21	+10	40	+08
Black	43	-13	07	+01	46	+10
Republican	27	-20	31	+14	39	+11
Independent	34	-11	18	+08	44	+06
Democrat	46	-09	10	+03	41	+09
White Evangelical	27	-12	29	+09	42	+09
White Mainline Protestant	36	-15	22	+12	40	+08
White Catholic	32	-19	18	+08	46	+10
Unaffiliated	38	-09	13	+07	44	+07

Source: Pew (2010b), "Growing Number of Americans Say Obama Is a Muslim," released August 19, 2010. The survey was conducted among a random national sample of 3,003 adults contacted by telephone between July 21 and August 5, 2010. Sample includes people contacted via landline and cellular telephones. The results from the full survey have a margin of sampling error of plus or minus 2.5 percentage points.

members sometimes express considerable doubts about the mainstream media (Rutenberg 2008).

Perhaps Obama could have done more to combat this perception that he may not be a Christian, which is not helpful to his public approval ratings. (Although the Constitution prohibits the establishment of any religious qualification for public office, the American populace is overwhelmingly Christian, and every president in American history has been a Christian.) Were he to choose to do so, the president could speak more about his Christian faith during his many public statements and make more public appearances with his family in churches on Sundays to resolve this important lingering public doubt about Obama's fundamental convictions. Of course, his previous efforts at outreach aimed at evangelical Christians—such as inviting Reverend Rick Warren to give an inaugural ceremony prayer in 2009—did not seem to generate much goodwill among Christian conservatives. Although biblical teachings suggest one should pray in private and not make too public a demonstration of one's religious devotion, practical political realities in the United States suggest otherwise. (Latter-day Pharisees, a group known for making loud, ostentatious displays of their religiosity, have often done well in US politics.)

Another issue raised by the president's critics is whether Obama was even eligible to be president. Perhaps he was born outside the United States, and therefore not a native citizen, these die-hard Obama opponents claimed. Apparently operating under the theory that late was better than never, Obama did release his Hawaii birth certificate in 2011 to try to quell the years-long controversy (Shear 2011). Even so, the debate over whether Obama was a genuine American continued into the 2012 presidential election (Parker 2012), further evidence that more aggressive efforts earlier on would have helped shield the president from such false charges.

One of the biggest mysteries about Obama, who has consistently appeared before the public in a cool and collected manner, is how such a mild public temperament and such a consensus-seeking governing strategy gives rise to such emotional reactions among his fellow citizens.

> Obama arouses both adulation and—not to put too fine a point on it—hatred. And these contradictory critiques run in parallel with contradictory behavior by voters—or if not contradictions exactly, sharp reversals in rapid sequence so precipitous that they might as well be contradictions. (Rockman and Rudalevige 2012:1)

We see from the above tables a couple of general findings relating to Obama's ability to shape political discourse within the United States about his policies and himself. First, Obama generally does not seek to, nor does he succeed in, dominating the US political discourse in the way some of his predecessors did. Obama's relatively quiet approach (for a president) to governing means that even fundamental personality questions are left unresolved in the minds of many voters years into his presidency.

The handling of policy matters likewise showed considerable public resistance to the new president's legislative agenda. To be sure, the highly partisan political environment that marked the Obama years undermines the president's ability to succeed in shaping the media and public discourse in ways to his liking. The same challenges that Bush faced with an unfriendly public policy narrative during his second term bedeviled Obama much sooner in his presidency, even during its opening months.

But Obama cannot fault the mainstream media for the problematic character narrative being spread by his enemies. A CMPA analysis found that 71 percent of the references to Obama's personality or character on ABC, CBS, and NBC were positive, as compared to 35 percent positive coverage of his policies. Obama even received 56 percent positive coverage of personality matters on Fox News's nightly newscast, where coverage of his policies was only 16 percent positive (Farnsworth and Lichter 2012b). (Of course, the talk shows on Fox News are another story altogether.) Clearly, presidents who emphasize personality in their appearances before the cameras do not hurt the tone of their coverage.

Examining International Television Coverage of Obama

Our Media Tenor content analysis of the first eighteen months of the Obama presidency addresses some key questions about the new president's international news coverage. Did Obama enjoy a presidential honeymoon in international media, as he did in the United States? If so, how long did it last, and did it last longer in some nations than others? Were international media generally more positive toward Obama, as one might expect given the higher levels of international mass public and elite support for the new president? How did international media outlets examine questions of character? Was this coverage more positive in international media than in US news reports?

These questions arise from the enthusiasm that greeted Obama's election in many nations, his aggressive international outreach efforts, and the greater access US news outlets have to a wide range of influential voices willing to criticize the president, particularly as the press-presidential "honeymoon" period erodes. Since foreign news reporters are at a considerable disadvantage compared to US reporters in their access to authoritative and critical sources, one might expect that White House spin may have an even greater advantage over alternative framing efforts regarding the United States by other political actors in international media (cf. Entman 2004; Hamilton and Jenner 2003; Hannerz 2004; Hess 2005).

As discussed above, presidents are often more effective at communicating positive character traits than their positions in contested public policy matters (cf. Farnsworth 2009; Farnsworth and Lichter 2006a, 2012b, 2013). A presidential-focused news approach seems particularly likely for international coverage of US affairs, since foreign audiences may have very limited interest in the details of US domestic partisan disagreements. Given the literature that points to high correlations between public preferences and news content, one would expect that the more positive a nation's public is toward US policies, the more positive the tone of news about Obama will be (cf. Hallin and Mancini 2004a).

Our analysis in this chapter is based on 29,834 statements relating to Obama on evening newscasts on five Arabic-language television outlets, two British and two German television outlets, as well as 46,890 statements on four US outlets (ABC, CBS, NBC, and Fox News). The sample period extends from January 1, 2009, through June 30, 2010, roughly corresponding to the first eighteen months of the Obama presidency. (Although presidents do not take office until January 20, the Media Tenor analysis includes the news relating to the president-elect from the start of the year.) Coders worked from taped newscasts, and a few broadcasts were missed because of technical glitches involved in the recording of broadcasts. The missing tapes are distributed randomly through the sample period, and there is no reason to suspect the missing tapes, if available, would skew the results. At least two broadcast outlets for each region are included here in order to gain a general sense of the overall news discussion in a given region.

The Middle East news outlets examined here include the evening newscasts of Al-Jazeera Arabic, an editorially independent news channel developed by the emir of Qatar; Al-Arabiyah, a Dubai-based affiliate of the Middle East Broadcasting Center (owned by a member of the Saudi royal family); Nile News of Egypt; the Lebanese Broadcasting Corporation (LBC); and Al-Manar TV, which is connected to Hezbollah (cf. Leenders 2007; Murphy 2006; Seib 2005).

The European news outlets used here include the 10 p.m. newscast on BBC1, Newsnight on BBC2, and the late evening newscasts of two state-owned German broadcasters, ARD Tagesthemen and ZDF heute journal. Unlike government-supported broadcasters in some other nations, both of these international media environments offer significant protection from government pressure regarding the news, though no such insulation can be absolute (Fraser 2000; Hallin and Mancini 2004a; Raboy 1996).

The European outlets considered here, based in nations where citizens are enthusiastic about Obama, therefore should be more positive than Arab media, located in a region where feelings about the United States are not as positive. The Pew Global (2010a, 2010b) data suggest that Germany's news might be slightly more positive than the BBC, given that Germans are marginally more enthusiastic about Obama. (Pew Global [2010a, 2010b] does not include all nations with media examined in this study in its international public opinion surveys, but survey evidence from other nations within the Middle East suggest that the populations of Britain and Germany generally were far more enthusiastic about Obama than were people in Muslim-majority nations.)

This expected pattern of media content also suggests that Arabic-language broadcasters will vary in their approaches, with Al-Manar, connected to the anti-US Hezbollah, the most negative. More positive news about Obama will likely come from Al-Arabiyah, a cable news outlet owned by a member of the royal family of longtime US ally Saudi Arabia. We would expect the tone of news at other Arab outlets to lay between these two more politically connected outlets.

Tone of International Coverage

The net tone ratings for the three media groups appear in table 3.4. As before, the net tone measure used by Media Tenor is the percentage of positive tone minus the percentage of negative tone. Most statements appearing on these television outlets are neutral or mixed in tone. A 0 percent net tone score represents an equal amount of positive and negative tone. (Tone that was 100 percent neutral

Table 3.4. News Coverage of Obama by Media Location

Location	Year	Net tone %	Negative %	Positive %	No clear rating %	N
Europe	2009	5.7	9.1	14.9	76.0	13,299
	2010*	−6.8	16.9	10.2	72.9	3,000
Arab	2009	7.7	9.5	17.2	73.4	9,976
	2010*	−4.0	15.8	11.8	72.4	3,559
US	2009	−8.0	15.3	7.4	77.3	35,989
	2010*	−12.0	18.9	6.8	74.3	10,901

* Data for 2010 through June 30.
N = Number of statements. Percentages might not sum to 100 because of rounding. This table is based on a content analysis of 29,834 statements relating to Barack Obama on nine international television news networks (ARD Tagesthemen, ZDF heute journal, BBC1 10 O'clock News, BBC2 Newsnight, Al-Arabiyah, Nile News, LBC, Al-Manar, and Al-Jazeera) and 46,890 statements on four US television news networks (ABC, CBS, NBC, and Fox News) from January 1, 2009, through June 30, 2010.

would also register as a zero in this classification system.) As before, the larger the positive number, the more positive the overall tone; the larger the negative number, the more negative the overall tone.

These overall results show an international honeymoon effect that resembles the honeymoon seen in US media. In all groups of media, reports on Obama were more positive during his first year in office than his second. But the international media were consistently more positive than the US media. Among all media groups, the Arab media stood out as the most positive (or least negative) toward the new president. This finding directly contradicts the assumption that the most critical media coverage would come from nations with the most critical mass publics.

Table 3.5 provides month-by-month comparisons of the tone of coverage for Obama on German, United Kingdom, Arab, and US television. The figures show a presidential honeymoon for all categories, though the era of good feelings lasted longer for some media outlets than others. Turning first to the international news, all three non-US media groups offered net positive results for the new president during 2009, Obama's first year in office. Looking at the monthly results, we see the Arabic-language media were the only media group to be positive about the new president for every one of the new president's first eight months. In contrast, the United Kingdom media's first net negative month was May 2009, five months in, when the tone was 5.2 percent net negative. The German media had their first negative month, albeit barely, in February 2009, the month after the new president was sworn in. The tone in the news reports on Obama that month was 1.5 percent net negative.

Over the entire eighteen-month period, the UK broadcasts were notably more negative than the German or Arabic television groups. Although the UK news reports on Obama were negative for only nine of the eighteen months examined here, four of those months were more than 10 percent net negative. Indeed, Obama's two worst monthly showings on international media were in the United Kingdom during May and June 2010. While the German media had as many negative months as the United Kingdom, nine of eighteen, only three of those months were more than 10 percent net negative. The Arabic-language media also had eight negative months, though none in double digits.

The Arab TV news data suggest the success of Obama's early outreach efforts to the region and the magnitude of the change that the new president was thought to represent. Five of the new president's first six months in office had net tone measures about 10 percent positive, as compared to only one such positive month during that same period on UK news and three on German television. Given these findings, perhaps Obama should have spent more time cozying up to German and UK publics and leaders as well!

Table 3.5.   Net Tone of News Coverage of Obama over Time

Month	Germany	UK	Arab	NBC	Fox
January 2009	18.5	12.2	19.3	10.2	–3.9
February	–1.5	3.8	14.8	–7.6	–7.1
March	0.6	7.5	10.6	–6.2	–13.4
April	18.3	3.2	12.0	7.1	–13.3
May	–0.9	–5.2	4.0	–6.8	–14.0
June	11.2	1.1	13.8	3.1	–15.9
July 2009	6.2	7.8	7.3	–9.0	–17.9
August	–5.5	–12.3	7.1	–4.4	–27.0
September	1.8	–5.0	–1.1	–10.7	–16.9
October	–4.1	11.0	6.1	–7.8	–16.4
November	1.6	1.5	–3.6	0.3	–13.7
December	–0.7	–2.4	–2.7	–1.2	–11.7
January 2010	–12.9	–14.5	–2.2	–8.6	–22.1
February	–13.8	–2.2	–6.8	–19.4	–20.1
March	9.1	10.7	–4.8	2.6	–8.0
April	8.0	–4.6	–5.1	–3.4	–10.6
May	–13.7	–25.6	2.3	–10.3	–15.3
June	–6.7	–26.8	–8.7	–8.4	–19.5
Net Tone 2009	7.7	3.2	7.7	–1.9	–13.5
2010*	–3.9	–12.1	–4.0	–6.3	–16.3

Figures are net tone percentages.
* Data for 2010 through June 30.
N = Number of statements. Percentages might not sum to 100 because of rounding. This table is
  based on a content analysis of 29,834 statements relating to Barack Obama on nine interna-
  tional television news networks (ARD Tagesthemen, ZDF heute journal, BBC1 10 O'clock News,
  BBC2 Newsnight, Al-Arabiyah, Nile News, LBC, Al-Manar, and Al-Jazeera), 8,188 statements on
  NBC News, and 22,725 statements on Fox News.

One of the most critical periods for Obama on the international news outlets occurred during the winter of 2010, when Scott Brown (R-Mass.) won the
US Senate special election to replace one of America's most visible liberals, US
Senator Edward M. Kennedy. Brown's election was seen as a blow to Obama's
political fortunes as well as a suggestion that the Democratic president's popularity was short-lived, even in one of the nation's most liberal states (Cooper 2010).
Brown served only briefly, as Democrat Elizabeth Warren won that seat back for
the Democrats in November 2012.

The international media were also relatively critical of Obama during the
spring of 2010, as Republican candidates appeared to be gaining strength as the
midterm elections that year drew near. In those midterm elections, Republicans

captured a majority of seats in the US House and reduced the size of the Democratic Party's Senate majority, largely based on public anger with Obama's economic and health care policies (Baker and Hulse 2010; Zeleny 2010). During the summer of 2009, when the Tea Party movement became more visible in its condemnation of Obama's health care proposal, international news coverage of the new president also trended downward.

The generally kind treatment Obama received from international media during most of his first eighteen months in office was quite different from the far more critical reporting in US media. But the US news about Obama was not all that negative at first. As table 3.5 shows, even on the conservative Fox network Obama received something approaching a honeymoon, at least in relative terms, during his two months in office. While his coverage was negative on Fox for all eighteen months of this study, it was least negative in January and February 2009. After that came the deluge—fifteen of the eighteen months we examined featured double-digit negative coverage. The most negative month for Obama on Fox was August 2009, when the anti–health care reform public hearings were at their most vocal and most visible. The news reports that month were 27 percent net negative, the worst month for Obama in any category listed in the table.

On NBC, the network whose evening newscasts attract the largest US audience, coverage was less negative than on Fox but still largely critical of the new president. NBC had positive coverage of Obama for five of the eighteen months, including when he was inaugurated in January 2009, and the months of his well-received trips to Istanbul (April 2009) and Cairo (June 2009). The other two positive months were marked by passage in the US House of Representatives of the first version of a health care reform bill in November 2009 and March 2010, the month when he secured final congressional approval of the health care bill and signed it into law. The most negative month on NBC for Obama, February 2010, came in the wake of Scott Brown's election, which cast doubt on the prospects for many of Obama's legislative initiatives, including health care reform.

Obama won the Nobel Peace Prize in October of 2009, but that was not a particularly good month for the president on either NBC or Fox. The month also marked the first time that the US unemployment rate exceeded 10 percent during the Obama presidency. It was one of his best months on UK television, with 11 percent net positive coverage, and a positive month on the Arabic-language media (6.1 percent net positive). The coverage was 4.1 percent net negative on German TV, still more positive than the US networks.

During Obama's first year, his coverage was net positive on the three international media groups and only slightly (1.9 percent net) negative on NBC. Fox News stood out in comparison, with reports on the new president that were 13.5 percent net negative. During the first half of Obama's second year, Fox News again stood out as the most critical, 16.3 percent net negative in tone. But the differences among outlets were not as great, as the UK media also soured on the new president, with reports that were 12.1 percent net negative in tone.

Table 3.6 presents the content analysis data separately for each of the nine international and four US news outlets. The table shows in greater detail how the new president's media "honeymoon" was notably more positive and longer lasting at many individual international news outlets. Not one of the five Arab media outlets—regardless of ownership—was as negative about Obama as any one of the four US news outlets. Indeed, it is striking how similar these very different Arab news outlets were in their treatment of the new president,

Table 3.6.   News Coverage of Obama by Media Outlet

News Outlet	Year	Net tone %	Negative %	Positive %	No clear rating %	N
ARD Tagesthemen	2009	7.4	10.5	17.9	71.6	3,400
	2010*	–3.3	13.5	10.2	76.3	993
ZDF heute journal	2009	7.9	10.0	17.9	72.0	4,145
	2010*	–4.6	14.3	9.7	76.0	966
BBC1 10 O'clock News	2009	0.1	6.6	6.7	86.8	2,870
	2010*	–8.1	18.4	10.2	71.4	528
BBC2 Newsnight	2009	6.2	8.8	15.0	76.2	2,884
	2010*	–16.2	27.1	10.9	62.0	513
Al-Arabiyah	2009	4.4	4.0	8.4	87.6	3,754
	2010*	–4.9	9.9	5.0	85.2	1,085
Nile News	2009	9.5	6.6	16.0	77.4	2,175
	2010*	–5.1	8.3	3.2	88.6	824
LBC	2009	2.4	5.0	7.4	87.5	755
	2010*	–1.1	1.1	0.0	98.9	265
Al-Manar	2009	6.3	21.4	27.6	51.0	1,770
	2010*	–4.0	32.9	29.0	38.1	835
Al-Jazeera	2009	17.5	15.4	32.9	51.7	1,522
	2010*	–2.0	19.8	17.8	62.4	550
ABC	2009	–2.0	9.6	7.6	82.8	7,157
	2010*	–7.1	13.7	6.6	79.7	1,789
CBS	2009	–5.1	14.6	9.5	75.9	5,465
	2010*	–8.6	16.8	8.2	75.0	1,566
NBC	2009	–1.9	11.1	9.2	79.7	6,359
	2010*	–6.3	13.5	7.2	79.3	1,829
Fox News	2009	–13.5	19.4	6.0	74.7	17,008
	2010*	–16.3	22.7	6.4	70.8	5,717

* Data for 2010 through June 30.

N = Number of statements. Percentages might not sum to 100 because of rounding. This table is based on a content analysis of 29,834 statements relating to Barack Obama on nine international television news networks and 46,890 statements on four US television news networks from January 1, 2009, through June 30, 2010.

with all providing mostly positive reports of his first year. Perhaps the region's media outlets anticipated that Obama might be a fairer mediator of the Israeli-Palestinian dispute than Bush was thought to be.

Al-Jazeera, which has been criticized for anti-US news coverage in the past, was the most positive outlet of all thirteen news organizations analyzed here, with coverage that was 17.5 percent net positive in 2009. Nile News, the Egyptian state broadcaster, was the second most positive outlet, with reports that were 9.5 percent net positive. (Obama's visit to Cairo might have helped with that assessment.) The two German newscasts were ranked third and fourth among these media outlets in their relatively positive treatment of Obama. Al-Manar, the voice of Hezbollah, ranked fifth overall and third among the Arabic-language media in upbeat assessments of Obama, with coverage that was 6.3 percent net positive. The two UK broadcasters lagged behind the German news reports. As with Arab media, however, all four European outlets were less critical of Obama than any of the four US outlets.

Very similar international coverage appeared during the first half of Obama's second year, again marked by relatively favorable treatment in Arabic-language and, to a lesser extent, German newscasts. Again, "favorable" is a relative term. All these outlets provided coverage that was roughly balanced or slightly negative. The most positive 2010 coverage came from the Lebanese Broadcasting Corporation (LBC), which was only 1.1 percent net negative. Al-Jazeera placed second, ARD Tagesthemen ranked third, Al-Manar fourth, and ZDF heute journal fifth.

Once again, the two UK broadcasters examined here were more critical than the German news reports. The most critical international news outlet was BBC2 Newsnight, with reports on Obama that were 16.2 percent net negative. This was the only international outlet with double-digit net negative reports during either period of the Obama presidency. The 10 O'clock News on BBC1 was the second most critical international outlet, with reports that were 8.1 percent net negative.

Fox News was the most negative outlet during both 2009 and 2010, though it edged out BBC2's Newsnight only narrowly as the most critical for the latter period. (Note that the Fox analysis includes the entire hour of *Special Report*, rather than the first half hour sometimes used by researchers. Because the second half hour contains more roundtable commentary, full hour results are likely more negative.) As we have discussed, relatively negative network television newscasts are the norm in the United States, where presidents face mostly harsh reports throughout their terms of office (cf. Farnsworth and Lichter 2006a).

Presidents are often thought to be particularly effective at marketing themselves, winning elections, and raising their public approval ratings by focusing attention on matters of personality and character (cf. Farnsworth 2009). In

Table 3.7.   News Coverage of Obama's Personality and Ability to Govern

News Outlet	Topic	Net tone %	Negative %	Positive %	No clear rating %	N
ARD Tagesthemen	Personality	14.4	8.8	23.2	68.0	125
	Govern	8.4	11.1	19.5	69.4	431
ZDF heute journal	Personality	19.8	8.2	28.0	63.8	207
	Govern	7.9	15.1	23.0	61.9	582
BBC1 10 O'clock News	Personality	10.4	10.8	21.3	67.9	240
	Govern	–8.0	11.2	3.3	85.5	338
BBC2 Newsnight	Personality	15.3	13.0	28.3	58.7	470
	Govern	–19.6	30.2	10.6	59.3	199
Al-Arabiyah	Personality	13.0	5.7	18.7	75.7	653
	Govern	3.9	5.4	9.3	85.3	129
Nile News	Personality	4.4	4.4	8.8	86.8	342
	Govern	0.0	0.0	0.0	100.0	41
LBC	Personality	0.0	2.1	2.1	95.7	281
	Govern	–*	–	–	–	–*
Al-Manar	Personality	7.5	11.7	19.1	69.1	94
	Govern	42.9	7.1	50.0	42.9	14
Al-Jazeera	Personality	19.4	14.4	33.8	51.9	160
	Govern	38.1	0.0	38.1	61.9	42
ABC	Personality	7.3	5.5	12.8	81.7	507
	Govern	–2.8	11.4	8.6	79.9	324
CBS	Personality	5.9	7.7	13.6	78.8	273
	Govern	–21.7	27.0	5.3	67.8	152
NBC	Personality	8.1	4.5	12.6	82.9	596
	Govern	–12.3	22.8	10.5	66.7	171
Fox	Personality	–8.4	17.5	9.2	73.3	633
	Govern	–16.2	22.7	6.5	70.8	612

* Insufficient number of cases to classify (less than ten).
N = Number of statements. Percentages might not sum to 100 because of rounding. This table is based on a content analysis of 29,954 statements relating to Barack Obama on nine international television news networks and 46,890 statements on four US television news networks from January 1, 2009, through June 30, 2010.

table 3.7 we see that character remains an effective part of the way Obama was presented in twelve of the thirteen outlets—only Fox News was more negative than positive in the assessments of his personality and character. The most positive reporting on presidential character appeared on international media, led by ZDF heute journal (19.8 percent net positive), Al-Jazeera (19.4 percent net positive), BBC2 (15.3 percent positive), and Al-Arabiyah (13 percent net positive). There was less of a distinction here among the European news outlets on this dimension, as the German and UK broadcasters were all net positive in the double-digit range.

There was more divergence within the Arabic-language group here than we have seen in other assessments of Obama, perhaps because issues of personality lend themselves more to interpretation than other matters. Obama's credibility, a part of the personality coverage category, seemed more suspect to the broadcasters located closest to Israel (LBC, Nile News, and Al-Manar). We will focus in considerable detail on news reports relating to US policies in the Middle East—perhaps the region with the most intractable foreign policy challenges for the United States—when we compare news reports on that topic in chapter 5.

US broadcast network news reports on Obama's personality and character during his first eighteen months in office were consistently positive, but less so than in most international outlets. Among those three outlets, the reports were quite similar in tone, ranging from 8.1 percent net positive on NBC to 5.9 percent net positive on CBS. Once again, Fox News gave a distinctly critical view on the Obama presidency—even in its news reports relating to the president's character—when compared to both the US broadcast networks and international media.

GOVERNING

General matters of governing are a different story. Even though we examined a time of Democratic Party control of both houses of Congress, the partisan disagreements that have marked the Obama presidency do not always look pretty, particularly when viewed from abroad. The deal making and compromises necessary to secure legislative approval for his stimulus bills, health care reform, and environmental legislation are not likely to inspire admiration regarding American politics in action. In parliamentary systems, a majority government faces far less obstruction from a minority than exists within the designed-for-conflict US political system (Jones 1994, 1995; Neustadt 1990). Even so, two Arab broadcasters often viewed as particularly critical of the United States—Al-Manar and Al-Jazeera—once again offered the most positive portrayals of Obama, with 42.9 percent net positive tone and 38.1 percent net positive treatment of his capacity for governing. Al-Arabiyah, a relatively pro-US news outlet, was slightly upbeat in this regard (3.9 percent net positive), though not as positive as the two German news outlets.

The six English-language news outlets were the most negative in their reports on Obama's governing. As expected, the US television programs, with their ready pool of authoritative critics on Capitol Hill, aired particularly critical reports. The most negative in this case was CBS, with 21.7 percent net negative coverage of governing. Fox News ranked third on this measure, with 16.2 percent net negative tone, behind CBS and BBC2 Newsnight (19.6 percent net negative tone). NBC was the fourth most negative news outlet when it came to discussions of Obama's governing performance, with reports that were 12.3 percent net negative.

Conclusion

This chapter offered a number of insights regarding news coverage of the first eighteen months of the Obama presidency. The new president enjoyed a generous honeymoon in international media, particularly during his first year. His reception was more positive on international television news than in domestic media. Reporting on the president's character was a major part of international news reports, and it was an area where Obama was highly regarded. All of these results conform to conventional wisdom.

In a departure from our expectations and past research, however, Obama received relatively favorable treatment in Middle Eastern media on all the topics examined here—often more positive reports than those found in European media. Likewise, the reports from the Arabic-language media were consistently more positive than the coverage the new president received from US media.

The most surprising aspect of this departure from past studies concerns the very positive treatment Obama regularly received on Al-Jazeera, a source of particular concern for Washington during the Bush years. The end of the Bush presidency and Obama's outreach efforts to Muslims appear to have triggered more enthusiasm for the United States than one would have expected based on relatively negative public opinion toward the United States (cf. Pew Global 2010a, 2010b). This suggests the need for some refinements in theories positing that television news caters closely to viewers' tastes. It also suggests that Al-Jazeera, at least as of 2009, might be viewed as a media outlet in the second or perhaps the third stage of development under the Stromback (2007) model. In other words, preferences of elites may matter more than audience desires for some of these outlets.

The European media, particularly German news reports, performed largely as expected. German news stories tended to be more positive on most measures than US and UK media, demonstrating the utility of examining news content in light of public perspectives in the nation where the media are based (cf. Hallin and Mancini 2004a). Of course, Obama's special outreach efforts to Germans, including his unprecedented appearance in Berlin in the midst of a presidential campaign (cf. Wright 2005a, 2005b), may also have continued to pay dividends in news content there.

Among the Arabic-language media, one might have expected a bit more favorable treatment from Al-Arabiyah, which is close to the Saudi royal family, a family closely aligned with the United States. Perhaps the Saudi regime's close ties with the Bush family made them a bit more skeptical of the new president than other Arabic-language media. And Obama's decision to emphasize building stronger ties with Egypt and Turkey, longtime potential rivals for influence in the region, may have given Saudi reporters pause.

Research involving additional nations—most notably Italy and France for the Europeans—can provide fuller tests of the various classification models proposed by other scholars, as well as untangle the explanatory factors when public approval of the United States closely corresponds with the level of support by political leaders (cf. Hallin and Mancini 2004a; Jones 2006; Pew Global 2010a; Stromback 2007; Stromback and Kaid 2008).

Finally, we examined only one president and one part of his presidential term. Given the significant declines in Obama's popularity during his second year in office—together with the highly challenging issues of Afghanistan, Iran, health care, the continuing economic crisis, and the BP oil spill—the findings presented here may represent the high-water mark for international news coverage of this new president.

The evidence for the international two-step flow idea was not particularly compelling. All the nations' media became more critical over time, but that seems more a natural outgrowth of moving from postelection euphoria to the prosaic realities of governing in the United States during highly partisan times. While the US media quickly became more critical of Obama, the international media did not closely track their domestic counterparts. Of course, this month-by-month comparison is not an optimal test for this idea. International journalists are almost certainly looking at the domestic news reports on a day-by-day basis. So changes in which issues to emphasize and what tone to take probably require a more precise day-by-day test than the general overview we have provided here.

In chapter 4, we examine news content of these same media outlets as they reported on President George W. Bush. We will search for similarities and differences in terms of Bush's coverage in comparison with Obama. Then, in chapter 5, we focus on a variety of specific policy issues of particular importance to the international community. These include America's standing in the world, the US-led wars in Afghanistan and Iraq, and US policies in the Middle East. That chapter features a head-to-head comparison of how international media portrayed these two presidents on these key policy matters.

CHAPTER 4

The George W. Bush Presidency: International Media Perspectives

While presidents routinely try to influence foreign coverage of the United States, few recent US presidents have sought to reshape the world politically as aggressively as did George W. Bush. Likewise, few presidents have faced so much international criticism for their "nation-building" and media-management efforts (Auletta 2004; Brooks 2006; Cohen 2008; Entman 2004; Farnsworth 2009; Kessler and Wright 2007; Mueller 2006; Pew 2006).

Throughout his post-9/11 presidency, the Bush administration struggled to frame US foreign and military policy as a global push toward greater democratization. From a variety of outreach efforts by the State Department (including "listening tours" in the Middle East by presidential confidante Karen Hughes) to pronouncements by Bush himself, Washington during the Bush years sought to fashion domestic and international perceptions of US Middle East policy in a more favorable light.

A 2006 Pew Global Attitudes survey, conducted roughly midway through the period we analyzed, found negative public attitudes in a number of allied countries regarding the United States. Some 60 percent of those surveyed in France and Germany had an unfavorable opinion of the United States, as did 56 percent in Pakistan, 73 percent in Spain, 76 percent in Turkey, and 85 percent in Jordan. Roughly one-third of the public in Great Britain, perhaps our closest ally, viewed the United States unfavorably (Pew 2006). Of the thirty-three countries surveyed by Pew in both 2002 and 2007, the United States was viewed less favorably in 2007 in twenty-six nations, more favorably in five, and about the same in two (Kessler and Wright 2007).

To determine what people in these countries were learning about the United States from their news media, we examined 43,811 international news statements related to George W. Bush on our familiar list of the international evening television news programs analyzed by Media Tenor. We also examine

85,762 statements relating to Bush on our regular complement of four US broadcasters (ABC, CBS, NBC, and Fox News). The data extend from January 1, 2005, through December 31, 2008, covering almost all of Bush's second term.

This period encompasses such key issues of the Bush presidency as growing resistance to the US-led occupation of Iraq, the administration's "surge" strategy there, growing international objections to the incarceration and treatment of suspected terrorists at the military base in Guantanamo, Cuba, as well as the widespread US voter rejection of Bush in the 2006 midterm elections, which returned Democratic majorities to both houses of Congress. Because our evidence on Obama's coverage data is limited to the first eighteen months of his term, any comparison with Bush's coverage is necessarily inexact. For example, we cannot examine possible international "honeymoon" coverage for Bush because we do not have fully comparable data for Bush's first eighteen months in office. So we must, to paraphrase Bush's first secretary of defense, analyze Bush with the data we have, rather than the data we might we wish we had. Thus, to provide a context for international news coverage of Bush, we will review his key foreign and military policies, along with US media coverage of those policies.

A Presidency Defined by 9/11, Afghanistan, and Iraq (and Their Aftermaths)

When the dust settled on the contentious and controversial 2000 presidential election, Americans thought they had a pretty good idea of what would come next. Bush, a Texas governor with no Washington experience beyond being the son of a former president, would focus on domestic policy issues as president (Ceaser and Busch 2001). He talked a good deal during the 2000 campaign about tax cuts, and he tried to distinguish himself from the Republicans who impeached Bill Clinton over the scandal involving Monica Lewinsky by calling himself a "compassionate conservative." Some moderate Republicans even imagined him as one of their own. While he was not as liberal as the first President Bush, and certainly not as internationally oriented as his father, many voters nevertheless viewed the younger Bush as likely to be a practical, result-oriented president (Abramson et al. 2002).

Before taking office, George W. Bush showed little interest in or affinity for international matters, once mocking a reporter who challenged him to identify the leader of Pakistan, an important US ally (Dowd 1999; Quirk and Matheson 2001). But perhaps America's dominant position in the world in 2000 meant that presidents did not have to worry about the world as much as they did during the decades of superpower rivalry during the Cold War. Americans could certainly not be faulted for thinking such things. After all, television news coverage of the 2000 campaign certainly did not spend much time on foreign matters. During the two months before the election, the three network television networks provided only ten stories that focused on international matters—out of more than 462 campaign news stories (Farnsworth and Lichter 2011a:39). The media's agenda-setting lesson was clear: the wider world no longer mattered as much to the United States.

How wrong America was! Whatever Bush's domestic policy plans might have been for cutting taxes, reforming education, privatizing Social Security, securing the nation's fiscal future, and preventing illegal immigration across the southern border with Mexico, the unexpected events of a single September morning created a presidency dominated by foreign (especially military) policy.

After a few uneven early steps on that fateful day, Bush soon found his voice. "I can hear you," Bush said to rescue workers who gathered around a wrecked fire truck in Lower Manhattan a few days after two hijacked passenger jets crashed into the Twin Towers of the World Trade Center and a third plane crashed into the Pentagon. "The rest of the world hears you. And the people who knocked these buildings down will hear all of us soon!" (Frum 2003:140). The roar of the crowd shouting "USA! USA!" echoed around the world via the global mass media in an instant. It was clear that the Bush presidency was not going to be defined by tax cuts or tinkering with Social Security.

The terrorist attacks altered the political environment in a way rarely seen in Washington. First, there was a massive change in US public opinion. For most Americans, questions of the legitimacy of Bush's presidency springing from the problematic ballot counting in Florida less than a year earlier vanished the moment the Twin Towers fell (Pfiffner 2004a, 2004b). Bush's approval rating just days before the planes hit the World Trade Center and the Pentagon stood at 51 percent; within in a week it skyrocketed to 86 percent (Dimock 2004; Pfiffner 2004a, 2004b). For comparison, consider the Cuban missile crisis of 1962, the closest the United States ever came to war with the Soviet Union. During that superpower standoff, President John F. Kennedy's ratings increased by only twelve percentage points (Pfiffner 2004a). One might think that the possible end of the world by nuclear holocaust would have triggered a somewhat larger "rally round the flag" effect in US public opinion! (Of course, comparing actual casualties with threats are not exactly an "apples versus apples" comparison.)

With the national crisis brought on by 9/11, Bush also had a dramatic reversal of fortune with Congress. Bush had faced a combative Congress, and even many Republicans were upset with the White House for his mishandling of Senator James Jeffords of Vermont, a Republican who left the party earlier that year, costing the GOP its Senate majority (Jeffords 2003; Tenpas and Hess 2002). After the attacks, though, Congress quickly passed the antiterrorism measures the president requested, including a bailout of the airline industry and the PATRIOT Act, which gave the government enhanced powers to investigate American citizens as well as potential terrorists abroad. In late 2002, Congress voted to authorize Bush to wage war on Iraq, even though the evidence regarding alleged weapons of mass destruction programs and links between Saddam Hussein and Al-Qaeda seemed unpersuasive to much of the national security community (Clarke 2004; Fisher 2004; Gaines 2002; Suskind 2004).

Traditionally, presidents have had far more success in shaping foreign and military policy than domestic policy, where Congress tends to care a great deal more about outcomes more likely to affect constituents directly. The difference is so stark that many political scientists actually talk of "two presidencies"—one foreign and one domestic. The president's generally greater latitude in foreign policy stems from three realities of Washington politics: the president has greater constitutional authority in that area, the White House can move more quickly in a crisis, and the executive branch has taken the lead in international matters going back to the nation's founding (Oldfield and Wildavsky 1989; Sullivan 2001; Wildavsky 1966).

Bush's forceful assertion of expansive executive branch authority, largely unchallenged at the time, was at least comparable to other wartime presidents (Fisher 2004). He established a military tribunal system, convinced Congress to approve virtually open-ended authorizations for the use of military force in both Afghanistan and Iraq, denied some US citizens constitutional protections (including access to a lawyer while in custody), rejected effective congressional oversight of military expenditures, and unilaterally exempted certain military detainees from the prisoner-of-war protections of the Geneva Convention (Baker 2002; C. Brown 2003; Fisher 2004). There was also the administration's authorization of waterboarding, an "enhanced interrogation" technique that critics regarded as a form of torture. Taken together, the administration's policies amounted to an effective state of emergency throughout most of the Bush presidency.

Bush's aggressive actions in the wake of 9/11 were broadly supported by the US public, and his approval ratings remained high during the early phases of the wars in Afghanistan and Iraq. Both of these wars were marked by early military victories—the Taliban leadership was rapidly dislodged from Kabul and Saddam Hussein was quickly dispatched in Iraq. (Several months later, US troops found Hussein hiding in a dirt hole, and he was tried and eventually executed by the Iraqis.) The interim leaders in both nations declared themselves in favor of the United States, and at first they gratefully accepted coalition efforts to help pacify their restive nation (Filkins 2001; Jacobson 2008).

But as so many military occupiers across the centuries have discovered, winning on the battlefield does not always lead to peaceful political transitions. Overly optimistic scenarios about the power the pro-US leaders in the region possessed (and even the extent of their expressed pro-American views) gave way to chaos in both Iraq and Afghanistan as the months passed (Tanter and Kersting 2008).

Even when the political backlash associated with these long-running wars cost the Republicans their congressional majorities in 2006, the newly empowered Democratic leadership hesitated to shut off funding for the military actions, as they could do under the shared power doctrine at the heart of Congress's constitutional authority (Lindsay 2003). They feared GOP attacks that the Democrats were not being tough enough on terrorists (Ceaser and Busch 2005).

Congress was, however, less deferential in the domestic policy realm. Democratic legislators rejected Bush's second-term economic stimulus plan and his proposal to allow oil drilling in the Arctic Wildlife Refuge. They also blocked some of his more controversial judicial nominees (Lindsay 2003). And Bush's plan to privatize a portion of Social Security likewise went nowhere, as neither Democrats nor Republicans in Congress wanted to champion that controversial initiative (Jacobs 2006).

Bush's use of terms such as the *axis of evil* and his frequent comparisons of 9/11 and the 1941 sneak attack on Pearl Harbor that plunged the United States into World War II helped stir patriotic feelings on the part of Americans, who have experienced few military attacks, much less invasions, in their nation's history. Since the Central Intelligence Agency and the Defense Department are under the control of the executive branch, the Bush team could pick and choose the national security evidence given to Congress, the media, and the public (Schmitt 2007). This gave the White House an immense framing advantage over its domestic and international critics, particularly in early news stories relating to 9/11 and the march toward war in both Afghanistan and Iraq.

Bush's patriotic exhortations to his fellow Americans, a key part of his rhetorical strategy, had a limited shelf life. That approach also may not travel well, becoming less effective in nations where occupations, invasions, or at least the threat of invasions are more common. But the approach can work in the United States. Indeed, Bush convinced voters to reject a number of Democratic lawmakers in 2002 and 2004—including Democratic presidential candidate and decorated military veteran John Kerry, who was charged with not being sufficiently supportive of the war in Iraq (Ceaser and Busch 2005).

Of course, the undeniable problems of the US-led Iraq occupation made the war a negative factor for Bush during his second term, as his poll numbers fell and his fellow Republicans were defeated in the 2006 midterm elections (Broder 2006; Milkis 2006). Ignoring this rebuke from the electorate, Bush escalated the war in Iraq in 2007 with his "surge" policy to add tens of thousands of troops in Iraq.

GEORGE W. BUSH AND A "REVISED CNN EFFECT": A TOP-DOWN PROCESS?

As we have discussed in earlier chapters, there has been considerable debate in recent years regarding what is known as the "CNN effect," which holds that real-time televised news reports of international crises can pressure governments to act via its impact on public opinion (R. Brown 2003; Gilboa 2005). Conversely, when international news coverage is limited or absent, there is little pressure for governments to act in response to crises in distant lands (Hawkins 2002).

In the case of the relatively heavily covered Bosnian crisis of the 1990s, for example, international intervention may have been encouraged by the horrific pictures of human suffering (Robinson 2002). But many other crises of the decade, including the limited response to the Rwandan genocide, demonstrate the limits of the "CNN effect" perspective (Power 2002).

In the wake of the 2003 US-led invasion of Iraq, some scholars argued that a president's command of the US mass media's attention during crises actually reverses the causal arrows of the alleged "CNN effect." For international military and intelligence matters, where reporters are heavily reliant on governmental information, government officials can try to build public sentiment for intervention through the selective release of information (Entman 2004).

While the CNN hypothesis suggests that outside voices can create counterframes to those offered by the White House, studies of recent military crises suggest that such critics are readily discounted and dismissed by reporters and the public, if such voices dare speak up at all (Bennett et al. 2007; Entman 2004). Once war breaks out, of course, Defense Department programs such as "embedding" journalists with military units help secure largely pro-military and pro-government coverage from reporters (Norris et al. 2003). Even so, the government's ability to shape the discourse of military matters erodes over time as the immediate crisis recedes and as more information comes to light (Bennett et al. 2007; Entman 2004).

As a result of the relative silence of potential critics (and the media's reduced interest in such voices) during times of crises, the executive branch dominates US political discourse to an ever greater extent than normal. When times are tough, a presidential administration can expand its huge framing advantages over Congress, other international figures, and even the reporters themselves in the tug-of-war over setting the news agenda and framing the stories reported (Entman 2004; Farnsworth and Lichter 2006a). During such periods of crisis, potential critics tend to have less access to relevant information and hesitate to risk being portrayed publicly by the president as disloyal (Entman 2004; Farnsworth 2009). International media, which do not have to respond to the demands of US viewers and readers, may be less constrained in their treatment of US government leaders and actions. But foreign reporters may not have access to any better information than what the administration released to US reporters.

A Center for Media and Public Affairs (CMPA) analysis of US network news coverage of President Bush during national crises bears out this general pattern of very distinct wartime coverage. Bush received coverage that was 63 percent positive (and 37 percent negative) in tone during the portion of 2001 after the terrorist attacks, as compared to 36 percent positive (and 64 percent negative) coverage during the first two-thirds of the year and 38 percent positive (and 62 percent negative) television coverage during 2002 (Farnsworth and Lichter 2006a:92).

Similarly, embedded reporters and the military successes in Iraq during 2003 sparked a period of relatively positive coverage: network news reports were 49 percent positive during roughly six weeks of actual combat in Iraq. But after Bush stood on the deck of an aircraft carrier in front of a sign announcing "Mission Accomplished" following the fall of the Saddam Hussein government, the coverage turned sour again: his coverage was only 32 percent positive in the six months following the May 1, 2003, announced end of major combat operations (Farnsworth and Lichter 2006a:92).

Other presidents received even more positive news coverage of their presidencies than Bush did during earlier military operations, including Bill Clinton during the 1999 Kosovo crisis and George H. W. Bush's 1991 military operation to remove Saddam Hussein's army from Kuwait (Farnsworth and Lichter 2006a).

BUSH, BIN LADEN, AND AL-JAZEERA

Scholars who studied international media in the wake of 9/11 focused on Al-Jazeera, the Qatar-based satellite news broadcaster that became highly visible internationally during the months following the attacks. The network was the only media outlet that had reporters in Taliban-dominated Afghanistan, and its coverage of the war offered a street-level perspective that focused on the events of late 2001 as a US invasion of a Muslim region (Jasperson and El-Kikhia 2003).

Al-Jazeera's reporters provided much less coverage of the military aspects of the Afghanistan war—which were covered in great depth by many Western media outlets—and instead focused on the human costs of the war. The sufferings of Afghan civilians and the collateral damage of Western bombing campaigns were standard fare for the network during that period (Jasperson and El-Kikhia 2003).

In addition, the network became the preferred place for Osama bin Laden to release his video and audio tapes to the world. While Al-Jazeera viewed itself as a prime example of democratic debate in a region where such discussions are in short supply, the channel faced much criticism in the West for allegedly becoming the "bin Laden network" (Bessaiso 2005; Seib 2005).

In the months following the Afghanistan invasion, the US government focused much of its public diplomacy efforts on Al-Jazeera, offering experts for interview programs to help promote its views on the Middle East (Zaharna 2005). Within a month of the 9/11 attacks, the US State Department appointed Charlotte Beers, a long-time advertising executive, as the department's under-secretary of state for public affairs and public diplomacy (Zaharna 2005). But the US rapprochement to the Arab network proved transient. The government rather quickly turned away from a media outlet it considered hostile and focused on other regional outlets where it felt Americans would get a more sympathetic hearing (Zaharna 2005).

Because it includes a detailed analysis of the content of several Middle East broadcasters, this chapter permits an examination of the effectiveness of US government efforts to reach out to the region's news outlets during Bush's second term, when it sought to defend US-led occupations of Iraq and Afghanistan to international publics highly suspicious of American motives and actions in the region.

BUSH AND IRAQ: US PUBLIC APPROVAL RATINGS

George W. Bush struggled to maintain his standing with the US public on his key issue area as his second term progressed, as shown in table 4.1. By January 2007, shortly after the midterm elections, the US public turned thumbs down on all major aspects of the president's plan to increase the number of troops in Iraq. Despite all of the Bush team's public relations efforts, fewer than three Americans in ten—29 percent—approved of Bush's handling of the situation in Iraq (Balz and Cohen 2007), a sharp drop from the roughly two-thirds of Americans who supported the Iraq War before it started (Entman 2004). There had been some positive video images, such as the stained fingers of Iraqis who cast ballots in the country's first free election, but the vast majority of the US media coverage of the Iraqi effort focused more on bombs wounding Americans rather than the rebuilding nation's unsteady path toward greater freedom.

Bush's plan to increase the number of troops in Iraq for a short period of time starting in 2007, known as the "surge," also generated little public support. Barely more than one out of every four people surveyed—28 percent—believed that the war in Iraq "contributed to the long-term peace and stability in the

Table 4.1.   US Public Opinion on President Bush's Iraq Policy, 2007

Question: "Do you approve or disapprove of the way Bush is handling the situation in Iraq?"

Approve	Disapprove	No opinion
29	70	1

Question: "Do you support or oppose Bush's proposal to send approximately 22,000 additional US military forces to Iraq?"

Support	Oppose	No opinion
34	65	1

Question: "Do you think Congress should or should not try to block Bush's plan to send more troops to Iraq?"

Should	Should not	No opinion
59	39	2

Question: (ASKED OF HALF SAMPLE) "Do you think the war with Iraq has or has not (ITEM)?"
a. Contributed to long-term peace and stability in the Mideast

Has	Has Not	No opinion
28	68	4

b. Encouraged democracy in other Arab nations

Has	Has Not	No opinion
36	59	6

c. Helped to improve the lives of the Iraqi people

Has	Has Not	No opinion
48	48	4

Question: "Which of these do you think is the better way to address the problems in Iraq—through diplomatic and political efforts, or through military efforts?"

Diplomatic/Political	Military	Both (vol.)	Neither (vol.)	No opinion
63	25	8	2	2

Source: Balz and Cohen (2007). This *Washington Post*-ABC News Poll was conducted by telephone January 16–19, 2007, among a random nationwide sample of one thousand adults. The margin of sampling error is plus or minus three percentage points for full-sample questions. TNS of Horsham, Pennsylvania, conducted the sampling and data collection.

Middle East," one of the administration's key justifications for the war. Just over one-third of those surveyed—36 percent—believed that the Iraq War encouraged democracy elsewhere in the region, another key justification for the war used by the Bush administration. US respondents were even divided over whether the Iraqis themselves were better off after the US-led invasion took place (Balz and Cohen 2007).

These results show the limits of Bush's ability to persuade the US public by the seventh year of his presidency. Bush's strongly pro-war appeals and the shaping of the prewar discourse helped him win the political debate in the 2002 midterm elections and start the war in 2003, but subsequent events took a heavy toll on the president's credibility. Overpromising may help win short-term political debates, but a president who disappoints is likely to lose status in the longer term, when the extent of White House deception and spin become clearer (Farnsworth 2009). Indeed, in that 2007 survey US respondents said they strongly favored diplomatic action, called for by the president's critics, over the largely military-oriented responses insisted upon by the Bush team (Balz and Cohen 2007).

Given past studies as well as the media patterns we have seen so far in this project, we expect the more critical a nation's government is of US policies, the more negative the tone of news about the US government (cf. Hallin and Mancini 2004a; Jones 2006). According to this perspective, German media should consistently be more critical than British media. In the Middle East, most nations refused to join the "coalition of the willing," Bush's preferred term for the US-led invasion of Iraq. Middle Eastern broadcasters should vary in their approaches, with the media outlet connected to the anti-US Hezbollah most negative in their news content, and far more positive coverage emanating from media outlets connected to long-time US ally Saudi Arabia.

We expected the tone of Bush's coverage to be more negative in international media than on US network television news, with the most critical nations those most opposed to US policies. This idea stems from the great influence the US government can bring to bear on the highly competitive US media when foreign and military matters are dominant (cf. Entman 2004). The contrasts between US and non-US media may be particularly sharp, in terms of both tone and topic selection.

Results

The tone of news coverage of George W. Bush during his second term is found in table 4.2. The net tone measure, calculated as the percentage of positive tonal assessments minus negative ones, shows that coverage of Bush was negative

Table 4.2.   News Coverage of George W. Bush by Media Location

Location	Year	Net tone %	Negative %	Positive %	No clear rating %	N
Germany	2005	–6.8	13.0	6.2	80.8	2,949
	2006	–12.4	15.3	2.9	81.7	2,131
	2007	–9.6	13.4	3.8	82.8	2,985
	2008	–17.0	22.7	5.7	71.7	2,057
UK	2005	–8.5	13.3	4.8	81.9	2,658
	2006	–13.4	15.5	2.2	82.3	2,464
	2007	–9.8	12.4	2.5	85.1	2,004
	2008	–9.0	13.6	4.7	8.17	2,277
Arab	2005	–9.2	10.9	1.7	87.3	5,548
	2006	–7.6	8.4	0.9	90.7	11,161
	2007	–9.8	11.4	1.5	87.1	5,355
	2208	–4.9	7.4	2.5	90.1	2,222
US	2005	–6.1	10.0	3.9	86.2	29,135
	2006	–5.4	8.4	3.0	88.5	29,365
	2007	–8.1	10.8	2.7	86.5	15,781
	2008	–7.3	10.4	3.1	86.5	11,481

N = Number of statements. Percentages might not sum to 100 because of rounding. This table is based on a content analysis of 43,811 statements relating to George W. Bush on nine international television news networks (ARD Tagesthemen, ZDF heute journal, BBC1 10 O'clock News, BBC2 Newsnight, Al-Arabiyah, Nile News, LBC, Al-Manar, and Al-Jazeera) and 85,762 statements on four US television news networks (ABC, CBS, NBC, and Fox News) from January 1, 2005, through December 31, 2008.

across the board—during every year in all four media groups. (As before, a 0 percent net tone score represents an equal amount of positive and negative tone.)

There were three instances of double-digit net negative coverage of the president: two years in German media and one in the United Kingdom. Year six of a presidential administration is often a difficult one, as Richard Nixon resigned over Watergate in 1974, Ronald Reagan faced the public disclosure of the Iran-contra affair that nearly wrecked his presidency in 1986, and Bill Clinton was impeached by the US House in 1998 (before being acquitted by the Senate). For Bush, 2006 was little better. His sixth year in office was marked by a particularly difficult military environment, as the instability in Iraq became particularly bloody. In addition, Democrats channeled deep public frustration with the president into significant victories in the 2006 midterm elections, robbing Bush of his Republican majorities in both houses of Congress.

Despite these problems, and despite the international controversy generated by Bush's military policies, 2006 was not a particularly rough year for Bush in

Arabic-language media reports, which were only 7.6 percent net negative, far less critical than the two European media groups that year. Bush also fared relatively well in US media in 2006 (5.4 percent net negative), even though his domestic political fortunes weakened throughout the year.

One would expect that the close attention that US media would pay to mid-term elections as a gauge of the president's popularity and a president's ability to help secure victories for friendly lawmakers would lead to more critical coverage than in international media. Beyond America's shores, after all, most individual House and Senate races would generate little attention. Perhaps that anticipated pattern emerges in specific issue areas rather than in the overall coverage examined at this stage.

In fact, the US news reports were least critical of Bush of the four media groups during all four years examined here. The worst year for Bush on US television was 2007 (8.1 percent net negative), when the president faced new Democratic majorities in Congress and as the highly unpopular "surge" of troops into Iraq got under way. With Democratic majorities come the opportunity and incentive to investigate a Republican president's policies. Such investigations, particularly in the deeply partisan times of recent years, often generate headlines critical of White House operations (Sinclair 2008).

The tone of European coverage was notably more critical in 2007, when Bush began to execute his plans to increase the number of US troops in Iraq (Abramowitz and Baker 2007; Abramowitz and Montgomery 2007). Even so, coverage of that year in international news was little more critical than domestic reports, with international assessments of Bush clustered closely within a narrow band just under 10 percent net negative range. This was also the year that featured the most critical Arabic-language media's coverage.

The news during 2007 was also marked by increasing conversations about expanding US efforts to counter Iran, with respect to both Iranian attempts to forge closer ties with allies in the Shiite-majority regions of Iraq and US efforts to thwart Iranian ambitions to develop a nuclear weapon. (Few of the Arabic-language news outlets examined here are based in countries or supported by organizations with friendly relations with Iran, and Saudi Arabia is particularly hostile.)

Overall, the UK media were the most critical group regarding Bush during 2006, and the Germans were most critical in 2008. The UK and Arabic-language media tied for most critical in 2007, with reports that were just under 10 percent net negative, while the Arabic-language television group was most critical in 2005, with reports that were 9.2 percent net negative.

UK media were most critical of Bush in 2006 when compared to other years. German coverage in 2008 was far more critical than German coverage in other years. Arabic-language media gave Bush more critical reviews in 2007 than in any other year, as did US media.

Strangely, not one media group treated Bush most critically during 2005, a year of increasing troubles in Iraq as well as Hurricane Katrina's devastation in New Orleans and the surrounding area triggered extensive criticism regarding the federal government's bungled response (Bennett et al. 2007). One factor that kept the coverage from being more critical that year was the January 30, 2005, parliamentary election in Iraq, where millions voted in defiance of insurgents who tried to disrupt the process (Wright 2005a, 2005b). That Iraqi election was seen, temporarily at least, as something of a vindication for Bush's policies. In addition, Bush's reelection in November 2004 may have diminished domestic and international criticism of the president for a while.

There may be other nation-specific circumstances for the relatively kind media treatment of 2005. Germany's public turned sour on Bush before the Iraq War started, and Chancellor Gerhard Schröder's government, with its somewhat critical views of Bush, lost a confidence vote in the German Bundestag in June 2005. With that defeat, German media attention began to focus on Angela Merkel, the conservative leader who subsequently replaced Schröder (Landler 2005). Merkel's less anti-American views were an important and newsworthy difference between the two party leaders (Landler 2005), and her increased visibility in German media during 2005 may help explain why the coverage of the United States was less critical that year. In US news, the president's Democratic critics may have held their fire for much of 2005, waiting until the midterm election year of 2006 (or at least until after the Katrina disaster) to unload on the increasingly unpopular president.

In a separate study (results not shown) of 210,944 statements relating to the US government, including those analyzed here that relate to Bush, on ten international media outlets (the nine discussed here plus Canada's CBC television network) and four domestic news programs from January 1, 2005, through March 31, 2007, we found considerable use of Bush and administration sources to explain administration policies (Farnsworth, Lichter, and Schatz 2008, 2010).

The proportions are roughly similar for the different media groups, though in many months the Middle East outlets were more likely to feature administration officials than were the Europeans. This suggests that the Bush administration efforts to make itself heard on Arabic broadcasters (cf. Kessler and Wright 2007) generated some success. As expected, given the language barriers, German TV consistently made less use of US administration sources than did television news in the United Kingdom.

But there were limits to the Bush administration's ability to shape the debate in its preferred direction. The often-expressed argument that US actions in the Middle East was primarily about democracy largely went unheard throughout the study period. In only one of the twenty-seven months examined in this study did discussion of democracy and elections exceed 10 percent of the total news reports. That month was November 2006, when the US midterm elections placed Democrats in control of both chambers on Capitol Hill for the first time in a dozen years. In other words, a partisan shift in Washington had far more to do with the spike in international coverage related to democracy than did the Bush administration's frequently stated commitment to reduce autocracy in the Middle East (Farnsworth, Lichter, and Schatz 2008, 2010).

Table 4.3 shows the tone of news content about President Bush over his second term. We examine here two German television outlets, two from the United Kingdom, two leading Arabic-language outlets (Al-Jazeera and Al-Arabiyah), and the three US broadcast networks, along with Fox News.

None of these outlets ever featured as much positive as negative coverage of Bush. The European outlets were the most critical, frequently producing double-digit net negative coverage. Two news outlets had news reports that were more negative than positive by double-digit margins in three of the four years (2006, 2007, and 2008): BBC2 Newsnight and ARD Tagesthemen. ZDF heute journal had two years of double-digit negativity (2006 and 2007), while the BBC1 10 O'clock News was only that negative during 2006.

Once again, Arabic-language media were quite modest in their criticisms of a US president when compared to the European news outlets examined here. Al-Jazeera had one double-digit net negative year in 2007, but only barely (10.4 percent net negative). In addition, that year appeared to be an aberration. Al-Jazeera was the single most favorable media outlet for Bush during both 2005 and 2006 (although its coverage was still 3 percent net negative for both years), even when US media are included. In 2008, Al-Jazeera ranked second only to Al-Arabiyah, which was 4 percent net negative. Al-Arabiyah's most negative year of the four was 7.3 percent net negative in its reports during 2007, which was still less critical than all four of the European media examined here for that year.

The influence a president can bring to bear in the tug-of-war over setting and framing the news agenda may help explain why US broadcasters were among those not particularly hostile toward Bush. Of the four US outlets, only CBS ever featured double-digit net negative coverage, in 2007 and 2008. In fact, in 2007 it was the most critical outlet of any outlet, at home or abroad. (CBS News has been the target of criticism over former CBS anchor Dan Rather's coverage of both the elder and the younger Bush during their presidential campaigns. The first controversy took place during the 1988 presidential primary season, over Rather's aggressive questioning of what George H. W. Bush [then vice president] knew about the Iran-contra affair. The second concerned CBS's ultimately discredited 2004 investigation of the younger Bush's National Guard records during the Vietnam years [Dionne 1988; Rutenberg and Carter 2001; Steinberg 2008].)

But CBS was the exception to a pattern of only modest negativity in the US media. During these four years of coverage of Bush, ABC and NBC looked

Table 4.3. News Coverage of George W. Bush by Selected Media Outlet

News Outlet	Year	Net tone %	Negative %	Positive %	No clear rating %	N
ARD Tagesthemen	2005	−6.0	11.6	5.6	82.9	1,297
	2006	−11.2	14.6	3.3	82.1	927
	2007	−10.5	14.7	4.2	81.2	1,460
	2008	−19.1	23.8	4.6	71.6	888
ZDF heute journal	2005	−7.3	14.1	6.8	79.1	1,652
	2006	−13.4	15.9	2.6	81.5	1,204
	2007	−8.7	12.1	3.5	84.4	1,525
	2008	−15.3	21.8	6.5	71.7	1,169
BBC1 10 O'clock News	2005	−7.3	14.3	7.0	78.6	754
	2006	−11.2	13.2	2.0	84.8	1,205
	2007	−7.9	10.8	2.9	86.3	797
	2008	−6.2	10.9	4.8	84.3	924
BBC2 Newsnight	2005	−9.0	12.9	3.9	83.1	1,904
	2006	−15.4	17.7	2.3	80.0	1,259
	2007	−11.1	13.4	2.3	84.3	1,207
	2008	−10.9	15.4	4.6	80.0	1,353
Al-Arabiyah	2005	−5.9	8.6	2.7	88.8	1,424
	2006	−4.7	5.7	1.0	93.2	3,257
	2007	−7.3	9.2	1.9	89.0	2,019
	2008	−4.3	8.7	4.4	86.9	794
Al-Jazeera	2005	−2.9	3.8	0.9	95.4	2,080
	2006	-3.0	3.2	0.2	96.6	2,986
	2007	-10.4	11.2	0.8	87.9	1,654
	2008	−4.6	5.9	1.3	92.8	1,406
ABC	2005	−7.1	10.5	3.4	86.1	4,003
	2006	−4.8	6.6	1.8	91.6	4,675
	2007	−8.3	10.9	2.7	86.4	3,830
	2008	−8.7	11.4	2.8	85.8	2,124
CBS	2005	−9.2	12.1	2.9	85.0	4,218
	2006	−5.2	7.3	2.1	90.6	4,321
	2007	−12.2	14.3	2.1	83.7	2,404
	2008	−11.5	14.6	3.1	82.4	1,174
NBC	2005	−7.4	10.2	2.9	86.9	6,010
	2006	−7.0	9.5	2.6	87.9	5,991
	2007	−7.3	9.7	2.4	87.8	4,743
	2008	−8.0	9.4	1.4	89.1	2,367
Fox News	2005	−4.5	9.1	4.7	86.2	14,904
	2006	−5.0	8.9	3.9	87.2	14,378
	2007	−6.8	10.1	3.3	86.6	4,804
	2008	−5.6	9.5	3.9	86.6	5,816

Note: Not all media outlets are shown in all years.
N = Number of statements. Percentages might not sum to 100 because of rounding. This table is based on a content analysis of 43,811 statements relating to George W. Bush on nine international television news networks and 85,762 statements on four US television news networks from January 1, 2005, through December 31, 2008.

more like Fox News than CBS. Overall, the US media evidence supports the claims of scholars who argue that government reporters in the United States are dependent on administration sources, particularly when foreign and military policy issues are highly salient, as they were during most of the Bush presidency. Journalists also pay relatively little attention to Congress during such times, and members of Congress tend to keep their criticisms to themselves during the early stages of military crises (Entman 2004; Farnsworth 2009).

Although the comparisons are not exact because they cover different parts of their presidencies, the news coverage of Obama during his first eighteen months in office was considerably kinder in nearly all media than the reports on Bush during his second term. As we saw in table 3.6, during the first year of Obama's presidency only one news outlet was double-digit net negative in its tonal treatment of the new president: Fox News. During the first half of Obama's second year, Fox was joined by BBC2 Newsnight. These findings suggest that the Fox network was far more critical of Obama than it was supportive of Bush, at least during the latter's second term.

Table 4.4 shows the coverage of Bush relating to his personality and his perceived ability to govern during the first eighteen months of his second term. (Again, our study falls short of an exact comparison with Obama's first eighteen months as president.)

Once again, we see the advantage that talking about character can make in the tone of presidential news coverage. Character and personality coverage was more favorable than assessments of Bush's ability to govern for all but one of these nine international and four domestic news outlets. From January 1, 2005, through June 30, 2006, coverage of Bush's personality and character was double-digit negative in only two news outlets. By far the most critical was Al-Manar, the voice of Hezbollah, with reports that were 44.8 percent net negative. BBC1, with reports on the president's character that were 14.3 percent net negative, was a distant second.

Coverage of Bush's personal side was positive in three outlets: Al-Arabiyah, with reports that were 7.9 percent positive in tone, led the pack, followed by ZDF heute journal. Al-Jazeera, whose surprisingly favorable coverage we noted above, was 5.9 percent net negative in assessments of Bush's character.

For the four American news outlets, character coverage was more negative than positive, but only barely so. Fox News, seen by many liberals as a propaganda instrument for Republicans, was actually the most critical of the four on this dimension, with reports that were 7.1 percent net negative in tone. The three US broadcast networks were almost identical in their modest level of criticism of Bush in this issue area, with coverage that was 3–4 percent net negative. The media negativity is seen far more clearly in coverage of Bush's ability to govern. All outlets were more critical than not of the second-term president. (The

Table 4.4.   News Coverage of George W. Bush's Personality and Ability to Govern

News Outlet	Topic	Net tone %	Negative %	Positive %	No clear rating %	N
ARD Tagesthemen	Personality	3.6	7.3	10.9	81.8	55
	Govern	–6.7	15.0	8.3	76.7	120
ZDF heute journal	Personality	4.1	10.8	14.9	74.3	74
	Govern	–11.2	18.7	7.5	73.9	241
BBC1 10 O'clock News	Personality	–14.3	22.4	8.2	69.4	49
	Govern	–18.5	24.6	6.2	69.2	65
BBC2 Newsnight	Personality	–7.9	14.7	6.8	78.5	251
	Govern	–18.0	21.0	3.0	76.0	167
Al-Arabiyah	Personality	7.9	5.7	13.6	80.7	140
	Govern	–9.5	14.8	5.3	79.8	243
Nile News	Personality	0	13.3	13.3	73.3	15
	Govern	–3.6	5.4	1.8	92.9	112
LBC	Personality	–*	–	–	–	–*
	Govern	–21.7	21.7	0.0	78.3	83
Al-Manar	Personality	–44.8	46.9	2.1	51.0	96
	Govern	–20.1	21.4	1.3	77.3	467
Al-Jazeera	Personality	–5.9	23.5	17.6	58.8	17
	Govern	–6.8	8.5	1.7	89.8	235
ABC	Personality	–3.5	7.0	3.5	89.5	314
	Govern	–18.9	21.3	2.4	76.4	127
CBS	Personality	–3.8	7.2	3.4	89.3	291
	Govern	–11.4	15.4	3.9	80.7	228
NBC	Personality	–3.6	8.1	4.5	87.4	419
	Govern	–17.6	22.0	4.4	73.6	227
Fox	Personality	–7.1	13.5	6.4	80.0	857
	Govern	–14.9	19.3	4.5	76.2	471

* Insufficient number of cases to classify (less than ten).
N = Number of statements. Percentages might not sum to 100 because of rounding. The results are based on a content analysis of 19,114 statements on evening newscasts from nine international television news providers and 43,276 statements on evening newscasts from four US television news providers from January 1, 2005, through June 30, 2006.

first eighteen months of Bush's second term was a time of unified Republican control of the White House and both houses of Congress.) The least hostile coverage was found on Nile News, with reports that were 3.6 percent net negative. Another Arabic-language broadcaster, Al-Jazeera, ranked third in its treatment of Bush's capacity to govern, after the German broadcaster ARD Tagesthemen; Al-Arabiyah ranked fourth. The other nine television news broadcasters, including all four US news outlets and the two UK news reports, were all double-digit negative regarding Bush's capacity to govern.

The most critical outlet was LBC, with reports that were 21.7 percent net negative. Al-Manar, with reports that were 20.1 percent net negative, ranked second. But that critical coverage on Al-Manar was not as bad as the coverage of Bush's personality, which was 44.8 percent net negative. Now that is a media outlet that really does not like a president! (In contrast to the Bush figures, Al-Manar's reports on Obama were 42.6 percent net positive on leadership and 7.5 percent net positive on character during his first eighteen months in office.)

As is often the case, the UK media were highly critical of US policies and leaders. BBC1 and BBC2 reports on Bush's ability to govern were 18.5 percent net negative and 18 percent net negative respectively. US media were in the same league, with the most critical domestic assessment coming from ABC, at 18.9 percent net negative, and NBC, with 17.6 percent net negative. Fox News was also relatively critical here, with reports that were 14.9 percent net negative. CBS was actually the least critical US news outlet we examined, with 11.4 percent net negative coverage.

In some cases, the US media were more critical of Obama during his "honeymoon" period than they were of Bush during his second term. As shown in table 3.7, coverage relating to the new president's ability to govern was worse on Fox News (16.2 percent net negative) and CBS (21.7 percent net negative). Coverage of Obama relating to this topic was better than the treatment of Bush, but still not all that enthusiastic, on NBC (12.3 percent net negative). Only on ABC, with reports that were only 2.3 percent net negative, was Obama's coverage significantly better than Bush's for that same issue area.

The US news findings in table 4.4 suggest two things. With respect to the domestic content, the higher level of interest an American audience would have in the midterm elections tends to generate stories that contain more critical discussion of a presidency. A more macro-level perspective on US news by international media outlets would not contain as much interest in the more parochial matters of specific US House and Senate elections.

On the question of a president's ability to govern, the news from domestic outlets is consistently bad. Although the two presidential periods examined are not fully comparable, the results here indicate that the governing question is a tough one for presidents at any point in their term of office. (Of course, it is also possible that both of these presidents were particularly bad at governing during the periods examined. A study of other presidents or other years would be required to assess this alternative explanation.)

For both domestic and international reports, presidential character coverage is more favorable. The more reporters focused on matters of character, the better for the president. That was true for both US and international media, whose reporters would be attending many of the same briefings and being subject to many of the same media manipulations attempted by a White House publicity operation. Of course, this assumes that the president's character has not become a political issue, as sometimes occurs in a scandal-ridden administration. Presidents as different as Richard Nixon and Bill Clinton found that negative character coverage overshadowed news reporting on their policy successes as their presidencies progressed. Policy goals are highly important to voters in their evaluations of presidents, to be sure. But given that not all goals can be realized, presidents often try to burnish their personal qualities before the media.

Conclusion

We identified some clear patterns in coverage of George W. Bush by foreign news outlets, which corresponded to their country's government policies and domestic public preferences. For example, Germany's media were generally more negative about the United States during the Bush years than were UK media. This is consistent with what we would expect from past studies (cf. Hallin and Mancini 2004a; Jones 2006).

Similarly, news coverage of Bush was more negative on state-supported or publicly funded media outlets in a Western country that did not send troops to Iraq (Germany) than in the United Kingdom, which has consistently been among the leading nations in the "coalition of the willing." This is consistent with Jones's (2006) study of the rhetoric of Abu Ghraib, which found that Germany's media were most critical of the United States, the United States was least critical of itself, and the media of the United Kingdom came down in the middle.

In some areas, though, UK news reports were more critical than German reportage. In particular, this pattern appears for issues such as Bush's ability to govern. Prime Minister Tony Blair was derided in the British media for being "Bush's poodle" (Rutenberg and Lyall 2007). The highly critical coverage of Bush in this area might also imply that perhaps the junior partner in the Anglo-American relationship is more competent and should be calling the shots. The articulate, urbane Blair, particularly in British media, was treated less harshly than news reports relating to the frontier cowboy persona engineered by the Connecticut-born, Harvard- and Yale-educated Bush (Sanger 2001). The American president's comments about Blair, such as the odd remark that the two men use the same brand of toothpaste (Sanger 2001), at a minimum would give UK audiences pause about the American president's judgment and the wisdom of following his lead. (In case readers are wondering, the toothpaste brand favored by the two world leaders was Colgate.)

This chapter again highlights differences among the Arabic-language television news channels. There were distinct variations among the media sources in the region, with some of the most negative and also the least negative coverage of Bush found in the region. These divergent perspectives among the region's media may be the result of ongoing events during our study period. Some of these outlets would be more concerned about Iran's increasing regional influence during the Bush years, for example, than other Arabic news outlets would be.

Our findings also demonstrate the utility of administration marketing efforts in the region, even by a relatively unpopular American president. Middle Eastern media were more likely to use Bush administration officials in their reports on the US-related policies than were the European media. Aggressive outreach efforts to key media outlets in the region—including Al-Jazeera and Al-Arabiyah—appear to have paid off. At a minimum, the coverage was notably less critical than coverage from television broadcasters originating in NATO allies in Europe.

Finally, the US television networks were somewhat less critical of Bush than were the European media. This suggests that wartime presidents continue to have, if not the upper hand, at least a stronger hand in US political discourse, even in an environment of considerable and growing public hostility to presidential policies.

In addition to these patterns in media coverage, our study sheds light on the so-called CNN effect on foreign policy. As originally conceived, the CNN effect suggests an upward pressure from the public on policymakers that encourages them to respond to humanitarian crises represented by emotionally compelling pictures on television. Our findings suggest the possibility of a somewhat different process. The tone of news coverage, at least for these public broadcasters, seems to reflect elite policy preferences in the home nation. Thus, media influence on foreign policy in Western nations seems to be as much top down as it is bottom up, as others have observed about US news, particularly during military crises (cf. Entman 2004).

Although this chapter revealed some important dimensions of international news coverage of George W. Bush, and established some significant differences with Barack Obama's coverage, some of the most compelling direct comparisons are still to come.

In the next chapter we compare international news reports of Bush and Obama on key foreign and military policy topics, including the United States' standing in the world, US policies in Iraq and Afghanistan, and US antiterrorism policies.

CHAPTER 5

US Foreign Policy and International News: Comparing Obama and Bush

George W. Bush and Barack Obama each sought to create positive feelings, both for the United States and for themselves, in the global political environment. But they ended up with somewhat different results. Even as George W. Bush engaged in policies that generated considerable discontent in the international arena, he also sought to build communication and foreign policy bridges in the international arena. Bush and his diplomatic team had only limited success, however, in those cross-border public relations efforts (Brooks 2006; Entman 2004; Kessler and Wright 2007; Mueller 2006; Pew Global 2006, 2010a; Zaharna 2005).

In a pattern that started during his months as a presidential candidate, Barack Obama sought to reverse the highly negative international views of the outgoing president through international travel and through highly publicized commitments to greater international cooperation (Shear and Sullivan 2009; Zeleny and Cowell 2009; Zeleny and Kulish 2008). Global public opinion polls and our media data suggest Obama did make the world view him and the country he leads more positively during his first years in office. This was a sharp contrast from the Bush years, which were marked by little success in generating international enthusiasm for US government policies or its president (Pew Global 2006, 2010a, 2010b).

Satellite and cable television news provide a key mechanism for reaching international mass publics, particularly in areas where online usage remains less widespread (Pew Global 2010b). Even in wired areas of the world, television news continues to command huge audiences, and its content influences much peer-to-peer online political communication (Pew Global 2010a, 2010b). Presidents frequently engage in high-profile, television-friendly efforts to secure positive international news coverage, ranging from making leading policymakers available to explain US initiatives to international reporters and their audiences

(Kessler and Wright 2007; Zaharna 2005) and to undertaking major presidential public addresses such as Obama's speeches in Egypt and Turkey in 2009 (Shear and Sullivan 2009).

The Bush Legacy and Obama's International Agenda

Few presidents entered office with as challenging an agenda as Barack Obama faced in 2009. In addition to domestic troubles relating to an underperforming economy, the deep federal budget deficits, and America's rapidly aging population, America had a full plate internationally. Obama inherited wars in Iraq and Afghanistan, which strained relations with many US allies, and Bush's promise to find Osama bin Laden "dead or alive" remained unfulfilled. Relations were deteriorating with Pakistan, a key ally in the "war on terror," and a nuclear-armed power facing its own insurgency from Muslim extremists. To make matters worse, a restive China and an increasingly self-confident Russia had considerable interest in reducing American influence in international relations. And to top things off, Iran was trying to develop nuclear weapons (Sanger 2010a, 2010b).

At home there was little prospect of bipartisanship. Republicans refused to cooperate with the new president, hoping that his failures and the nation's suffering would install a Republican regime in Congress in 2010 and a Republican president in 2012 (Calmes 2011a; Sinclair 2012).

Where's the good news for this new president? Well, many people around the world liked the fact that Obama, rather than Bush, was running America (Pew Global 2010a, 2012). Surveys showed Americans also were eager to turn the page on Bush's international agenda. And most people seemed likely to give Obama credit for any improvement, whether he deserved that credit or not, as a result of Bush's profound unpopularity.

Like many presidents before him, Obama energetically grabbed the reins of America's foreign policy agenda. "'The day I take the oath of office, the world will look at us differently,' the candidate confided to his wife early on" (quoted in Wolffe 2009:20). As America's first African American president—and one who spent a significant part of his childhood in Indonesia and Hawaii, one of America's most multicultural states—Obama seemed more familiar with—and open to—the world than some previous American presidents. Above all, the new president tried to send the message to the world that he was more interested in international collaboration than Bush was. It didn't hurt that Obama physically personified the multicultural role that he said America would play in international relations going forward.

Once Obama became president, the world, generally speaking, liked what it saw and liked what it heard. Stung by comments about "Old Europe," traditional allies in the Western democracies rejoiced at the change in the direction of America viewing itself as part of a multilateral world (Singh 2012). Frustrated by having their concerns largely ignored in Washington, Palestinians and other Muslim peoples looked forward to a very different presidency, one much more open to hearing from all peoples in the middle of one of the world's most intractable crises (Sanger 2010a). Even Americans, who generally think about international matters as little as possible, were hopeful that this young, new, internationally oriented president could get America out of some of the military tar pits the United States was stuck in at the end of 2008 (Pew Global 2010a; Singh 2012).

Of course, practical political realities constrained the new president. A more multipolar foreign policy was essential for a nation facing significant budgetary constraints. Post-Bush America simply could not afford to finance an expansive international foreign and military policy in the years ahead without a significant increase in allied support and ever-greater cost-sharing agreements with US allies (Kupchan 2012; Zakaria 2008). This is not to say that Obama and Hillary Clinton, Obama's secretary of state, envisioned abandoning America's traditional leadership role in international relations. Rather, they believed American leadership could be retained with an agenda that had greater global consensus than the Bush foreign policy agenda did (Singh 2012).

Critics within the United States, such as James Ceaser of the University of Virginia, saw the personality-oriented Obama doctrine of collaboration as a recipe for American decline.

> This kind of soft power realism hardly bespeaks a foreign policy conducted on the basis of "a decent respect for the opinions of mankind," where principles are set down as markers designed to help open eyes to the rights of man. It represents instead a foreign policy based on an indecent pandering to an evanescent infatuation with a single personality. (quoted in Singh 2012:275)

In addition, hopes for peace were constrained by military realities. Obama saw the war in Afghanistan, which in June 2010 became the longest war in American history, as a necessary response to 9/11. In 2009, he sent an additional thirty thousand troops to Afghanistan, hoping to use a "surge" of his own to support the troubled Karzai government, to train more extensively the Afghan army, and to reverse Taliban gains in many of the nation's rural areas. More US troops were sent in 2011, with the hope of being able to reduce the US military presence in the region in the coming years. This continuation of the war looked—at least to some liberal critics and some elites abroad—more like a continuation of

Bush's strategy than the "change" that many had expected as a result of Obama's election. NATO allies were clamoring for an end date that always seemed to be just beyond the horizon (Baker 2010; Woodward 2010).

Nor did Obama shy away from unilateral military action. The US raid inside Pakistan to kill Osama bin Laden was undertaken without providing any advance notice to Pakistani authorities because of concerns that bin Laden would be notified or that the Pakistani military would otherwise undermine the operation (Schmitt, Shanker, and Sanger 2011). Bin Laden's location in one of the most militarized regions of that nation also raised questions about whether key elites in the Pakistani military and government were keeping the location of the world's most famous terrorist secret from their American allies (Gall 2011; Gall and Schmitt 2011).

In addition, Obama's policies of increasing the use of Predator drone strikes in the region, including some unmanned attacks within Pakistan that resulted in casualties, generated considerable frustration in that nation and in the larger region (Singh 2012).

Obama also has had little success in dealing with the Israeli-Palestinian impasse. Within the Middle East, Obama's decision to visit Cairo—but not Tel Aviv—during his first months in office was seen as a powerful snub to Israel. It also undermined his efforts to convince Israel to undertake swaps of land for peace, a precursor to the two-state solution that has been a key goal of US negotiations in the region for years. But Arabic voices liked the shift in emphasis that this travel schedule appeared to represent (Singh 2012).

Obama's efforts to deal with Iran also met with little success. Obama used economic sanctions and international efforts at isolating the regime to deter the nation from developing nuclear weapons. Both sanctions and saber rattling do not appear to have convinced Iran to follow a more peaceful course—at least not yet (as of this writing).

The most important bright spot for the Obama administration in international affairs was the steady drawdown of US forces in Iraq. The campaign promise to get US troops out of that nation was under way during Obama's first term and was fulfilled before Obama had completed three years as president (Arango and Schmidt 2011). But the news, once again, was not all good. US troop departures have not ensured peace in that long-suffering nation (Healy 2012).

Taken together, the Obama military policies proved less of a departure from the Bush years than many of his supporters might have hoped for in the wake of the 2008 presidential election. Indeed, some experts suggest that Obama's first-term approach to military matters resembled the Bush second term more than the Bush second term resembled the Bush first term (Singh 2012). Of course, supporters of Obama may take solace in the fact that the new president did not take the United States into *another* discretionary war (at least not yet).

DATA AND EXPECTATIONS

These events and policies provide the backdrop for understanding Obama's international media coverage during the eighteen-month period from January 2009 and through June 2010. This period was marked by Obama's selection for a Nobel Prize, but also by a decline in Obama's international popularity and a flare-up of Middle East tensions after Israeli commandos killed nine civilians on a Turkish ship near the Gaza strip in late May 2010 (Shear 2010). We examine news coverage of Obama overall as well as reports linking his administration to specific areas of evaluation, including America's standing in the world, the Iraq and Afghanistan wars, US antiterrorism policies, and initiatives in the Middle East.

We also compare these international findings with the tone of coverage of George W. Bush and his advisers during the eighteen-month period from January 2005 through June 2006. While the time periods are not fully comparable—one involves an incoming president and the other the start of a president's second term—the Bush-era results do provide important context for understanding the international news coverage of Obama. (Although occurring at different points in presidential terms, neither of the two periods examined here involved divided government in Washington. Obama enjoyed Democratic majorities in Congress during his first two years in office, and Bush enjoyed Republican majorities on Capitol Hill during the first two years of his second term.) Comparing Obama's first eighteen months in office with Bush's first eighteen months, even if we had fully comparable data, would be problematic. That earlier period included 9/11, which created a very distinct political and media environment for most of Bush's first term.

The news analysis relating to the Obama administration is based on a total of 172,739 statements relating to the United States on our now-familiar complement of five Arabic-language television outlets, two British, and two German television outlets. The analysis relating to the Bush administration is based on 138,379 statements relating to the United States from those same outlets. In addition, we supplement part of this chapter's analysis with a focused look on a portion of that total international news sample that directly assessed the two presidents and their policies. In that portion of the chapter, the Bush results are based on a content analysis of 19,114 statements on evening newscasts from nine international television news providers and 43,276 statements on evening newscasts from four US television news providers (ABC, CBS, NBC, and Fox News) during the first eighteen months of his second term. The Obama results in that portion of the chapter are based on a content analysis of 29,834 international news statements and 46,890 statements on US newscasts during his first eighteen months in office.

Given our findings so far, we expected that Obama would enjoy more positive coverage during 2009–2010 than Bush did during 2005–2006. We expected that the tone of the Obama administration's coverage would be more positive on matters relating to the US standing in the world than coverage of specific policies, and Obama coverage in all policy areas would be more positive than international reports on those same policies during 2005–2006. Once again, we expected that the more positive a nation's public and elites are toward US policies, the more positive the tone of news about a given administration would be.

Our expectations about what the data should reveal draw upon the enthusiasm that greeted Obama's election in many nations, his aggressive international outreach efforts, and the general international discontent with Bush. They also draw on the challenges foreign news reporters face in their access to authoritative and critical sources in the United States, challenges that give White House spin an advantage over alternative framing efforts by other political actors in international media (cf. Hamilton and Jenner 2003; Hannerz 2004; Hess 2005). That presidential marketing advantage seems most effective at the general level rather than at the level of specific policy initiatives, where actual events on the ground may undermine attempts at White House spinning of the news.

The European outlets considered here, based in nations where citizens are enthusiastic about the Obama administration, should be more positive than Arab media, located in a region where feelings about the United States are far less positive. The Pew Global (2010a) data suggest that Germany's news might be slightly more positive than the BBC's, given that Germans are marginally more enthusiastic about Obama. (Pew Global [2010a] does not include all the nations examined in this study in its international public opinion surveys, but survey evidence from other nations within the Middle East suggests that the populations of Britain and Germany generally were far more enthusiastic about the Obama administration than citizens in Muslim-majority nations.)

We expect that Middle Eastern broadcasters will vary in their approaches, with Al-Manar, which is connected to the anti-US Hezbollah, being the most negative. More positive news about both administrations seems most likely to come from Al-Arabiyah, a cable news outlet owned by a member of the royal family of long-time US ally Saudi Arabia. We expected the other Arab outlets to lie between these two more politically connected outlets. In the European context, higher elite support for the US government in the United Kingdom (as evidenced by their all-in approach to following the US lead in Iraq and Afghanistan) as compared to the somewhat less congenial relations between Washington and Berlin would lead to more positive coverage from British media.

Because the public opinion and elite perspectives suggest different results of comparisons between German and British media, the results here will offer a test of divergent interpretations of the connections among the media and elites and the mass public. If elite preferences matter more in Germany, as one would expect (cf. Hallin and Mancini 2004a), then coverage in German outlets should be more critical than that of the UK outlets. If public preferences matter more in the United Kingdom, as one would also expect (cf. Hallin and Mancini 2004a), then UK coverage should be more critical.

Results

We start here with an examination of news content relating to the two presidents themselves. Table 5.1 provides information about this coverage on the four European and five Arabic-language media outlets during the two eighteen-month study periods. The table also reports findings from a separate study of evening news coverage of Bush and Obama on four US television networks (ABC, CBS, NBC, and Fox News) during those same periods. As one would expect, the volume of US coverage of a US president on any US broadcast network far exceeds the amount of coverage of that president on any international news outlet. The net tone ratings for the two presidents in these thirteen news outlets appear in table 5.1. As in the previous chapters, the net tone measure is the percentage of positive tone minus the percentage of negative tone.

As already discussed, the findings show an international honeymoon coverage effect for Obama. Coverage by all international media outlets was more positive (or less negative) during Obama's first eighteen months in office than during the start of Bush's second term four years earlier. Eight of the nine international news outlets were more positive than negative in their treatment of Obama. Only the evening newscast on BBC1 was on balance negative, and only barely so. Coverage of Obama on Al-Jazeera, the satellite news provider so frequently identified as the source of anti-American news content during the Bush years, was the most positive of all.

By contrast, all nine international news outlets were negative overall in their treatment of Bush during 2005–2006. The gap between the Obama coverage and the Bush coverage exceeded ten percentage points for seven of the nine international news outlets. Only Al-Arabiyah, a news provider owned by the Saudi royal family (a royal family particularly close to the Bush family), and the Lebanese Broadcasting Corporation failed to cross that threshold. Perhaps the heavy Saudi investment in and influence over LBC helps explain this similarity in coverage (Kraidy 2012).

The claim that Al-Jazeera was notably anti-American in its sentiments during the Bush years is not borne out by this study. Coverage of Bush during this study period was barely negative on that broadcaster's evening news programs,

Table 5.1.   Television Coverage of Obama and Bush in International and US News Outlets

Period	Outlet	Net tone %	Negative %	Positive %	No clear rating %	N
2009/2010	ARD Tagesthemen	4.9	11.2	16.2	72.7	4,393
2005/2006		−7.7	12.5	4.7	82.8	1,626
2009/2010	ZDF heute journal	5.5	10.8	16.4	72.8	5,111
2005/2006		−7.7	13.6	5.8	80.6	2,112
2009/2010	BBC1 10 O'clock News	−1.2	8.4	7.2	84.4	3,398
2005/2006		−10.1	15.2	5.1	79.7	1,284
2009/2010	BBC2 Newsnight	2.8	11.6	14.4	74.0	3,397
2005/2006		−10.7	14.6	3.8	81.6	2,449
2009/2010	Al-Arabiyah	2.3	5.3	7.6	87.0	4,839
2005/2006		−5.1	7.6	2.5	89.9	2,431
2009/2010	Nile News	5.4	7.0	12.5	80.5	2,999
2005/2006		−8.5	9.6	1.1	89.3	1,229
2009/2010	LBC	1.5	4.0	5.5	90.5	1,020
2005/2006		−6.9	8.3	1.4	90.3	787
2009/2010	Al-Manar	3.0	25.1	28.1	46.9	2,605
2005/2006		−18.5	20.4	1.9	77.7	3,486
2009/2010	Al-Jazeera	12.3	16.6	28.9	54.5	2,072
2005/2006		−2.6	3.3	0.6	96.1	3,710
2009/2010	NBC	−2.8	11.6	8.8	79.6	8,188
2005/2006		−7.3	9.9	2.6	87.5	8,676
2009/2010	ABC	−3.0	10.4	7.4	82.2	8,946
2005/2006		−6.7	9.6	2.9	87.5	6,246
2009/2010	CBS	−5.9	15.1	9.2	75.7	7,031
2005/2006		−7.5	9.9	2.4	87.6	6,506
2009/2010	Fox News	−14.1	20.2	6.1	73.7	22,725
2005/2006		−4.8	9.2	4.4	86.3	21,848

N = Number of statements. Percentages might not sum to 100 because of rounding. The Bush results are based on a content analysis of 19,114 statements on evening newscasts from nine international television news providers and 43,276 statements on evening newscasts from four US television news providers from January 1, 2005, through June 30, 2006. The Obama results are based on a content analysis of 29,834 international news statements and 46,890 statements on US newscasts from January 1, 2009, through June 30, 2010.

and the reports were the least negative of the nine international news outlets examined here. The most negative assessments of Bush were found on Al-Manar, the voice of Hezbollah, and on the two news programs from the BBC included here.

The three traditional US evening news programs, such as the international media outlets discussed above, were less negative in their comments about Obama than they were about Bush. Of the thirteen news outlets we examined, only Fox News was more critical of Obama than of Bush. By contrast, the tone of coverage of Obama on Fox was far more negative than on any one of the twelve other news outlets. Five of the news outlets examined here were negative on balance toward Obama—the four US media outlets and BBC1. Even Al-Manar, the voice of the anti-American group Hezbollah, had more positive things to say about Obama than the four US news outlets.

The Obama honeymoon, as discussed in chapter 3, was deeper and longer lasting in international media than in US television news reports. That period of relatively favorable coverage likewise marked a powerful departure from more normal coverage, as measured by the 2005–2006 comparison. In a pattern that reflects public opinion in these nations, international news coverage of Bush was particularly harsh, and coverage of Obama was particularly positive, in part because of the change that Obama's election was thought to represent. US media, in contrast, avoided each extreme, sticking with a negative treatment of both presidents during both study periods (cf. Farnsworth and Lichter 2006a). (The analysis of Fox News in this project includes the entire hour of *Special Report*, rather than the first half hour sometimes used by researchers. Because the second half hour contains more roundtable commentary, full-hour results are more negative.)

Part of the explanation for the difference between US and international news coverage is likely the much more extensive coverage a US president receives on US news: the number of assessments of Obama on the four US outlets was 57 percent greater than the number of assessments of Obama on the *nine* international news outlets. For Bush, the number of assessments on those four US outlets was double the amount of attention he received on those nine international news outlets. The more extensive coverage of the White House in US media involves more granular coverage of the president's legislative struggles with Capitol Hill, controversies that tend not to place any president in the best of lights. Because international media have less interest in incremental, day-by-day actions in Washington, coverage of the president's domestic critics is reduced in news aimed at non-US audiences (cf. Farnsworth, Soroka, and Young 2010). How many international news viewers would even know who Senate Minority Leader Mitch McConnell (R-Ky.) is, and how many of them would have much interest in what he has to say about Obama?

Table 5.2 compares the international news coverage of the Obama administration with that of the Bush administration on assessments of America's standing in the world. News in this category includes broad assessments of America's global influence with respect to both hard and soft power. News stories that focus on specific policy matters, such as the wars in Afghanistan and Iraq or the various US initiatives to lessen tensions in the Middle East, are not included in this measure. They are discussed later in the chapter. (We have not conducted comparable US news content analyses for the Obama and Bush administrations' policies on the specific international dimensions that are the focus of the rest of this chapter. The remaining tables provide comparisons only among the nine international news outlets examined here.)

Obama's efforts to rebuild the American brand in the international arena appear to have paid dividends across the board, according to the results found in table 5.2. Eight of the nine international media outlets offered mostly positive statements relating to the US role in global affairs during the Obama administration's first eighteen months in office. The one exception was Al-Arabiyah, and it was only slightly more negative than positive. Al-Jazeera was the most pro-US world leadership in its coverage during 2009–2010, followed by the four European news outlets. In 2005–2006, in contrast, seven of the nine media outlets offered mostly negative assessments of the United States' standing in the world. The differences between the two periods were striking, with six of the nine outlets offering double-digit swings in a more positive direction.

Only Nile News, controlled at the time by then-president Mubarak and his allies, was more positive in its treatment of the Bush administration during 2005–2006 than the Obama administration four years later. The Obama administration's increasing pressure for democratic reform in Egypt may have reduced the positive treatment of the new president's team by that state broadcaster. In addition, Egypt, a close US ally ruled at that time by an authoritarian, secular government, would be far less troubled by the continuing occupation of Iraq and Afghanistan during the Bush years than were other voices in the Arab world. But arguing for political reform while within Egypt, as Obama did, could be a problem for the sclerotic Mubarak regime. And it was.

News coverage of the wars in Afghanistan and Iraq, reported in table 5.3, generated the most negative reviews of the two administrations found in this study. In 2005–2006, for example, negative assessments outpaced positive assessments by at least an eight-to-one margin. Britain may have been an ally in both of those engagements, but the news coverage of the Bush administration during this time was highly negative there as well. (This earlier study period, it should be noted, did coincide with some of the greatest instability during the occupation of Iraq.) Both BBC1 and BBC2 were 26.3 percent net negative in their news stories during the start of Bush's second term. Of course, the

Table 5.2. International News Coverage of America's Standing in the World

Period	Outlet	Net tone %	Negative %	Positive %	No clear rating %	N
2009/2010	ARD Tagesthemen	7.6	16.0	23.6	60.4	457
2005/2006		-1.4	9.1	7.7	83.2	519
2009/2010	ZDF heute journal	7.4	14.6	22.0	63.4	610
2005/2006		-3.0	14.2	11.2	74.6	571
2009/2010	BBC1 10 O'clock News	7.7	8.1	15.8	76.2	768
2005/2006		3.3	15.9	19.2	64.9	271
2009/2010	BBC2 Newsnight	8.6	8.3	16.9	74.8	1,630
2005/2006		-7.2	15.2	8.0	76.8	638
2009/2010	Al-Arabiyah	-1.4	8.7	7.3	84.0	3,934
2005/2006		-11.8	23.4	11.6	65.0	577
2009/2010	Nile News	2.2	13.1	15.4	71.5	1,919
2005/2006		9.9	6.4	16.3	77.3	141
2009/2010	LBC	-2.3	12.5	10.2	77.3	176
2005/2006		-6.2	14.4	8.2	77.3	97
2009/2010	Al-Manar	0.8	34.9	35.7	29.4	2,269
2005/2006		-21.3	29.6	8.3	62.1	1,127
2009/2010	Al-Jazeera	10.6	24.9	35.5	39.6	1,926
2005/2006		-11.0	20.8	9.8	69.3	336

N = Number of statements. Percentages might not sum to 100 because of rounding. This table is based on a content analysis of 138,379 statements about the United States on evening newscasts from nine international news outlets from January 1, 2005, through June 30, 2006, and 172,739 statements about the United States from January 1, 2009, through June 30, 2010.

Table 5.3. International News Coverage of Obama and Bush Policies in Iraq and Afghanistan

Period	Outlet	Net tone %	Negative %	Positive %	No clear rating %	N
2009/2010	ARD Tagesthemen	−25.9	31.3	5.4	63.3	313
2005/2006		−46.6	47.5	0.8	51.7	712
2009/2010	ZDF heute journal	−26.4	30.2	3.8	65.9	364
2005/2006		−43.2	43.5	0.4	56.1	843
2009/2010	BBC1 10 O'clock News	−4.0	12.8	8.8	78.4	1,234
2005/2006		−26.3	29.9	3.6	66.5	669
2009/2010	BBC2 Newsnight	−2.1	10.3	8.2	81.4	1,675
2005/2006		−26.3	28.2	1.9	69.9	1,647
2009/2010	Al-Arabiyah	−10.9	12.4	1.5	86.1	1,227
2005/2006		−32.7	34.1	1.4	64.6	1,766
2009/2010	Nile News	−22.3	24.5	2.2	73.2	538
2005/2006		−42.0	42.7	0.7	56.6	848
2009/2010	LBC	1.0	5.7	6.7	87.6	105
2005/2006		−35.3	37.8	2.5	59.6	669
2009/2010	Al-Manar	−58.3	61.9	3.7	34.4	544
2005/2006		−40.4	41.2	0.8	58.0	4,280
2009/2010	Al-Jazeera	−42.1	48.7	6.6	44.6	708
2005/2006		−34.0	35.6	1.6	62.8	2,575

N = Number of statements. Percentages might not sum to 100 because of rounding. This table is based on a content analysis of 138,379 statements about the United States on evening newscasts from nine international news outlets from January 1, 2005, through June 30, 2006, and 172,739 statements about the United States from January 1, 2009, through June 30, 2010.

German media were even more critical, with coverage 46.6 percent net negative on ARD Tagesthemen and 43.2 percent net negative on ZDF heute journal during 2005–2006. Higher levels of criticism may have been more palatable in Germany, as that nation was not part of the "coalition of the willing" in Iraq.

The different Arabic-language media had relatively similar perspectives on Bush's handling of Iraq and Afghanistan, ranging from 32.7 percent net negative on Al-Arabiyah to 42 percent net negative on Nile News. Within the group, Al-Jazeera's coverage was less critical than three other Arabic-language outlets—though at 34 percent net negative it was plenty critical in its own right.

The Iraq and Afghanistan war coverage was also quite negative during the Obama administration's first eighteen months on the job. But it was markedly less negative than the earlier period for seven of the nine media outlets—excepting only Al-Manar and Al-Jazeera, which were highly critical of both administrations' efforts in the region. There was a fifteen-percentage-point swing or more in the Obama administration's direction for seven of the nine media outlets. These findings suggest that changing circumstances and a new president's outreach efforts can help persuade the media regarding even unpopular policies.

Table 5.4 shows coverage of US antiterrorism policies. This topic includes coverage of the sometimes-controversial activities of the US Department of Homeland Security, the tightening restrictions on visitors to the United States, and the continued incarceration of some suspected terrorists at a US military installation in Guantanamo Bay, Cuba.

The Guantanamo story was the arena in which Obama's international charm offensive most clearly failed to bear fruit. Although Obama promised to turn the page on the Bush administration's unpopular policies, he sometimes has found it hard to do so. Obama did not keep his promise that he would close the Guantanamo antiterrorist jail and bring detainees to trial. With respect to international visitors and immigrants, Obama talked about making access to America less problematic for outsiders. But would-be visitors and immigrants report continued severe obstacles to getting visas to work or study in the United States (Semple 2010). Obama did, however, ban the military's widely criticized practice of waterboarding, which was considered internationally (but not by the Bush administration) to be torture (Shane 2009).

The Obama administration's international news coverage in the antiterrorism area was even more negative than the Bush administration's in four media outlets—BBC2's Newsnight, Nile News of Egypt, Al-Manar, and Al-Jazeera. Although coverage of the Obama administration was more favorable in three of the four European outlets, negative coverage continued to exceed positive coverage by a three-to-one margin in all four cases.

Europeans clearly do not see as great a need for such aggressive homeland security efforts in the United States as Washington does, regardless of who is

Table 5.4. International News Coverage of US Antiterrorism Policies

Period	Outlet	Net tone %	Negative %	Positive %	No clear rating %	N
2009/2010	ARD Tagesthemen	-16.0	23.0	6.9	70.1	692
2005/2006		-26.6	28.7	2.1	69.2	812
2009/2010	ZDF heute journal	-17.6	22.1	4.5	73.4	910
2005/2006		-24.9	26.0	1.1	72.9	1,281
2009/2010	BBC1 10 O'clock News	-12.5	16.3	3.7	80.0	1,284
2005/2006		-17.5	20.3	2.8	76.9	1,006
2009/2010	BBC2 Newsnight	-18.1	25.3	7.2	67.5	2,157
2005/2006		-12.0	13.7	1.7	84.7	2,646
2009/2010	Al-Arabiyah	-9.8	13.7	3.9	82.4	1,506
2005/2006		-15.3	16.5	1.3	82.2	2,853
2009/2010	Nile News	-12.4	18.2	5.8	76.1	869
2005/2006		-9.4	10.2	0.8	88.9	1,065
2009/2010	LBC	0.9	0.4	1.3	98.3	235
2005/2006		-11.8	13.4	1.6	84.9	922
2009/2010	Al-Manar	-40.1	50.3	10.2	39.6	2,027
2005/2006		-24.5	25.3	0.9	73.8	4,562
2009/2010	Al-Jazeera	-25.3	35.7	10.4	53.9	1,587
2005/2006		-12.0	12.6	0.5	86.9	2,060

N = Number of statements. Percentages might not sum to 100 because of rounding. This table is based on a content analysis of 138,379 statements about the United States on evening newscasts from nine international news outlets from January 1, 2005, through June 30, 2006, and 172,739 statements about the United States from January 1, 2009, through June 30, 2010.

president. For this issue it may be that increased international expectations led to disappointment regarding the amount of change Obama engineered. Television reports in the United Kingdom, which has had significant experience with terrorism via bombings by Al-Qaeda and before that by the Irish Republican Army, were less critical of US policies in this regard than were the German broadcasters. With respect to their own borders, the nations of the European Union have agreed to open up Germany, the United Kingdom, and other member countries to international population movements that would have been unimaginable a few decades ago. (Of course, how warmly these international population movements have been received is perhaps a different story.)

The Obama administration fared only slightly better than the Bush team in coverage of Middle East initiatives as well (see table 5.5). This issue area includes US policies relating to the core regional players of the Israeli-Palestinian dispute: Israel, the Palestinian territories, Lebanon, and Syria. (Egypt and Jordan, other influential nations in the region, already have peace agreements with Israel and have been far less involved in the regional instability during the periods we studied.) The Obama administration tried to take a tougher line with Israel than Bush did regarding new settlements in contested areas, and he tried to revive the peace process. Those efforts, though not generating much progress toward the two-state solution favored by many in the region, appeared to result in improved news coverage of US efforts in the region in the Arabic-language media. All five Arabic-language media and the two British media were less negative of Obama on the Middle East crisis, but the differences between the two periods tended to be modest. In contrast, the two German media outlets examined here were more critical of the Obama administration's policies in the region than they were of efforts by the Bush team, perhaps because Germany's particularly close political alliance with Israel made them more sympathetic to Bush's perspective (Dempsey 2011a, 2011b).

The good news for the Obama team was the evenly balanced assessments of US policies in the region by all the Arabic-language media except Al-Manar, the voice of Hezbollah. Four years earlier, negative assessments were outweighed by positive ones by a three-to-one margin in all five Arabic-language outlets.

The final table in this chapter examines environmental issues. As shown in table 5.6, US environmental policies are yet another area where Obama does not fare better than Bush in the international news arena. In fact, the Obama administration received more negative reviews than the Bush team did four years earlier.

It may seem strange that the Obama team, which viewed man-made climate change as an international crisis, received more negative notices in three out of four European media outlets than did the Bush administration, which did little in this policy area but try to tone down scientific reports about climate change

Table 5.5. International News Coverage of US Policies in the Middle East

Period	Outlet	Net tone %	Negative %	Positive %	No clear rating %	N
2009/2010	ARD Tagesthemen	-12.9	20.5	7.7	71.8	365
2005/2006		-8.3	8.3	0.0	91.7	48
2009/2010	ZDF heute journal	-6.7	15.3	8.6	76.1	255
2005/2006		0.9	0.9	1.9	97.2	107
2009/2010	BBC1 10 O'clock News	-2.3	2.3	0.0	97.7	218
2005/2006		-4.0	4.0	0.0	96.0	50
2009/2010	BBC2 Newsnight	-1.6	3.7	2.1	94.2	191
2005/2006		-3.3	7.4	4.1	88.4	121
2009/2010	Al-Arabiyah	-0.6	4.5	3.9	91.6	1,742
2005/2006		-4.0	5.7	1.7	92.6	721
2009/2010	Nile News	-1.7	10.0	8.3	81.7	1,555
2005/2006		-4.6	5.7	1.2	93.1	418
2009/2010	LBC	0.3	2.1	2.4	95.5	380
2005/2006		-10.5	10.8	0.3	89.0	353
2009/2010	Al-Manar	-14.4	33.5	19.0	47.5	1,802
2005/2006		-18.0	19.3	1.3	79.4	1,615
2009/2010	Al-Jazeera	-0.8	22.8	22.0	55.2	1,193
2005/2006		-7.6	10.7	3.1	86.2	458

N = Number of statements relating to US policies involving Israel, the Palestinian territories, Lebanon, and Syria. Percentages might not sum to 100 because of rounding. This table is based on a content analysis of 138,379 statements about the United States on evening newscasts from nine international news outlets from January 1, 2005, through June 30, 2006, and 172,739 statements about the United States from January 1, 2009, through June 30, 2010.

Table 5.6. International News Coverage of US Environmental Policies

Period	Outlet	Net tone %	Negative %	Positive %	No clear rating %	N
2009/2010	ARD Tagesthemen	-31.7	40.8	9.1	50.2	895
2005/2006		-20.2	25.4	5.3	69.3	114
2009/2010	ZDF heute journal	-38.5	45.7	7.1	47.2	898
2005/2006		-17.8	19.8	2.0	78.2	101
2009/2010	BBC1 10 O'clock News	-41.9	47.3	5.4	47.2	754
2005/2006		-19.2	26.7	7.5	65.8	120
2009/2010	BBC2 Newsnight	-9.1	23.1	14.0	62.9	1,142
2005/2006		-14.7	18.4	3.8	77.8	320
2009/2010	Al-Arabiyah	-29.1	30.6	1.6	67.8	258
2005/2006		-39.5	42.1	2.6	55.3	38
2009/2010	Nile News	-27.5	33.0	5.5	61.5	109
2005/2006		*	*	*	*	*
2009/2010	LBC	-22.0	22.0	0.0	78.0	50
2005/2006		*	*	*	*	*
2009/2010	Al-Manar	-30.5	47.5	16.9	35.6	59
2005/2006		*	*	*	*	*
2009/2010	Al-Jazeera	-30.8	40.8	10.0	49.2	130
2005/2006		-36.4	38.6	2.3	59.1	44

* Too few cases to classify (n < 10).

N = Number of statements relating to US policies involving the environment. Percentages might not sum to 100 because of rounding. This table is based on a content analysis of 138,379 statements about the United States on evening newscasts from nine international news outlets from January 1, 2005, through June 30, 2006, and 172,739 statements about the United States from January 1, 2009, through June 30, 2010.

(cf. Clayton 2007; McCright and Dunlap 2003; Revkin 2005, 2006; Rich and Merrick 2007). But whatever the Obama administration's preferences regarding environmental policies, pro-business majorities in Congress have blocked the most significant climate change efforts proposed by the new president (Broder 2010). Obama's promises may have led to more critical assessments of policy outcomes that fell short of the rhetoric. Those negative evaluations would still come Obama's way in broad-brush media reports, even if Obama himself is not responsible for the discrepancy between what Obama said he would do and what Congress refused to authorize. Even though the president's stimulus bill did include significant investments in "green" energy, the constraints of domestic public opinion—and the financial troubles experienced by some of those programs supported in the bill—limited Obama's ability to trumpet efforts in that area (Broder 2012; Fletcher 2009).

The negativity was pronounced in all the outlets examined here. Even in the Arabic-language media, which tended not to emphasize this topic in news reports, the coverage of the US government's environmental policies was markedly negative. The BBC1 news reports were most critical of Obama, with reports that were 41.9 percent net negative, while ZDF heute journal was not far behind, with reports that were 38.5 percent net negative. There was far less coverage of the Bush administration's environmental issues for these two outlets; there were more than five times the number of Obama stories as Bush stories in this issue area.

The least critical outlet for Obama regarding the environment was on BBC2, where coverage was 9.1 percent net negative. It was the only one of the outlets examined here that was not double-digit net negative. The second most critical outlet was LBC, at 22 percent net negative. All of Bush's evaluations were net negative by a double-digit margin. Three of the four European outlets were more critical of Bush (all except BBC2).

The two Arabic-language broadcasters that produced enough environmental coverage in both time periods to allow for valid comparisons were more critical of Bush in both instances. Coverage for Bush regarding the environment was most critical on Al-Arabiyah, with 39.5 percent net negative, and Al-Jazeera, with 36.4 percent net negative.

The lengthy, problematic US government response to the BP oil spill in the Gulf of Mexico helps explain some of the negativity relating to the environment news coverage of Obama. Although the company was first blamed for the disaster, media attention increasingly focused on the federal government's inability to help BP cap the flow of oil, leading to very negative evaluations of Obama and his administration. This pattern was particularly pronounced in UK media, the home nation of BP (Maltese 2010; Schatz 2010b).

Another problematic issue for Obama in the environmental arena was the failure of the international community to make progress at the Copenhagen environmental summit in December 2009 (Gawthorne 2010). A Media Tenor study of thirty international television news outlets around the Copenhagen conference revealed there was little news coverage leading up to the meeting, which led to relatively little public pressure on policymakers to reach an agreement. The lack of agreement also drew relatively little attention.

In the four quarters of 2009 and the first two quarters of 2010, a period that included both the BP spill and the uneventful Copenhagen summit, the Media Tenor study revealed that environmental news failed to draw even as much attention as did sports, much less the economy or foreign affairs (Gawthorne 2010).

Conclusion

Obama enjoyed a powerful honeymoon in international media, and this pattern is particularly apparent when compared to coverage of George W. Bush at the start of his second term. The most positive international treatment of Obama was in the areas he emphasized in his public presidency—coverage of himself as president and the general discussion of the role the United States can play in world affairs. With respect to some specific issue areas, the Obama administration routinely received better coverage during his first eighteen months than the Bush team did during the first eighteen months of his second term, with the biggest gaps found in international news coverage of the high-profile wars in Afghanistan and Iraq. Despite the improvement, however, overall coverage of the US-led wars was mainly negative under both presidents.

In some issue areas, such as the environment and antiterrorism policies, international coverage was actually more negative for Obama. This appears to represent some frustrations in international circles that US policies did not change as much as candidate Obama had indicated they would.

European media were more positive than most of the Arabic-language media with respect to Obama generally. They were also more positive regarding America's standing in the world, presumably because of Obama's promise to engage in a more collaborative foreign policy, a sharp departure from the "Old Europe" ally bashing that sometimes took place during the Bush years (Bernstein 2003). Those results are consistent with the idea that the closest allies and those with mass publics more supportive of the US government would offer the most positive news coverage. But this pattern was less consistent when we looked at media coverage of specific issue areas, including the wars in Iraq and Afghanistan, Middle East policies, and the environment.

In a departure from our expectations based on past research, President Obama received relatively favorable treatment in Middle Eastern media on many topics. Arabic-language newscasts often contained more positive reports than those found in at least some European media. The most surprising aspect of this departure from past studies concerns the very positive treatment Obama received for himself, for America's standing in the world, and for Middle East policies on Al-Jazeera, a news outlet of particular concern for Washington during the Bush years.

The end of the Bush presidency and Obama's outreach efforts to Muslims appear to have triggered more enthusiasm for the United States than one would have expected given publics in the region, who were relatively critical in their assessments of the United States (cf. Pew Global 2010a). Of course, the continuing highly critical coverage of US policies relating to wars and antiterrorism efforts demonstrates the limits of an American president's public appeals. These results suggest the need for some refinements in theories positing that television news caters closely to viewers' tastes, at least where international news regarding the United States is concerned. It may also suggest that Al-Jazeera, at least in 2009–2010, might be viewed as a media outlet in the second or perhaps the third stage of development under the Stromback (2007) model.

Previous comparative media studies suggested that Arabic-language media might be aligned from the most pro-US elites (Al-Arabiyah, owned by a part of the Saudi royal family) to the most opposed (Al-Manar, connected to Hezbollah). As expected, Al-Manar was in fact the most critical of the five Arabic-language media examined here in three of six cases: the wars in Afghanistan and Iraq, US antiterrorism policies, and US Middle East policies. Al-Arabiyah, thought to be the most positive of this group because of its links to the Saudi royal family, finished in the middle of the pack and was not the most positive in any of the six comparisons here. The Lebanese Broadcasting Corporation was the most positive in four of six cases, and Al-Jazeera was the most positive in two others. LBC's performance is not entirely unexpected, as Lebanon does have a large, pro-Western political dimension to its politics, but the relatively pro-US coverage found in Al-Jazeera does represent a departure from what many government officials have been saying about that news outlet for years.

The European media outlets sometimes performed as expected and sometimes did not (cf. Hallin and Mancini 2004a). Obama's special outreach efforts to Germans during the 2008 campaign had only limited long-term impact on specific policy coverage. While the German media treated Obama positively and had mostly positive assessments of the US role in the world under the new president, German media were quite critical when it came to controversial policies such as the US-led wars in Afghanistan and Iraq, US antiterrorism policies, the new president's initiatives in the Middle East, and US environmental policies.

The UK media also were largely positive in their treatment of Obama and of the US standing in the world under the new president, but they were less negative than the German media on US-led wars in Afghanistan and Iraq. The difference in the news coverage coming out of those two NATO allies is probably explained by the fact that the United Kingdom has played a key role in both international efforts, while the German military played a smaller role in Afghanistan and was not part of the Iraq War and occupation. But there are limits to even the extremely tight US-UK alliance. The British media were critical of US antiterrorism policies, barely differing from the German media, and BBC1 was even more critical than German media of US environmental policies.

Although candidate Obama was a very appealing choice to many mass publics and governments around the world in 2008, our findings are reminders that political realities trump personal popularity. Regardless of who sits in the Oval Office, the US government often engages in policies that are viewed critically beyond America's borders. Obama's election and efforts in the international public presidency had a significant influence in how the United States is evaluated around the world—particularly in terms of overall assessments regarding the president and America's global role. But US policies that are unpopular internationally, such as the wars in Afghanistan and Iraq, keeping the Guantanamo Bay prison open, retaining many Bush-era antiterrorism policies, and doing relatively little to combat global warming, continue to weigh down international news coverage of the United States, regardless of who the president may be.

Administrations may not change foreign policy as much as promised—or as much as many in the Middle East or Europe would like. Many overseas media outlets remain focused on those policy areas where the United States is seen to fall short of the preferences of their audiences. That should not be surprising: criticism of authority is a key media function, and criticism of a distant government is hardly the most politically sensitive thing an international news provider could do. Many international reporters, in other words, would rather criticize US government policy than attack one's own government. For reporters working at some state media outlets, doing so would be problematic.

One limitation of the comparative aspects of this chapter is that the first eighteen months of a first term is not the same as the first eighteen months of a second term. Even so, Bush administration coverage offers a useful context, demonstrating that Obama's coverage improved on a number of policy dimensions—but not all of them. Finally, given the significant declines in Obama's popularity in the United States as the midterm elections approached—together with the highly challenging issues of Afghanistan, Iran, Iraq, and Pakistan, the continuing global economic crisis, and an unusually restive Middle East—the generally positive findings presented here may represent the high-water mark for international news coverage of this new president (Diehl 2012; Morton 2006/2007; Sanger 2010b, 2012).

CHAPTER 6

International News Perspectives on the 2008 US Presidential Election

When Americans select their presidential candidates and their presidents, people across the globe have more than a passing interest in the outcome. Never was this truer than in 2008, when America chose a successor to George W. Bush, who received particularly negative international evaluations throughout most of his presidency (Pew Global 2006). Add the first viable African American and female presidential candidates to the 2008 nomination campaign, not to mention the first female Republican vice presidential nominee, and you have an election season of extraordinary interest at home and abroad (Abramson, Aldrich, and Rohde 2010; Burden 2010; Ceaser et al. 2009; Nelson 2010).

This chapter examines international television news coverage of the nomination and general election phases of the 2008 presidential campaign, as seen through the media found in two key European allies: the United Kingdom and Germany. Four UK and two German television news sources are examined here. Using Media Tenor's content analysis, this study examines the amount and tone of coverage received by the leading Democratic and Republican candidates, as well as the amount and tone of coverage for the leading candidates on key issues of policy, leadership, and campaign dynamics. The Media Tenor content analysis codebook created for elections is drawn from previous studies of US presidential nomination and election campaign content in US media by the Center for Media and Public Affairs (cf. Farnsworth and Lichter 2003, 2006b, 2008, 2011a, 2012a). Extensive similarities in content analysis methodologies allow for European news to be examined in the context of how US television news covered the same campaign. (But the approaches are not identical, as we discuss below.)

While presidential campaigns are waged primarily for and to a domestic audience, news coverage of potential presidents abroad can offer international audiences valuable insights into the American democratic system and the individuals who might lead it. Indeed, such coverage can help shape the ability of a newly elected US president to persuade international leaders and publics to think more positively about the United States and to support a new president's policies in contentious international matters (Pew Global 2010a, 2010b). As a candidate, Barack Obama took European public opinion very seriously. He waged an unprecedented international tour after he secured the presidential nomination that included a speech to hundreds of thousands gathered in Berlin in July 2008 (Heilemann and Halperin 2010; Zeleny and Kulish 2008).

This chapter examines the potential problems identified in US television news coverage of presidential campaigns and seeks to determine whether the problems associated with US election news also appear in international news coverage.

US Presidential Campaign News: Coverage Patterns and Problems

Few political institutions have been criticized as frequently and as vehemently in the United States as the mass media. Politicians of all parties and all ideological stripes regularly rail against the media's role in the political process, reserving their harshest judgments for media coverage of national elections. While their complaints might be self-serving, they are often supported by scholarly studies of media performance, critiques by in-house media analysts, and even the *mea culpas* of reporters and editors.

While scholars most often focus on how journalists cover general elections, their concerns about news content are at least as relevant to primary campaigns. Citizens depend most heavily on the media during the presidential nomination process, a time when most candidates are not well known, when the selection process often takes place quickly, and when voters cannot use partisanship as a cue to choose among competitors from the same political party (Busch 2008; Cohen et al. 2008; Lengle 1981; Mayer and Busch 2004; Polsby 1983). International audiences likewise need effective media content to get to know the leading rivals for arguably the world's most important office.

Researchers have identified four key problems with mainstream US news coverage of campaigns and elections: (1) there is not enough coverage of campaigns; (2) the coverage is misdirected, focusing on the horse race rather than how the candidates would address important issues if elected; (3) the coverage is not fairly allocated among the candidates; and (4) the tone of news coverage is unfair, as reporters treat some candidates more harshly than others (Adatto 1990; Alter 1992; Cappella and Jamieson 1997; Dautrich and Hartley 1999; Farnsworth and Lichter 2011a; Iyengar 1991; Owen 2009; Patterson 1994).

THE HORSE-RACE FOCUS

The conventional scholarly view of US media coverage is that its usefulness depends on whether it focuses on matters of substance or ignores public policy in favor of campaign hoopla, ephemeral campaign trail controversies, and "horse race" reports on the latest surveys. US reporters frequently vow that they will improve future campaign coverage by making it more substantive, but research shows that few keep that promise (cf. Alter 1992). With polls released daily in the weeks before pivotal contests such as the New Hampshire primary, every day can be a poll-reporting day for correspondents who are tempted to provide horse-race journalism of the presidential campaign at the expense of more substantive news focusing on what the candidates would do, policywise, if elected (Farnsworth and Lichter 2003, 2006b; Smith 2004).

Indeed, horse-race coverage in the news has been dominant on US network television news during the last three primary campaign cycles for which we have data: 71 percent of the primary coverage in 2008 focused on the horse race, just slightly below the 78 percent recorded in 2000 and 77 percent in 2004 (Farnsworth and Lichter 2012a). The 1988 nomination contest was the least oriented toward the daily rankings of the candidates of the last six nomination cycles, with 49 percent horse-race coverage (Farnsworth and Lichter 2012a). So, at best, roughly half the primary campaign news provides little information to help voters learn what the candidates would do if elected. In the worst of times, issue coverage loses to horse-race journalism by a three-to-one margin on the US evening newscasts.

Horse-race coverage has also dominated the mass media's general election discourse. During the last three general election campaigns for which we have data, 41 percent of the general election coverage in 2008 focused on the horse race, as compared to 48 percent recorded in 2004 and 71 percent of the reports on the razor-thin content in 2000 (Farnsworth and Lichter 2011a). Even in the best of times, in other words, nearly half the campaign news provides little information to help voters learn what the candidates would do if elected. In the worst of times, issue coverage loses to horse-race journalism by a huge margin on the US evening newscasts. A Project for Excellence in Journalism study of newspaper, cable, radio, and online reports on the presidential campaign in 2008 likewise found media reports focused on polling results (Farnsworth and Lichter 2011a).

The relative absence of issue coverage can be particularly troubling during the fast-moving primary campaigns. Such contests often involve several viable but little-known contenders. The differences among candidates of the same party are likely to be far more subtle than differences between candidates of opposing parties. This increases the value of news reports examining the candidates' issue positions during the early primaries for all but the most sophisticated online searchers of political information.

A key issue in much US media coverage of primary candidates involves the horse-race questions of whether they "beat the spread"—that is, whether they do better or worse than pre-primary polls suggested they would do. In the last *USA Today*/Gallup poll taken during 2007 among likely Democratic voters, Hillary Clinton was favored by 45 percent of those Democrats expressing a preference, as compared to 27 percent for Obama and 15 percent for John Edwards. In the Republican poll at the end of 2007, Rudy Giuliani was favored by 27 percent of partisans expressing a preference, as compared to 16 percent for Mike Huckabee and 14 percent each for John McCain, Mitt Romney, and Fred Thompson (Reiter 2009). In other words, neither of the pre-season favorites emerged as the nominee.

Previous studies suggest US election news tends to be more horse-race focused than election news in some other countries. A comparison of the coverage of election news in US newspapers during the 2004 presidential campaign with that of three Swedish newspapers during the 2002 national elections found the US media were far more inclined to focus on politics as a strategic game at the expense of issues (Stromback and Dimitrova 2006). Likewise, researchers who have examined news coverage of US and Canadian national elections and party nomination contests found more extensive coverage of substantive policy issues in north-of-the-border news reports (for instance, Andrew et al. 2006, 2008; Farnsworth, Lichter, and Schatz 2009; Gidengil 2008; Gidengil et al. 2002).

TONAL DIFFERENCES IN COVERAGE

Media attention can reward or punish nomination candidates in three different ways: by the amount of news coverage a candidate receives, by the selection of the topics that are emphasized in news reports, and by the tone of the news coverage. Since most candidates are relatively unknown nationally (and internationally, for that matter), a key early challenge is to build name recognition. If a candidate does not have much money, and most campaigns do not until they start doing well in the polls, news coverage (known by campaigns as "free media") is the best way to become better known (Mayer 2004).

Past studies of news coverage of nominations suggest that a form of journalistic triage takes place well before the first votes are cast in Iowa and New Hampshire. Robinson and Sheehan (1983) found that for purposes of allocating scarce media resources, candidates are categorized as "hopeless," "plausible," and "likely." The likely nominees, also known as front-runners, get a lot of coverage by virtue of their status as favorites. In the middle category are the plausible candidates, who get some coverage, but not as much as likely nominees. If these midrange campaigners exceed expectations, though, they may suddenly receive a lot more media attention, and even become likely nominees themselves. Then there are the hopeless candidates, who get little news coverage unless their campaigns show some signs of life—which probably won't happen, since reporters are ignoring them.

Thus, once Barack Obama emerged as the key nomination rival to one-time favorite Hillary Clinton, both the volume and the tone of his coverage improved. Obama's coverage during the 2008 primary season (measured in that study as the period from December 16, 2007, through March 22, 2008) was 75 percent positive and 25 percent negative. He fared considerably better in the media than Hillary Clinton, the eventual second-place finisher, who received 53 percent positive coverage during that same campaign period (Farnsworth and Lichter 2011a:113).

On the Republican side, US network news coverage once again reflected the compensatory coverage model (Robinson and Sheehan 1983). Huckabee's rise to become McCain's major rival provided him with significant attention and more positive press than McCain, who emerged as the party's front-runner following his New Hampshire primary victory. Huckabee received 58 percent positive coverage during the period from December 16, 2007, through March 22, 2008. That was better than John McCain, the eventual nominee, who received 46 percent positive coverage, and former Massachusetts governor Mitt Romney, who obtained 44 percent positive coverage (Farnsworth and Lichter 2011a:115). The harshest news coverage was reserved for the candidate who failed to meet the media's projected odds: the fast-falling campaign of Rudy Giuliani, with only 16 percent positive coverage (Farnsworth and Lichter 2012a:145). (To convert the CMPA findings to the Media Tenor scale, Obama's coverage was about 20 percent net positive, Clinton's coverage was about 2 percent net positive, and Edwards was about 13 percent net positive. For the Republicans, Huckabee's coverage was roughly net 6 percent positive, McCain's coverage was roughly 3 percent net negative, Romney's coverage was about 5 percent net negative, and Giuliani's coverage was about 24 percent net negative. The comparison remains only approximate, however, as the CMPA figures exclude the horse-race assessments that are used in the overall calculation of tone in the Media Tenor data.)

Uneven treatment of presidential candidates is also a problem in general election campaign coverage of the US media. Barack Obama received the most positive treatment of any presidential candidate on network news during the past six presidential election campaigns, according to CMPA's data. Obama's coverage during the 2008 general election season (measured in that study as the period from August 23, 2008, through November 3, 2008, the day before Election Day) was 68 percent positive (and hence 32 percent negative). Obama fared considerably better in the media than John McCain, who received 33 percent positive coverage (and 67 percent negative) during that same campaign period (Farnsworth and Lichter 2011a:99). The thirty-five-percentage-point gap between the two major party presidential nominees was the largest CMPA recorded over the past six presidential elections. The second most positively treated presidential candidate over the six presidential elections going back to 1988 was 2004 Democratic nominee John Kerry, who received 59 percent positive coverage, as compared to 37 percent positive coverage of then-president George W. Bush (Farnsworth and Lichter 2011a:99).

In 2008, running mate Sarah Palin did not help McCain, at least in terms of US mainstream media coverage during the entire campaign. Coverage of Palin on network television was 34 percent positive in tone, almost exactly as negative as the network news reports on McCain (Farnsworth and Lichter 2011a:99). (To convert—roughly, mind you—the CMPA findings to the Media Tenor scale, Obama's general election coverage in the United States was about 11 percent net positive, McCain's coverage was about 10 percent net negative, and the reports on Palin were also about 10 percent net negative. As noted above, the comparison remains only approximate, however, as the CMPA figures exclude the horse-race assessments that are used in the overall calculation of tone in the Media Tenor data.)

DATA AND EXPECTATIONS

Given the general similarities between US and international news coverage seen in previous studies, one would expect that international news reports of the Democratic and Republican nomination contests would reflect patterns of coverage similar to those seen in US media, with the highest volume of coverage directed at the most viable candidates and the most positive coverage directed at those candidates who do better than expected, such as Obama, McCain, and Huckabee. Along these sane lines, the most critical coverage would be directed at the candidates who do worse than expected, such as Clinton and Giuliani.

Also consistent with US media content, one could expect that international news coverage of campaign dynamics, including the horse race, would be greater in volume than coverage of policy issues or candidate character. The nomination campaign coverage patterns predicted for the German and UK media reflect the same basic patterns seen in previous studies of US television campaign coverage in recent decades: most notably the "triage" and compensatory coverage first emphasized by Robinson and Sheehan (1983), and the heavy reliance on the game schema emphasized by Patterson (1994). Patterson noted that journalists turn critical when they have to explain public shifts away from candidates who had been described as favorites in earlier news stories. These patterns were reflected in recent nomination campaigns, including the two party contests of 2008 (Farnsworth and Lichter 2011a, 2012a).

The 2008 nomination campaign results are based on a Media Tenor content analysis of 2,169 statements about the leading Republican presidential candidates and 5,314 statements about the leading Democratic presidential candidates on evening newscasts from two German television news providers and four UK television news providers between December 16, 2007, and March 22, 2008. This time frame corresponds to previous studies of US network television coverage of the 2008 primary campaign season (Farnsworth and Lichter 2011a). This period begins roughly two weeks before the Iowa Caucus and continues until the competitive phase of the Democratic primary was effectively over. By March 22, Obama had a significant lead in delegates and a consistent lead in national polls, advantages that Clinton could not overcome during the rest of the nomination season. McCain effectively wrapped up his nomination even earlier (Ceaser et al. 2009).

The general election results are based on a Media Tenor content analysis of 5,256 statements about the Obama campaign and 3,991 statements about the McCain campaign on evening newscasts from two German television news providers (ARD Tagesthemen and ZDF heute journal) and four UK television news providers (BBC1 10 O'clock News, ITV News at Ten, BBC World, and BBC2 Newsnight) between August 23, 2008, and November 3, 2008, the day before Election Day. This time frame corresponds to previous studies of US network television coverage of the 2008 general election season (Farnsworth and Lichter 2011a) and includes the two national party conventions as well as the most intense period of the general election campaign.

Because Sarah Palin received an unusual amount of network news attention in the United States, we also included her in this study. Palin received a total of 2,032 statements during the campaign on these six European news outlets, or roughly half the number of assessments received by the GOP presidential nominee. By contrast, the Democratic vice presidential nominee, Joe Biden, received only 305 tonal assessments. That figure is 15 percent of the number of assessments Palin received, and less than 6 percent of the assessments Obama received. (Because of the limited amount of coverage Biden received, he is not included in the analysis that follows.)

Nomination Campaign News

Table 6.1 identifies the amount and tone of coverage the leading candidates received in German and UK media during the nomination campaign. First, the

Obama-Clinton race generated far more media attention than did the Republican field. The two front-runners on the Democratic side had roughly equal amounts of coverage, as measured by the statements relating to them on the four UK and two German outlets. On the Republican side, McCain received far more coverage than did his Republican rivals—more than his three leading rivals combined. Even so, McCain's coverage totals were far below those of the two leading Democratic candidates. The four other candidates receiving at least a minimal amount of coverage—Giuliani, Huckabee, and Romney for the Republicans and Edwards for the Democrats—lagged far behind in terms of news attention. There is greater interest in the nomination campaigns among UK media than German news outlets, as one would expect given the particularly close alliance between the United States and the United Kingdom. A common language also facilitates coverage of US news in the United Kingdom.

All things being equal, one would expect that the four media outlets in the United Kingdom would produce double the news on the campaigns that two German outlets would. But the cross-national ratio exceeds that level for all candidates, with the biggest gaps relating to the least well-known candidates.

In the tone of their coverage, there were also sharp differences among the candidates. Obama was exceedingly well received by European television, with coverage at 27.6 percent net positive for German media and 20.9 percent net positive for UK media. For Clinton, the positive and negative coverage were roughly equal in volume, adding up to reports of 3.5 percent net positive for UK news and 0.5 percent net positive for German news. John Edwards, the third Democratic candidate, received far less coverage. Nevertheless, it was more positive than Clinton's in Germany and more negative than either of the other Democrats in the United Kingdom. The US patterns also favored Obama over Edwards in news coverage, with Clinton receiving more negative than positive news. (As before, the Media Tenor tonal measures calculate net tone as the percentage of positive minus the percentage of negative tone.)

For the Republicans, the two candidates who came from behind to end up as finalists for the nomination received consistently positive coverage. McCain had the most positive treatment among the four leading Republicans in UK news (27.5 percent net positive), with Huckabee second (20.3 percent net positive). In German news, the positions were reversed, with Huckabee getting the most favorable notices (25.9 percent net positive) and McCain placing second (19 percent net positive). Romney's coverage was slightly negative on German news (5 percent net negative), and Giuliani's was slightly upbeat, at 1.5 percent net positive. Romney's coverage was neutral on UK television, and reports on Giuliani were overwhelmingly negative in tone for the UK news sources examined here. In the US news broadcasts, only Huckabee received net positive coverage. Giuliani also stood out as an outlier, albeit in the opposite direction, with the most negative assessments of the field on US television.

Table 6.1. Amount and Tone of Television News Coverage of Nomination Candidates by Nation

Candidate	Nation	Net tone %	Negative %	Positive %	No clear rating %	N
McCain	Germany	19.0	9.3	28.3	62.5	237
	UK	27.5	10.6	38.2	51.2	1,101
Giuliani	Germany	1.5	16.9	18.5	64.6	65
	UK	–21.0	31.2	10.2	58.6	157
Huckabee	Germany	25.9	10.3	36.2	53.5	58
	UK	20.3	12.3	32.6	55.1	227
Romney	Germany	–5.0	22.5	17.5	60.0	80
	UK	0.4	16.0	16.4	67.6	244
Edwards	Germany	20.6	2.9	23.5	73.5	34
	UK	–9.7	18.7	9.0	72.3	155
Clinton	Germany	0.5	16.5	17.1	66.4	762
	UK	3.5	17.3	20.9	61.8	1,655
Obama	Germany	27.6	6.6	34.2	59.2	848
	UK	20.9	11.9	32.7	55.4	1,860

N = Number of statements. Percentages might not sum to 100 because of rounding. The results are based on a content analysis of 2,169 statements about the leading Republican presidential candidates and 5,314 statements about the leading Democratic presidential candidates on evening newscasts from two German television news providers and four UK television news providers between December 16, 2007, and March 22, 2008.

Table 6.2, which separates the coverage for Republican candidates for the party's nomination by individual outlet, demonstrates that McCain's positive coverage was consistently strong across all six UK and German media outlets examined here. Huckabee's coverage was a bit less positive on ITV and BBC World than with the other four outlets, but it was still net positive for all six. Romney's overage was the most inconsistent of the four candidates, with relatively positive treatment on BBC World, but markedly more negative on BBC1. ZRD Tagesthemen was the most negative outlet of the six for the former Massachusetts governor. Giuliani's coverage was particularly negative on ITV and BBC World, but it was more consistently negative across the four British media than was Romney's.

Table 6.3 examines the tone by outlet for the leading candidates for the Democratic presidential nomination. Here we see high consistency regarding the international news coverage relating to Obama, which was uniformly positive across the six outlets, and to Clinton, which was generally neutral overall. All six media outlets treated Obama at least twice as positively as they treated Clinton. For Clinton, the results were not all that negative, with four of the six outlets

Table 6.2. Amount and Tone of Television News Coverage of Republican Candidates by Outlet

Candidate	Outlet	Net tone %	Negative %	Positive %	No clear rating %	N
McCain	ARD Tagesthemen	16.7	10.2	26.9	63.0	108
	ZDF heute journal	20.9	8.5	29.5	62.0	129
	BBC1 10 O'clock News	31.0	13.2	44.1	42.7	213
	ITV News at Ten	29.3	12.1	41.4	46.5	157
	BBC World	28.3	4.8	33.1	62.1	375
	BBC2 Newsnight	23.9	14.6	38.5	46.9	356
Giuliani	ARD Tagesthemen	*	*	*	*	*
	ZDF heute journal	7.0	14.0	21.1	64.9	57
	BBC1 10 O'clock News	-10.7	25.0	14.3	60.7	28
	ITV News at Ten	-33.3	45.5	12.1	42.4	33
	BBC World	-26.3	26.3	0.0	73.7	38
	BBC2 Newsnight	-15.5	29.3	13.8	56.9	58
Huckabee	ARD Tagesthemen	20.0	16.0	36.0	48.0	25
	ZDF heute journal	30.3	6.1	36.4	57.6	33
	BBC1 10 O'clock News	29.2	4.6	33.9	61.5	65
	ITV News at Ten	10.8	23.1	34.6	42.3	26
	BBC World	9.5	20.6	30.2	49.2	63
	BBC2 Newsnight	24.7	8.2	32.9	58.9	73
Romney	ARD Tagesthemen	-27.3	50.0	22.7	27.3	22
	ZDF heute journal	2.8	12.1	15.5	72.4	58
	BBC1 10 O'clock News	-11.3	27.4	16.1	56.5	62
	ITV News at Ten	*	*	*	*	*
	BBC World	11.8	5.9	17.7	76.5	102
	BBC2 Newsnight	-2.8	18.3	15.5	66.2	71

* Too few cases to classify (n < 10).
N = Number of statements. Percentages might not sum to 100 because of rounding. The results are based on a content analysis of 2,169 statements about the leading Republican presidential candidates on evening newscasts from two German television news providers and four UK television news providers between December 16, 2007, and March 22, 2008.

Table 6.3. Amount and Tone of Television News Coverage of Democratic Candidates by Outlet

Candidate	Outlet	Net tone %	Negative %	Positive %	No clear rating %	N
Edwards	ARD Tagesthemen	0.0	8.3	8.3	83.3	12
	ZDF heute journal	31.8	0.0	31.8	68.2	22
	BBC1 10 O'clock News	-30.4	30.4	0.0	69.6	23
	ITV News at Ten	30.0	10.0	40.0	50.0	10
	BBC World	0.0	7.6	7.6	84.9	53
	BBC2 Newsnight	-15.9	24.6	8.7	66.7	69
Clinton	ARD Tagesthemen	2.3	15.5	17.7	66.8	310
	ZDF heute journal	-0.7	17.3	16.6	66.2	452
	BBC1 10 O'clock News	2.7	14.3	17.0	68.8	448
	ITV News at Ten	7.5	20.6	28.1	51.3	398
	BBC World	-7.5	22.6	15.0	62.4	226
	BBC2 Newsnight	5.7	15.4	21.1	63.5	583
Obama	ARD Tagesthemen	35.4	6.8	42.1	51.1	311
	ZDF heute journal	23.1	6.5	29.6	63.9	537
	BBC1 10 O'clock News	15.9	11.6	27.4	61.0	467
	ITV News at Ten	35.4	8.7	44.1	47.2	381
	BBC World	23.5	12.8	36.3	50.9	289
	BBC2 Newsnight	15.4	13.4	28.8	57.8	723

N = Number of statements. Percentages might not sum to 100 because of rounding. The results are based on a content analysis of 5,314 statements about the leading Democratic presidential candidates on evening newscasts from two German television news providers and four UK television news providers between December 16, 2007, and March 22, 2008.

positive on balance, but the tonal contrast between the competitors' coverage was striking.

Table 6.4, which examines the amount and tone of the coverage of the leading Republican candidates by topic, reveals a heavy diet of campaign and polling news on German and UK media. (Because of small cell sizes, the six media outlets are combined for the results reported in the next three tables.) For McCain, campaign news and polls/horse-race matters edged out any discussion of policy matters. Those two categories ranked first and second as well for the other three Republican candidates.

Horse-race news assessments about McCain were extremely positive in tone (56.9 percent net positive), as befits his come-from-behind victory. The same was true for reports on the leadership dimension (55.4 percent net positive), which reflects his decisive temperament as well as his senior position in the Senate and within the GOP. Huckabee, who also did far better than pre-season polls suggested, received very high marks for poll/horse-race coverage (50.7 percent net positive). He also did quite well in the personality category, with 28.6 percent positive, and he tied with Romney for first place among the GOP in tone of coverage for personality assessments. McCain also scored positively in this category, with 13.6 percent net positive comments.

The most negative assessments were found for the boom-to-bust Giuliani campaign, with 34.4 percent net negative coverage of poll/horse-race matters and 21.8 percent negative coverage of campaign matters. His rapid decline in public support, coupled with his problematic decision to bypass the early nomination states of Iowa and New Hampshire to concentrate on Florida, doomed his campaign and contributed to the negative notices he received from European reporters. (The former New York City mayor did not have the minimum of ten assessments we require to make an assessment of tone in either the leadership or personality categories.)

Turning to the Democrats, whose coverage by topic is examined in table 6.5, we once again see the huge roles that campaign and polls/horse-race coverage play in European news. Those were the top two categories in terms of volume for both Obama and Clinton. The campaign and horse-race categories ranked first and third for John Edwards, who exited the race relatively early on. Policy issue coverage ranked second for Edwards, who received only a tiny fraction of the news focusing on the Democratic field, while policy matters ranked third in volume for the two front-runners. Thus, just as we saw in US nomination campaign news, media discussion of the sport of politics trumps reporting of more substantive matters (Farnsworth and Lichter 2012b).

The most positive category devoted to Obama concerned polls and the horse race (46.2 percent net positive). The second most positive category for the Democrats also related to Obama's coverage, in this case the personality-oriented

Table 6.4. Amount and Tone of Television News Coverage of Republican Candidates by Topic

Candidate	Topic	Net tone %	Negative %	Positive %	No clear rating %	N
McCain	Policy Issues	-0.5	11.4	11.0	77.6	219
	Leadership	55.4	1.8	57.1	41.1	56
	Campaigning	31.3	6.4	37.8	55.8	233
	Polls/Horse Race	56.9	7.6	64.4	28.0	225
	Personality	13.6	13.6	27.1	59.4	155
Giuliani	Policy Issues	*	*	*	*	*
	Leadership	0.0	0.0	0.0	100.0	17
	Campaigning	-21.8	25.5	3.6	70.9	110
	Polls/Horse Race	-34.4	53.1	18.8	28.1	32
	Personality	*	*	*	*	*
Huckabee	Policy Issues	0.0	0.0	0.0	100.0	20
	Leadership	6.7	0.0	6.7	93.3	15
	Campaigning	11.5	14.1	25.6	60.3	78
	Polls/Horse Race	50.7	13.0	63.8	23.2	69
	Personality	28.6	0.0	28.6	71.4	42
Romney	Policy Issues	-10.5	15.8	5.3	79.0	19
	Leadership	38.5	7.7	46.2	46.2	13
	Campaigning	-9.4	20.8	11.5	67.7	96
	Polls/Horse Race	-13.7	35.3	21.6	43.1	51
	Personality	28.6	3.6	32.1	64.3	28

* Too few cases to classify (n < 10).
N = Number of statements. Percentages might not sum to 100 because of rounding. The results are based on a content analysis of 2,169 statements about the leading Republican presidential candidates on evening newscasts from two German television news providers and four UK television news providers between December 16, 2007, and March 22, 2008.

Table 6.5.   Amount and Tone of Television News Coverage of Democratic Candidates by Topic

Candidate	Topic	Net tone %	Negative %	Positive %	No clear rating %	N
Edwards	Policy Issues	-8.0	8.0	0.0	92.0	25
	Leadership	*	*	*	*	*
	Campaigning	-3.4	13.6	10.2	76.3	59
	Polls/Horse Race	20.0	15.0	35.0	50.0	20
	Personality	*	*	*	*	*
Clinton	Policy Issues	-2.5	9.4	6.9	83.7	202
	Leadership	20.1	14.4	34.5	51.2	174
	Campaigning	0.2	15.2	15.4	69.4	818
	Polls/Horse Race	6.2	23.9	30.0	46.1	486
	Personality	15.2	14.5	29.7	55.8	138
Obama	Policy Issues	0.6	11.4	12.0	76.6	367
	Leadership	11.2	22.4	33.5	44.1	161
	Campaigning	14.8	8.4	23.2	68.3	723
	Polls/Horse Race	46.2	10.0	56.2	33.7	489
	Personality	32.8	4.6	37.4	58.0	238

*Too few cases to classify (n < 10).
N = Number of statements. Percentages might not sum to 100 because of rounding. The results are based on a content analysis of 5,314 statements about the leading Democratic presidential candidates on evening newscasts from two German television news providers and four UK television news providers between December 16, 2007, and March 22, 2008.

assessments (32.8 percent net positive). Hillary Clinton also did well in the personality category (15.2 percent net positive), her second most positive category. She received her most positive assessment in the leadership category (20.1 percent net positive), one of the few places where her treatment in European media was more positive than Obama's (11.2 percent net positive).

In table 6.6, we examine coverage by specific issue area. Because policy coverage was only a small fraction of each candidate's coverage, we could only compute results for McCain, Clinton, and Obama in the leading issue areas. The four other candidates examined so far in this chapter—Giuliani, Huckabee, Romney, and Edwards—did not have ten tonal assessments in any one of the five top policy areas examined here. We therefore look at coverage of the three most newsworthy candidates relating to the issues of foreign policy, Iraq, war and military matters more generally, terrorism, and the economy.

As we see from table 6.6, policy coverage for the three leading candidates focused on foreign policy generally and Iraq specifically. Terrorism, which played such a huge role in US policy throughout the George W. Bush presidency, received far less attention than those two topics during this early phase of the 2008 campaign. The economy, which would come to play such a powerful role in the general election that followed these nomination campaigns, also received little attention from these international campaign news reports.

Foreign policy, McCain's strong suit in terms of his Senate expertise, was also his most positive area of news attention. His 15.2 percent net positive rating edged out Clinton's 13 percent net positive rating for foreign policy and both far exceeded Obama's neutral coverage. All three candidates received net negative assessments relating to Iraq, an unpopular war in both the United Kingdom and Germany. Coverage of war and military matters generally (which excludes the separate categories of Iraq, terrorism, and foreign policy) was marked by far more upbeat coverage relating to Obama (11.5 percent net positive) than to Clinton (5.3 percent positive) or McCain (with a neutral rating). Though there was little coverage on the topic, Obama was also portrayed very positively in news reports on economic matters. His 14.3 percent net positive coverage was far ahead of McCain's neutral coverage and Clinton's 6.7 percent net negative rating.

General Election Campaign News

Once the nominations are decided, news coverage of presidential campaigns often enters a summer lull before the party conventions. Our coverage of the general election begins in late August, just before the conventions and the fall sprint to the early November finish line.

Table 6.6. Amount and Tone of Television News Coverage of Leading Nomination Candidates by Issue

Candidate	Issue	Net tone %	Negative %	Positive %	No clear rating %	N
McCain	Foreign Policy	15.2	6.1	21.2	72.7	33
	Iraq	-2.1	12.8	10.6	76.6	47
	War/Military	0.0	7.7	7.7	84.6	26
	Terrorism	0.0	7.1	7.1	85.7	14
	Economy	0.0	7.7	7.7	84.6	13
Clinton	Foreign Policy	13.0	0.0	13.0	87.0	46
	Iraq	-11.1	18.5	7.4	74.1	27
	War/Military	5.3	5.3	10.5	84.2	19
	Terrorism	*	*	*	*	*
	Economy	-6.7	6.7	0.0	93.3	15
Obama	Foreign Policy	0.0	12.9	12.9	74.3	101
	Iraq	-6.3	18.8	12.5	68.8	48
	War/Military	11.5	15.4	26.9	57.7	26
	Terrorism	-9.1	18.2	9.1	72.7	11
	Economy	14.3	0.0	14.3	85.7	14

Note: The four other candidates analyzed in previous tables (Giuliani, Huckabee, Romney, and Edwards) had less than ten evaluative statements in all of the categories examined above.

N = Number of statements. Percentages might not sum to 100 because of rounding. The results are based on a content analysis of 2,169 statements about the leading Republican presidential candidates and 5,314 statements about the leading Democratic presidential candidates on evening newscasts from two German television news providers and four UK television news providers between December 16, 2007, and March 22, 2008.

Table 6.7 identifies the amount and tone of coverage McCain, Palin, and Obama received on television broadcasts in Germany and the United Kingdom. Coverage of Obama far exceeded that of his Republican rival. Once again, there was greater interest in the campaign among UK media than German news outlets, as one would expect given the trans-Atlantic alliance as well as the results from the primary news comparisons earlier in the chapter. All things being equal, one would expect that the four media outlets in the United Kingdom would produce double the news on the campaign as would the two German outlets. But the cross-national ratio for the amount of coverage exceeds that level for all three candidates examined here.

The enthusiasm Obama received during the nomination phase continued, albeit to a lesser degree, in the general election campaign coverage. The enthusiasm McCain received in the early 2008 struggle for the GOP nomination, however, was not replicated during the fall campaign (Farnsworth, Lichter, and Schatz 2012, 2013). Obama's coverage was more positive in German news than in UK news. But both media groups gave Obama a double-digit margin over McCain, as did the US media figures calculated by CMPA. Obama's coverage of 11.6 percent net positive in German media was a particularly large gap from the 13.2 percent net negative coverage that McCain received. The relatively positive coverage of Obama in German media may be a reflection of Obama's 2008 visit to Germany, which included a massive campaign rally in Berlin, a sharp contrast from the Bush administration's sometimes cavalier dismissal of "old Europe."

Palin's coverage was almost exactly equivalent in tone to that of Obama. The coverage in both the German media (11.4 percent net positive for Palin versus 11.6 percent net for Obama) and the UK media (4.2 percent net positive for Palin versus 4.1 percent net for Obama) were nearly identical. And both candidates' reports represent huge differences from that of McCain's treatment in European media.

At first glance, this highly positive coverage of Palin seems to be something of a surprise. Her highly critical coverage in US media might have offered some guidance for European media examining a candidate who had little national or international exposure before being named to the ticket. Coverage of Palin on the big three US television networks was more negative than positive by a roughly two-to-one margin (Farnsworth and Lichter 2011a). The 34 percent negative/66 percent positive coverage identified by CMPA for Palin represents a roughly 10 percent net negative assessment by US media when the CMPA results are converted to the Media Tenor coding scale. The far more negative US figures represent a sharp contrast from the positive coverage Palin received in these international news programs.

If there really is an "international two-step flow" in news coverage of the United States (cf. Farnsworth, Soroka, and Young 2010), one would expect a

Table 6.7. Amount and Tone of Television News Coverage of General Election Candidates by Nation

Candidate	Nation	Net tone %	Negative %	Positive %	No clear rating %	N
McCain	Germany	-13.2	28.9	15.7	55.4	983
	UK	-10.2	19.6	9.4	70.9	3,008
Palin	Germany	11.4	22.9	34.3	42.8	621
	UK	4.2	16.2	20.5	63.4	1,411
Obama	Germany	11.6	16.5	28.1	55.5	1,435
	UK	4.1	14.3	18.4	67.3	3,821

N = Number of statements. Percentages might not sum to 100 because of rounding. The results are based on a content analysis of 3,991 statements about the McCain campaign, 2,032 statements about the Palin campaign, and 5,256 statements about the Obama campaign on evening newscasts from two German television news providers and four UK television news providers between August 23 and November 3, 2008.

small-state governor's sudden national star turn to produce a heavy US influence on international news coverage. In addition, Palin's unsteady discussion of international matters during the campaign might also lead to even greater derision from the international media (cf. Heilemann and Halperin 2010). But overall, the tone of the coverage of Palin was surprisingly positive. The international coverage of McCain and Obama was far more similar to the US treatment of the two presidential nominees than the very divergent paths trod by US media and international media in their discussion of Palin.

Table 6.8 shows the overall trends for each candidate across all six international television outlets. McCain's negative coverage, for example, ranged from 8.5 percent net negative to 16.6 percent net negative. There was a greater variation for Obama, with coverage ranging from 2.3 percent net positive to 14.9 percent net positive. For Obama, ZDF heute journal was his most positive outlet, while BBC2 Newsnight was his least positive.

The greatest variation, though, came in the reports on Palin, where three of the six outlets were net positive and the three others were net negative. The differences in tone for Palin ranged from a net of 6.1 percent negative to 19.4 percent positive. Partisanship does not appear to be at work here: the most negative news outlet for McCain (ZDF heute journal) was also the most positive outlet for Palin. Likewise, the second most negative outlet for McCain (BBC2 Newsnight) was also the second most positive outlet for Palin. Perhaps there was something approaching compensatory coverage (cf. Robinson and Sheehan 1983) within the GOP field!

Table 6.9, which examines the amount and tone of the coverage by topic, reveals a heavy diet of campaign and polling news on German and UK media. For both McCain and Palin, campaign news and polls/horse-race matters exceeded any discussion of policy issues, while policy issues played a far larger role in Obama's coverage. The single most frequently mentioned issue for McCain was leadership, while policy issues ranked first for Obama, and coverage of personality issues was the most commonly discussed matter regarding Palin. Even so, there was more horse-race material on the US news.

As one would expect from Obama's consistent lead in US surveys from mid-September onward, his horse-race coverage was highly positive (39.9 percent net positive in tone), while McCain's coverage was highly negative (24.1 percent net negative). Palin's presence on the campaign trail, where she generated enthusiastic crowds, was seen as helping McCain's horse-race prospects. Thus, Palin's horse-race coverage was 27.9 percent net positive. These very different evaluations had a heavy influence on the overall evaluations. Without this category, other coverage of the three candidates ranged from 12.1 percent net negative to 10.9 percent net positive.

Table 6.8. Amount and Tone of Television News Coverage of General Election Candidates by Outlet

Candidate	Outlet	Net tone %	Negative %	Positive %	No clear rating %	N
McCain	ARD Tagesthemen	-10.4	26.8	16.4	56.9	530
	ZDF heute journal	-16.6	31.4	14.8	53.9	453
	BBC1 10 O'clock News	-8.5	19.6	11.1	69.2	790
	ITV News at Ten	-11.3	24.6	13.3	62.2	505
	BBC World	-13.2	21.8	8.6	69.5	197
	BBC2 Newsnight	-16.5	17.7	7.4	74.9	1,516
Palin	ARD Tagesthemen	5.2	25.7	30.8	43.5	347
	ZDF heute journal	19.4	19.3	38.7	42.0	274
	BBC1 10 O'clock News	-0.2	21.4	21.1	57.5	426
	ITV News at Ten	-1.3	16.6	15.3	68.1	307
	BBC World	-6.1	15.9	9.9	74.2	132
	BBC2 Newsnight	13.6	11.9	25.5	62.6	546
Obama	ARD Tagesthemen	8.4	17.8	26.2	56.0	725
	ZDF heute journal	14.9	15.1	30.0	54.9	710
	BBC1 10 O'clock News	5.2	16.0	21.3	62.7	1,073
	ITV News at Ten	6.1	16.5	22.6	60.9	744
	BBC World	5.2	12.9	18.1	69.0	287
	BBC2 Newsnight	2.3	12.5	14.9	72.6	1,717

N = Number of statements. Percentages might not sum to 100 because of rounding. The results are based on a content analysis of 3,991 statements about the McCain campaign, 2,032 statements about the Palin campaign, and 5,256 statements about the Obama campaign on evening newscasts from two German television news providers and four UK television news providers between August 23 and November 3, 2008.

Table 6.9. Amount and Tone of Television News Coverage of General Election Candidates by Topic

Candidate	Topic	Net tone %	Negative %	Positive %	No clear rating %	N
McCain	Policy Issues	-9.5	14.7	5.2	80.1	331
	Leadership	10.9	17.5	28.4	54.0	1,154
	Campaigning	-11.8	18.2	6.4	75.4	939
	Polls/Horse Race	-24.1	43.2	19.1	37.7	639
	Personality	1.8	19.3	21.1	59.6	223
Palin	Policy Issues	-12.1	22.1	10.0	68.0	231
	Leadership	-4.7	31.5	26.8	41.7	235
	Campaigning	0.3	17.9	18.2	63.9	402
	Polls/Horse Race	27.9	23.1	51.0	26.0	104
	Personality	9.2	13.5	22.7	63.8	437
Obama	Policy Issues	-8.0	15.7	7.7	76.6	1,420
	Leadership	-4.6	30.4	25.8	43.8	345
	Campaigning	4.2	11.5	15.8	72.7	875
	Polls/Horse Race	39.9	13.2	53.1	33.7	665
	Personality	-0.5	16.4	15.9	67.7	548

N = Number of statements. Percentages might not sum to 100 because of rounding. The results are based on a content analysis of 3,991 statements about the McCain campaign, 2,032 statements about the Palin campaign, and 5,256 statements about the Obama campaign on evening newscasts from two German television news providers and four UK television news providers between August 23 and November 3, 2008.

The bright spot for McCain was clearly the leadership category. Not only did he rank first in the number of media assessments, but it was also his most positive category (10.9 percent net positive). McCain's long years of public service as a naval officer, a prisoner of war during the Vietnam conflict, and a leading voice for Republicans in the US Senate were clearly recognized by the international reporters. This category also demonstrated a major distinction between McCain and both Obama and Palin, each of whom (unlike McCain) received more negative than positive notices with respect to leadership. Both candidates were relatively new to the political scene, which tends to work against claims of experience and leadership. (Obama first gained national attention with a keynote speech at the Democratic National Convention in 2004. Later that year he was elected to the US Senate. Palin was an obscure first-term governor of a remote state in her second year in office when named to the GOP ticket in 2008.)

Policy issues generated more negative than positive evaluations for Obama (8 percent net negative). But even that downbeat coverage was less critical than that relating to McCain and policy issues (9.5 percent net negative) or Palin (12.1 percent net negative). The coverage of the two presidential nominees was relatively similar in terms of tone across these six European television outlets, and even Palin's numbers were not that far from those of Obama and McCain. One might have expected a somewhat more critical tone of coverage of Palin's views regarding policies in international news, particularly in the wake of her highly publicized and uneven news interviews with the network evening news anchors on CBS and ABC.

Palin's clear advantage on the European television news shows came in the personality category, which was 9.2 percent net positive in tone. That figure compares quite favorably with the 1.8 percent net positive in tone for McCain in personality and the 0.5 percent net negative in tone for news reports regarding Obama's personality.

Taken as a whole, we see that candidate efforts to shape US news coverage have international news consequences. The McCain campaign's chief argument was the senator's exceptional background, particularly his long years of political experience and leadership, and the European television programs focused on that area. Obama argued that his policy visions were the reason to elect him, and he received relatively positive coverage in that area. Palin, arguably a force of nature on the campaign trail, basked in the warm glow of positive personality-oriented coverage on European television news. Her large, enthusiastic crowds were catnip to international television reporters speaking any language.

In table 6.10, we examine coverage by specific substantive issue area. Because policy coverage comprised only a small fraction of Palin's coverage, and her total coverage was less than that of the presidential nominees, we could only

Table 6.10. Amount and Tone of Television News Coverage of General Election Candidates by Issue

Candidate	Issue	Net tone %	Negative %	Positive %	No clear rating %	N
McCain	Foreign Policy	-2.4	13.4	11.0	75.6	127
	Iraq	-42.4	42.4	0.0	57.6	33
	War/Military	12.3	8.2	20.4	71.4	49
	Terrorism	-3.4	10.3	6.9	82.8	29
	Economy	-19.3	22.2	3.0	74.8	441
	Tax Policy	-6.0	7.5	1.5	91.0	133
	Budget	-6.8	10.8	4.1	85.1	74
	Employment/Jobs	0.0	0.0	0.0	100.0	10
	Energy/Environment	-1.4	5.7	4.3	90.0	70
	Health Care	-6.9	6.9	0.0	93.1	58
Palin	Foreign Policy	-20.0	23.1	3.1	73.9	65
	Iraq	-23.5	23.5	0.0	76.5	17
	War/Military	*	*	*	*	*
	Terrorism	*	*	*	*	*
	Economy	-6.7	6.7	0.0	93.3	15
	Tax Policy	*	*	*	*	*
	Budget	*	*	*	*	*
	Employment/Jobs	*	*	*	*	*
	Energy/Environment	0.0	13.0	13.0	73.9	23
	Health Care	*	*	*	*	*
Obama	Foreign Policy	-8.6	15.1	6.5	78.5	186
	Iraq	2.9	11.4	14.3	74.3	35
	War/Military	0.0	22.4	22.4	55.2	58
	Terrorism	-11.1	15.6	4.4	80.0	45
	Economy	2.0	6.1	8.1	85.8	458
	Tax Policy	-31.1	32.2	1.1	66.7	177
	Budget	-18.6	18.6	0.0	81.4	59
	Employment/Jobs	-20.8	20.8	0.0	79.2	24
	Energy/Environment	-2.0	10.0	8.0	82.0	50
	Health Care	-5.9	5.9	0.0	94.1	85

* Too few cases to classify (n < 10).
N = Number of statements. Percentages might not sum to 100 because of rounding. The results are based on a content analysis of 3,991 statements about the McCain campaign, 2,032 statements about the Palin campaign, and 5,256 statements about the Obama campaign on evening newscasts from two German television news providers and four UK television news providers between August 23 and November 3, 2008.

assess the tone of her coverage in four of the ten leading policy areas examined here. Both Obama and McCain could be evaluated for all ten categories.

The economic crisis that enveloped America and much of the rest of the world during the fall of 2008 emerged as the leading topic for European news coverage of both the McCain and the Obama campaigns. By a margin of more than two-to-one, evaluations of economic news matters trumped any other issue for the two presidential nominees. The related issues of tax and budget policies were also important matters, as much of the early conversation regarding responses to the economic crisis involved discussion of tax cut extensions and potential new stimulus measures. Obama enjoyed a substantial advantage in coverage of overall economic matters: his coverage on that topic was net 2 percent positive, as compared to 19.3 percent net negative for McCain. Palin received far less coverage in this area, but her 6.7 percent net negative tone was less negative than that of McCain.

Obama fared significantly worse than McCain on three separate economically related categories, however. His coverage on tax policy, budgets, and employment/jobs ranged from 18.6 percent net negative to 31.1 percent net negative. McCain's coverage in those areas, in contrast, ranged from neutral to 6.8 percent net negative. (There were not ten tonal assessments of Palin in any of those categories, the minimum necessary for valid assessments in a given issue area.) Obama's favorable treatment concentrated in the general discussion of economic matters, while the more experienced McCain was presented in news reports as having the edge where more specific policy details were concerned.

As for other leading domestic matters, the two major party nominees received similar, slightly negative assessments on energy/environmental issues and health care, which would become a major issue during Obama's first two years in office. Contrary to what one might anticipate from European media, Palin's "drill, baby, drill" oil production campaign rhetoric did not lead to negative notices in these evening newscasts. Her coverage on environmental/energy matters was neutral overall.

As one would expect, foreign policy concerns were an important part of campaign coverage in German and UK television news reports. With respect to the war in Iraq, coverage of Obama—who had been highly critical of the effort since before it even started—was slightly positive (net 2.9 percent positive). The Republican ticket was far more supportive of Bush's policies in Iraq, and the European news notices were quite negative as a result. Coverage of McCain on this topic was highly critical (42.4 percent net negative), and Palin also received largely downbeat coverage (23.5 percent net negative). McCain fared a bit better than Obama on coverage of war and military matters (a category that includes Afghanistan), with coverage that was 12.3 percent net positive, as compared to neutral coverage of Obama. (Palin had only five statements relating to war and military matters.)

Both of the above categories were far less significant in terms of volume of coverage than the overall foreign policy category. While all three candidates received somewhat negative notices, McCain's foreign policy reports were somewhat less critical than those of Obama. The really bad press, though, went to Palin, who received foreign policy coverage that was 20 percent net negative. Her limited knowledge of foreign policy matters appeared not to endear her to German and European reporters who had spent several previous years deriding an incumbent president for his combative and sometimes ill-informed foreign policy commentary (cf. Entman 2004; Farnsworth, Lichter, and Schatz 2010; Heilemann and Halperin 2010; Jones 2006; Nelson 2010; Pew Global 2006).

Conclusion

INTERNATIONAL NOMINATION NEWS

As expected, the international news coverage of the two parties' nomination campaigns did not differ greatly from that found on US network television of those same contests (cf. Farnsworth and Lichter 2011a, 2012a). Most of the international coverage was directed at those candidates with the best political prospects, as is the case in US nomination news. Close-fought competition spurs great interest in both nations, with the showdown between the first viable African American presidential nominee and the first viable female presidential nominee generating much more attention on both sides of the Atlantic than the less dramatic and quicker victory of McCain on the Republican side. In terms of tone, the candidates doing better than had been predicted in early polls benefitted from the most positive coverage. The early front-runners, who slipped back in the pack, received the harsher notices. Overall, these results suggest support for the old Robinson and Sheehan (1983) model of media "triage" of candidates, even for US candidates portrayed in European media.

News outlet comparisons demonstrated consistency for the candidates treated most positively (McCain and Huckabee for the GOP and Obama for the Democrats), but far greater variation in tone of coverage for the candidates who ended up farther back in the pack (particularly Giuliani and Romney for the GOP and Edwards for the Democrats). There was no consistent national pattern here, as was suggested by some previous research (cf. Hallin and Mancini 2004a; Stromback 2007). German media were more positive in some cases, UK media in others. Perhaps the general antipathy for Bush at this point at both the public and the elite levels in these two nations made the distinctions suggested by these models undetectable.

As we have seen in US coverage of nomination campaigns, coverage of campaigning and the horse race dominates the European campaign coverage as well. By contrast, policy issues received very little attention. Even in cases where there was a sufficient amount of issue coverage to analyze, the modest volume of issue coverage fell far short of the coverage of campaigning and the horse race.

The coverage of candidate personalities tended to be quite positive, though not all candidates received much attention. Matters of character are an important part of introducing little-known political figures to a television audience, and personality issues tend not to generate the controversy found in policy debates or even in discussions of the wisdom of various campaign strategies. Personality coverage of McCain was somewhat less positive than Clinton, but both fell far short of the very positive tone of Obama's personality coverage. That enthusiasm for who Obama was as a candidate was found in both the United States and the trans-Atlantic coverage. This lends support to the idea that presidential candidates and presidents try to emphasize personality and character matters whenever they can, as it can generate positive news reports in a wide variety of outlets (cf. Farnsworth 2009).

As one would expect, US foreign policy attracted the greatest interest from European news outlets. In addition to the relatively high volume of coverage compared to other policy matters, all candidates received neutral to positive notices in that issue area. This is likely a response to the feeling in some European circles that all the alternatives in 2008 might be more appealing than the incumbent. (A separate Media Tenor analysis of the tone of President George W. Bush's foreign policy coverage on these six outlets during the same time period was 8.6 percent net negative.) The modest coverage on issues that did exist showed a great deal of fatigue with the Iraq War, with all the three Democratic candidates generating net negative coverage. (Bush's comparable coverage on Iraq was 8.3 percent net negative—not as critical as the assessments involving Clinton!)

INTERNATIONAL GENERAL ELECTION NEWS

European TV coverage of the general election was particularly noteworthy for being very close to the American TV coverage in the tone adopted toward the presidential nominees. Using the Media Tenor calculation of tone, the converted CMPA data demonstrate that ABC, CBS, and NBC were about as pro-Obama and about as anti-McCain as the German and UK broadcasters examined here. The most striking departure, of course, was the coverage of Palin, which was far more positive in European media than in the US media. (Although the Media Tenor data include horse-race measures in the calculation of tone and CMPA does not, excluding the negative evaluations of McCain and positive evaluations of Obama in the European outlets would further narrow the gap between the two candidates.)

Taken together, these results regarding tone of coverage during the general election suggest a general pattern of following US news trends, as is suggested by the "international two-step flow" theory (Farnsworth, Soroka, and Young 2010) at the presidential nominee level—but not for Palin. Perhaps the European media are less closely aligned to US news than Canadian television news. Or perhaps coverage of campaigns differs more than coverage of governance, at least for celebrities like Palin. Palin's unique position in attracting media attention when compared to other vice presidential nominees makes it difficult to generalize.

Although the European media did no worse (and arguably a bit better if we exclude horse-race assessments) than US media on the question of tonal bias, they were not as even-handed in the amounts of coverage of the two campaigns. In this case, novelty seems to be even more important for European news than it is for the US news outlets. This suggests some of the downside risks associated with the media-dominated campaigns during the fourth stage of media influence (cf. Stromback 2007; Stromback and Kaid 2008). As the first African American major party nominee, and one whose election would signal a major departure from the status quo, the Obama campaign received far more European media attention than the McCain campaign. Palin, the first female Republican nominee for vice president, likewise generated extensive interest from both domestic and international reporters.

Thus, if one combines the amount of McCain and Palin coverage, the amount of media attention received by the GOP ticket on these news programs exceeded that of Obama and running mate Joe Biden, the subject of only 305 statements on these six international outlets. If McCain chose Palin in part to bring excitement and a lift to media coverage of his campaign, that strategy worked, albeit on the wrong side of the Atlantic!

When we examined the results of international outlets individually, there did not appear to be any consistent national pattern of tonal differences, as suggested by some previous research (cf. Hallin and Mancini 2004a; Stromback 2007). German and UK media generally reflected very similar results when looking at both Obama and McCain. There was a bit more variation among the outlets in their treatment of Palin, but the volume of her coverage was well below that of the two presidential nominees. Perhaps the general antipathy for Bush by this point at both the public and the elite levels in these two nations made the distinctions suggested by these models undetectable in this study.

International TV news compares favorably with US network news insofar as coverage of campaigning and the horse race did not dominate all other topics. Coverage of policy issues received considerable attention, as did issues of leadership. CMPA found that 41 percent of the US network news stories contained a horse-race focus in 2008. In contrast, the combined campaigning and polls/horse-race categories in the Media Tenor analysis of the six European news outlets accounted for 32 percent of the tonal assessments of the three candidates. Again, the relative lack of international interest in incremental developments on the campaign trail may explain the more issue-oriented and personality-oriented reports on the European news outlets examined here.

American foreign policy, as one would expect, attracted the greatest interest among policy matters covered by those European news outlets. And in the special circumstances of 2008, the candidates' plans for dealing with a global economic slowdown were of great interest to viewers not only in the United States but also in two of Europe's largest economies. The modest coverage of other issues showed a willingness to focus on key policy matters of greatest relevance for each country's own audience, as one would expect.

CHAPTER 7

Globalization, International News, and the US Government

Barack Obama's election in November 2008 generated huge changes in international public opinion regarding the United States. Those more positive international evaluations about America have remained in place throughout the first term of the Obama presidency, as demonstrated by the discussion of Pew polls in the early chapters of this book. But the new president's impact on international news content was neither as sharp nor as long-lasting a departure from the previous presidency as it was on international opinion. There was clearly a media honeymoon for Obama personally—and one that lasted longer on television news abroad than in the United States. But television coverage of the United States more generally and many of its policies changed less than one might think. More positive coverage of the United States during the early days of Obama's presidency related more to the president than the country, and more to the man than the policies.

Part of the difficulty every American president faces with international media is America's highly influential place in the world. Even a president who reaches out to international publics and leaders and tries to develop a more collaborative international framework must deal with the frustrations expressed in international television broadcasts. Some US presidents try to work more with the international community, while others want to reduce those ties and act more unilaterally. But either way, a number of media outlets—particularly European ones—present news stories that express considerable frustration with the United States and its dominance over global politics. Of course, an American president can only cooperate so much with allies before the president's domestic audience starts to object.

Patterns of News Coverage:
The Kindness of (Relative) Strangers

Several key findings emerge regarding the coverage patterns in the nations we studied, and how that coverage of the United States differs from one region and one nation to another. The most unexpected—and arguably the most important—finding of this work is how favorably Arabic-language media often treat the United States and its leaders, in spite of widespread frustrations in the region with US policies. Despite wars, years of military occupations of parts of the Middle East, and what many Arabic-language news consumers would consider a too-cozy relationship between the United States and Israel, these very diverse broadcasters often treated the United States and President Obama better than did media from countries closely allied with America. One might have expected the region's media to revile George W. Bush over his decision to invade Iraq (based on WMD claims that turned out not to be true) and the botched and bloody occupation that followed. Yet Bush's coverage in Arabic-language news was less critical than his coverage in some allied nations. The Arabic-language media may have been in a position to emphasize the changes in the region (such as the withdrawal of US troops from Iraq), while the European media may have been in a better position to emphasize the things that did not change, such as the continuing operation of Guantanamo and the escalation of the US troop levels in Afghanistan.

Although the volume of coverage of issues relating to the United States was lower than in other parts of the world, television reports from the region's leading news outlets nevertheless provided a relatively even-handed treatment of the United States. The efforts by successive US governments to try to justify American policies to the journalists and the peoples of the Middle East may help explain this surprising finding.

Clearly, however, there is more at work here than effective US salesmanship of its policies. By itself, marketing seems insufficient to explain the relatively kind coverage of the United States by the Arabic-language media during the years we examined. There is great diversity of perspectives among the region's broadcasters, yet the findings demonstrate considerable sympathy for American policies and presidents. Al-Jazeera, the region's dominant broadcaster and the source of so much anxiety in Washington over media bias, actually produced news about the United States that was often positive (or at least less negative) than many other outlets in the region and even in Europe. Criticism of this highly visible broadcaster in the United States, our research suggests, has been overblown.

Al-Arabiyah, the closest thing to Al-Jazeera's rival for viewers, sometimes gets preferential treatment in Western capitals because of its connections to the

Saudi royals, as well as concerns about the presumed bias of Al-Jazeera. But our evidence shows that Al-Jazeera has often been at least as positive in its treatment of the United States as Al-Arabiyah, particularly during the Obama years. Both the larger size of the Al-Jazeera audience and its relatively kind treatment of the Obama administration suggest that the administration would be wise to pay more attention to the region's most dominant media voice.

Other Arabic media outlets, less likely to receive sustained US attention than these two larger broadcasters, also showed patterns of relatively US-friendly news. It also is important to note that even an Arabic-language media outlet that has the greatest reasons to be hostile to the United States is less negative than one might think. Al-Manar is the voice of Hezbollah, an organization the United States defined as a terrorist entity during both the Bush and the Obama presidencies. Even so, Al-Manar was not as consistently critical as one might expect (although coverage of US antiterrorism matters and policies in the Middle East were powerful exceptions during both administrations). Overall, Fox News has been more critical of Obama than Al-Manar has been.

The fact that we found a pattern of relatively friendly US coverage across the Middle East region's media is not to suggest that White House marketing efforts aimed at the Arabic-language media should be reduced or discontinued. Our findings indicate that such efforts clearly do not hurt, and they probably help. Obama sought to turn the page on Bush's poor relationship with the region, and those efforts paid off in more positive coverage. During Bush's years in the White House, his administration also often reached out to the Arabic media, and those efforts appeared to keep the coverage of the region from becoming overwhelmingly critical. Indeed, Arabic media were consistently less critical than European media in their treatment of Bush and his policies.

Although the coverage could have been far worse, there is significant room for improvement in media relations during Obama's second term. In an interview, Arab broadcast journalist Nadia Bilbassy of MBC-TV complained that despite Obama's promises of accessibility, the working relationship between reporters and the White House has not improved in recent years:

> When President Obama was elected [in 2008] he campaigned on the ticket of openness and transparency, therefore the expectations were high and most journalists were disappointed to find out that his administration is more closed to the media than the Bush administration. There is a constant battle for access, information is not easily available, and officials at the senior and mid-level do not answer emails. (Bilbassy 2010:42)

In addition to the relatively positive treatment of Obama in the Middle East media, another media group culturally distant from the United States also provided a surprising amount of very positive coverage for the United States and its presidents. South African broadcasters were, comparatively speaking, very up-beat regarding the United States during both the Bush and the Obama presidencies. There was less coverage of the United States in South African media than in Europe, but South African television coverage of the United States was routinely among the most favorable in its reports. While there were specific areas where the US coverage was highly critical (particularly war and antiterrorism policies during the Bush years), South African news reports on the United States were comparatively kind overall, regardless of which president was in office. This may be partially an Obama effect, but one can also see a consistent pattern of public opinion very supportive of democracy in South Africa and many other nations in sub-Saharan Africa (Schatz 2009). As a relatively new multicultural democracy, South Africa may look particularly favorably on the United States.

The European media, to be sure, were a different matter entirely.

The nations whose people we think know America best were far from the most understanding. One could imagine that media in the United Kingdom, a nation sharing an extremely close military alliance, a common language, a common law-based legal system, and many other common cultural touchstones, might be more understanding of the United States, its one-time colony. One might think that the shared language gives US policymakers greater opportunities to be heard in UK media. One might expect that those linguistic advantages would infuse UK coverage of the United States with a deeper understanding and sympathy that befits both a century of deep trans-Atlantic partnership and shared global burdens.

One would be wrong.

George W. Bush, who seemed a stereotypical American frontier rube (or worse) to many British eyes, was clearly not their cup of tea. So perhaps UK media would gush over his successor, who was very popular with the British public and who promised greater multilateralism and a rapid end to the wars that proved so costly in blood and treasure to both nations (and to so many others). In point of fact, however, UK media sometimes gave Bush and Obama the most critical coverage of all the international outlets we studied.

There were some bright spots for Obama in the UK coverage, though, mainly in comparison to his predecessor. BBC1 and BBC2, like the US mass media and many international news outlets examined here, were rougher on Bush during his second term than they were to Obama during his first eighteen months in office. Coverage of America's standing in the world, for example, was more positive during the Obama years, and Obama received very positive reviews during his time as a presidential candidate. But in most cases, UK coverage was more critical than that of either Arabic-language broadcasters or German news reports. Even so, it was less critical than US news reports from the same time periods.

German media reports stood out as highly critical in the places where one would expect, most notably in the coverage of US policies in Afghanistan and Iraq. The German media were perhaps freer to be more critical, as Germany was not part of the "coalition of the willing" that drove Saddam Hussein from power in Iraq, and German involvement in Afghanistan was far smaller—and far less deadly for its troops—than was the UK experience there.

In addition, Germany has taken relatively aggressive steps to combat global warming (Dempsey 2012), so it should come as no surprise that German media were highly critical of America's much higher use of energy per capita and the nation's lagging efforts to develop renewable energy resources. But more often than not, the German media were more complimentary of Obama than were the UK media, though both nations frequently featured less positive media coverage than the Arabic-language group.

We have had less to say about other European media in this book, but our limited story-level analyses of the news from four other European nations (France, Spain, Italy, and Switzerland) during 2007 and 2009 suggested a mixed picture across the major nations of the continent. The tone of news coverage in France and Italy tended to be highly critical of both American presidents—very closely aligned with the reports from the United Kingdom and Germany. The media of Spain and Switzerland, on the other hand, joined in the harsh condemnation of the United States during the Bush years but were much more positively disposed toward the United States than other European media during Obama's first year in office. Turkey, on the edge of Europe, was somewhere in the middle between these two media patterns: less critical than most of these news outlets, but more critical than Spain and Switzerland.

A key explanation for the range of criticism in these nations may come from long-standing trans-Atlantic rivalries that existed long before George W. Bush's presidency and, from this vantage point, seem likely to survive Barack Obama's presidency more or less intact. But this is not simply trans-Atlantic churlishness, in our view. Elite concerns in these societies that focus on the negative aspects of the US human rights record in both presidencies over what Bush called "the war on terror" seems particularly salient to the negativity in the media of these two nations, as well as in some others. Nations with publics highly focused on questions of civil rights seem particularly negative where these past two administrations are concerned. Reporters tend to be familiar with elite opinion, even if they are not elites themselves, and they can hardly ignore this perspective as they produce their news segments.

Of course, one cannot eliminate the possibility of envy's impact entirely. A nation that plausibly can be hoisted on its own petards will be so treated in today's global political and media environments. These days, no one expects much in terms of government adherence to human rights in Russia or China, to be sure.

But America, well, that is another matter entirely. To buttress this argument, it is striking to observe that the European nations most likely to view the United States as a political, economic, and/or cultural rival—for example, the United Kingdom, Germany, and France—are more critical of Obama than the European states we examined that historically have expressed relatively little concern over these potential forms of US domination: Switzerland, Spain, and Turkey.

TESTING THE THEORIES

Altogether, the findings across these chapters raise questions about the applicability of some social science models that divide Western media into three groups in order to explain patterns of international news coverage (Hallin and Mancini 2004a). According to this perspective, the Liberal media environments (such as the United States and to a lesser extent the United Kingdom) respond primarily to commercial interests, while the Democratic Corporatist nations (like Germany) are most responsive to organized social and political groups. The third group, the Polarized Pluralist countries, is marked by a strong central state and relatively weak development of commercial media (such as in Italy and, to a lesser extent, in France).

As we have seen at several points in this project, this framework is not entirely successful in explaining differences in tonal coverage of news about the United States. Certainly the international media honeymoon Obama enjoyed at the start of his presidency reflected public and elite preferences, as well as the political preferences of leaders such as France's President Sarkozy. But the more critical coverage in Germany and especially the United Kingdom during Obama's second year did not reflect massive declines in international public opinion during that same time period. (As late as the spring of 2012, we saw only marginal declines in international support for Obama when compared to the 2009 survey.) Indeed, the high levels of public support for Obama in Europe in 2012 (table 1.1 and table 1.2) might suggest that the media honeymoon should still be going strong. But the European public's love for Obama was rarely reflected in international news coverage of the new president. Toward the end of the Bush presidency, one might have expected more positive treatment of the United States, at least in Italy, where the government remained more supportive of the Bush-led coalition than most of its fellow European states (Fisher 2004). But it appears that public anger over the outgoing American president may matter more to the media than a prime minister's fondness for America's chief executive.

If public opinion plays a role in shaping the tone of international news content, the Arabic media should be consistently more critical than the news in

Europe. There should also be huge gaps in the tone of coverage between the two presidents, with Bush faring far worse than Obama. Yet neither of these patterns emerged. If the preferences of political leaders are highly salient to international news content, there should be much greater differences among media outlets in the Arabic-language group, with Al-Arabiyah consistently more positive than its rivals. That expected pattern did not materialize. Leader preferences would also have suggested far larger tonal gaps favoring Obama over Bush in these media outlets. That expected pattern did not materialize either.

Thus, the tripartite model of Hallin and Mancini (2004a) has some utility, but much of our evidence marks a departure from the patterns it leads one to expect. We suspect that the main reason the general model did not work better stems from the very distinct area of our investigation: we looked only at news about the United States. As we have noted earlier, this topic represents a fraction of the news coverage of these nations. While US news is an important part of international news, we did not look at all international news from the nations whose media we examined. Nor did we examine the domestic news content of the media operating in the United Kingdom, or Germany, or the other European nations. A more comprehensive analysis, one not limited to international coverage of the United States, would likely provide a better empirical test of this model.

Nor do we consider here the domestic news from the home nations of these Arabic-language broadcasters. This data limitation also works against an effective test of the model. News about the United States, after all, would not likely be an area where a government in a Polarized Pluralist media environment would be most interested in exercising its influence. News about matters closer to home would be of far greater concern. Perhaps more critical news about the United States functions as an escape valve for a government that would rather not have critical public pressures directed inward. A case in point would be a recent Italian prime minister (and domestic media mogul) who regularly faced allegations of corruption and other misconduct (Donadio and Povoledo 2011). Better to report on American missteps, a leader considering his personal foibles may believe.

Even more important in explaining the similarities of news coverage by many of these outlets may be the growing international convergence regarding cross-Atlantic journalistic norms (Donsbach and Patterson 2004; Esser 2008; Stromback and Kaid 2008). The consistently high levels of criticism of presidents and government actions on US television news, with the exception of a brief Obama honeymoon, would not be lost on European journalists, particularly those whose professional responsibilities involve reporting on the United States. The original development of the "international two-step flow" (cf. Farnsworth, Soroka, and Young 2010) hypothesized that news adjustments in one nation, say, an increasing emphasis on a given issue area by domestic media, would be followed by greater attention being paid to that same issue by international reporters. The findings here, at least with respect to Europe, suggest that the highly critical perspective that US reporters train upon American politicians would be echoed if not amplified by international media covering the United States. The traditional Fleet Street media culture of London, after all, was not known for genteel reporting of political news (Donsbach and Patterson 2004).

Since international reporters get little cooperation from US politicians, who focus mainly on answering the queries of US reporters, critical coverage does not hurt their information gathering much. So these reporters have little to lose by being particularly hard on the Americans (cf. Fraser 2007; Goldbloom 2007). Such highly critical reporting also may please the editorial bosses back home.

If reporters really want to be working in public relations, why do so while working for a television station? In many newsrooms, softball reporting would earn you the contempt of your colleagues. And you could make a lot more money doing PR in the private sector—in-house for a politician, perhaps—than in the poorly paid world of journalism. Perhaps this congenital distrust of authority on the part of so many journalists helps explain why the tone of international coverage of the United States does not always parallel movements in domestic public opinion in the home nation of a given newscast. Apparently, public opinion toward Obama is more forgiving than reporters and editors are, particularly in Germany and the United Kingdom.

The US President: A Global "Spinner in Chief"?

Throughout this project we have focused on White House efforts to make the president look good. Although these efforts are aimed primarily at reporters and voters in the United States, one of our major research questions was how much those marketing efforts affect coverage of the United States in international news. We found that such efforts at presidential promotion had considerable impact on international news broadcasts. Perhaps the key difference to remember when comparing United States and international news is the difference between micro reporting and macro reporting. US newscasts focus almost entirely on US matters, leaving considerable time for news reports on incremental political movements in Washington. Will the Senate vote on the president's bill? Did the Republican alternative get out of the Ways and Means Committee? What did the president just say about the economy, the campaign, or US troop levels in Afghanistan? How did Wall Street respond today?

International reporters, in contrast, care far more about delivering the big picture from America. Political developments of modest interest to a US audience might have no interest at all for an international audience. Despite its global influence and its considerable self-regard, the United States is hardly an obsession for most people in other nations. In the three years we examined (2002, 2007, and 2009—key years for the United States in international news), not one nation in any one year devoted even 20 percent of its international news to developments in the United States. When considered as a percentage of all news, including the domestic news in the home country, the US share of the newscast is far smaller.

Given this relatively limited interest in US news, the stories that make the cut for broadcast internationally are not going to be about legislation inching its way through the labyrinth of Congress. Nor are they going to be discussing the "he said, she said" dynamics of partisan sniping between a president and an opposition party. Major stories involving the president, the US military, crime, and the offbeat features that give global audiences a taste of American life and culture can satisfy a modest global appetite for US news. The result is that the president's legislative critics, so commonly used in US domestic news stories, make less of an appearance on international television. Certain details simply are not visible—or perhaps not even worth seeing—from thirty thousand feet (or 9,144 meters).

Of course, if European reporters and news audiences had a greater understanding of the heavy bias toward the status quo in US politics, and the important role that partisan gridlock plays in legislation, they might be less inclined to overstate America's influence in the world and less troubled by America's international activities. Indeed, they might also be less critical of a presidential administration that faces the sharpest political divisions seen in US politics in decades.

Clearly, the international news coverage dynamics seen here can work to a president's great advantage, at least relative to the political communication capacities of other political actors in Washington. Our data indicate the area where presidents are likely to have the greatest impact on international media reports relates to personal character, the same area where presidents have high levels of influence in shaping domestic news coverage. International public opinion results suggest that such broad-brush matters may help explain the high levels of international public approval for Obama, who has sought to charm foreigners like few other presidents in American history.

Our evidence is part of a growing number of studies that question the validity of the "CNN effect," the idea that pictures of human suffering cause mass publics to pressure political leaders to take action. Proponents of the "CNN effect" theory can find relatively few examples of the expected pattern from our data. Indeed, a preponderance of the evidence seems to suggest public apathy, rather than public calls to action, results from horrific images of devastation human suffering around the world (Power 2002). Widespread bloodletting in the Balkans, Syria, and South Sudan are only the best-known and most recent examples of the pattern of inaction that suggests the absence of a mass-influenced political culture supporting military intervention to protect international human rights. These long-suffering locales are not all that well known to global publics anyway, further evidence of the problems inherent in trying to find evidence of a traditional "CNN effect" of public pressure for international humanitarian actions by governments, particularly in the US context.

In short, what we find here, as others have, is that the causal arrow runs in the opposite direction: from the powerful to the public. Public leaders are far more likely to try to mobilize public support for their intended policies by careful, limited release of information to the media that would be helpful to their cause than to feel pressed to respond to a groundswell of public demands for action (Bennett et al. 2007; Entman 2004). Whether presidents succeed in generating significant gains in public support for their preferred actions remains unclear (Edwards 2003, 2004).

White House marketing, in other words, can take an administration only so far. It is hard to imagine the inward-looking US electorate selecting a president who showed more concern for the sensibilities of the Middle East and the international community generally than Barack Obama. Although Obama won the 2008 election primarily on economic concerns, his international orientation has been a constant source of trouble for Obama in domestic politics. US critics have charged throughout his time on the national stage that he is too European, too internationalist, or just plain not American enough to lead this country (Kristof 2012; Milbank 2012; Westen 2012).

Three of the last four presidents—and all three of those elected after the end of the Cold War—were first elected primarily by voters who focused on domestic policy matters. The exception was George H. W. Bush, a vice president elected president in November 1988, as the Soviet Union was about to crumble. Even so, the first President Bush's expertise in the foreign policy realm—he was a former ambassador to the United Nations and to China and a former CIA chief—did not help him much in US politics. Despite his effective handling of the breakup of the Soviet Union and the military liberation of Kuwait, the elder President Bush lost his reelection bid in 1992. His strong suit, politically speaking, was also his undoing. Bush lost largely because Bill Clinton convinced many Americans that Bush wasn't paying enough attention to the economic hardships of ordinary Americans and because Ross Perot convinced many that Bush was selling out the United States with his free-trade agreement with Mexico (Ceaser and Busch 1993).

Perhaps one might want to add George W. Bush's 2004 reelection to the very short list of internationally oriented presidential victories in recent years.

Concerns over terrorism and the ongoing wars in Iraq and Afghanistan were particularly significant in that election (but note that those international matters also had powerful domestic components). Perhaps 1988 and 2004 belong together. Even so, by the time the younger President Bush left office in January 2009 he faced the same charges hurled at his father sixteen years earlier: that he failed to spend enough time dealing with the US economy's health (Fiorina 2008; Sinclair 2008).

So, if Obama is about the most internationally oriented president who could possibly be selected by the largely inward-looking US electorate, why are European media still not happy?

The disparity between the tone of Obama's coverage and the tone of reports on US policies gives us an important clue. Reporters treat presidents far more kindly as individuals, as we see from our analysis of character coverage. That same president's policies, though, generate far harsher words on the evening news.

Indeed, the political culture in the United States is quite different from its fellow Western democracies. European nations and Canada have had national health insurance for decades. Yet even Obama's health care plan—one that left the private insurance industry in control of most aspects of health care—was attacked within the United States as socialistic, if not communistic (Maraniss 2012; Milbank 2012). The political weakness of American unions and the relative political inattention to working-class concerns in the United States also baffle many Europeans (Birnbaum 2012). The level of gun violence in the United States troubles Europeans, who wonder why the stricter gun control laws (and the much lower homicide rates) of Europe are not appealing on this side of the Atlantic.

The critical media coverage emanating from some of the most influential nations in Europe may be partly due to a continental cultural gap that cannot be bridged by any president, no matter how popular he or she is abroad. Even among the advanced democratic allies we studied, the media coverage we found reinforced the sometimes-expressed idea that Americans are from Mars and Europeans are from Venus (cf. Turner 2003/2004).

Indeed, the answer to this dilemma may simply be that the role the United States carves out for itself in the world makes it unpopular in many places (Kagan 2003). America's policies may not change as much as some would like—or expect—when a new president takes office. Americans are often disappointed themselves about how little change a new president can bring about, after all. Many Europeans, with their more centralized political authority, lament that America does not change more dramatically when a new president takes the international stage. Certainly nations weaned on efficient parliamentary democracies, such as the United Kingdom, which often enjoy majority governments;

or Germany, with its powerful chancellor; or France, apart from the occasional inconvenience of a *cohabitation* government of divided authority, must view America's gridlocked legislative system with astonishment. How can such a dysfunctional political system have such a global influence? Or, to put the same basic idea of a cultural gap in a more pro-American way, the United States simply may be too rich, too globally influential, and too distrustful of centralized authority in Washington to be well understood, much less loved, in some parts of Europe. (There may also be an aspect of "getting even" in European news reports. What little coverage European reporters see of their home nations in US news focuses on critical reports that emphasize the dysfunctional aspects of the Eurozone, which would hardly encourage frustrated journalists to produce positive reports on the United States.)

Even so, unilaterism in US foreign policy can trouble even close allies (Mulroney 2003/2004). Of course, the alternative of a revived American isolationism may be even more problematic for the international community than the often-unpopular actions that US presidents take, as one experienced American observer noted during the early months of the Iraq War:

> The US is becoming not only a lonely superpower, but increasingly a frustrated and reluctant one, hesitant to assert singlehandedly the burdens of a 21st century Rome. And yet, ironically, both American leadership and engagement are required more than ever if we are to achieve a semblance of world order. The gravest risk of all would be a retreat by the US into a new strain of isolationism. (Mulroney 2003/2004:8)

As this former Canadian prime minister observed, international pessimism about the United States can be overstated. One of the major new foreign policy crises of the Obama years has been the rebellion in Libya. Here, it seems, Obama's efforts to secure international collaboration bore fruit. Europeans took the lead in assisting the Libyan rebels to oust Muammar al-Qaddafi, with a comparably small US footprint on the operation (Knowlton 2011).

It would have been hard to imagine George W. Bush convincing international leaders to take such an active role in another Muslim nation after the difficulties the US-led coalitions faced in Iraq and Afghanistan. But Obama did so, and all public indications are that the new president did not need to lean very heavily on our European allies to accomplish this collaborative effort. Indeed, it would have been hard to imagine any US president obtaining such international support in the wake of US policies in the region over the past decade. No US ground troops fought in Libya during the uprising as the United States achieved its aims (as did the Europeans) of deposing an internationally despised dictator at a relatively small cost (Knowlton 2011). Of course, it was not without cost, as four Americans—including the ambassador to Libya—were killed in a subsequent attack on a US consulate in Benghazi during the fall of 2012 (Gordon and Schmitt 2012).

Given the severe problems facing this president in the highly challenging and volatile international arenas of Afghanistan, Iran, North Korea, and Pakistan, our mixed findings regarding international news on matters of war and peace may represent the high-water mark for Obama's efforts to make the United States better understood abroad—and to make the world more comprehensible to his fellow American citizens.

Of course, any miscommunication is rarely the fault of only one party to the conversation. US journalists can also learn a good deal from looking at how domestic coverage of the president and the world differs from the international coverage. Our finding, that the United States fails to provide sufficient coverage of international matters—excepting nations that the United States has invaded and close allies such as the United Kingdom—is hardly a novel observation. But the consequences are nonetheless worth reiterating. If the US media fail to do an adequate job of covering the world, it should come as no surprise that few Americans believe international matters should play a significant role in a president's policy agenda. Nor do most Americans have any sense of the deeply troublesome, if not intractable, nature of many international problems. Indeed, the media-fueled misperception of a president's deep involvement with international issues likewise leads to great public frustration with presidents who are seen as spending too much time on global matters.

Journalists everywhere have two major functions. The first is the crucial civil society task of telling viewers and readers what they need to know in order to go about their lives. That process ranges from accurate weather reports to information necessary to evaluate the people engaged in government activity and the policies they propose. The second task, which relates more to a journalist's professional survival than the health of democratic debate, is telling viewers and readers what they want to know. Some critics of US commercial media believe that a globalized world requires the delivery of far more extensive and comprehensive international news to US audiences (cf. Entman 2004). While we agree in principle, one must also consider the incentive system in which US journalists find themselves. International reporting is breathtakingly expensive, and the domestic audience for such news is relatively small. (Indeed, US journalists can even justify undercovering the world by noting that the people who care the most about international news are also likely to be sufficiently savvy to be able to find what they desire online.)

Asking US journalists to downplay coverage that maximizes the financial health of their employers in favor of creating a more educated public conversation about the world is not going to bring about change in the heavily domestic focus of US news. The one thing consistently shown to increase international reporting in domestic media—a war involving the United States—is a cure worse than the disease. Perhaps the 24/7 demand for news on cable and online will encourage greater international coverage. Low-cost stringers can be used more extensively to bring news of the world to America's television screens. But all such efforts accomplish little if American viewers turn their attention elsewhere.

Reporters on both sides of the Atlantic can learn from the findings here. European media tend to offer news that is arguably too presidency focused, making it harder for their audiences to appreciate the extent to which American presidents are constrained by a political system that is designed to make it difficult for any administration to enact major changes. The American system's bias toward the status quo in nearly every legislative matter is well known to US residents, but the presidency-focused news provided abroad may lead to greater cynicism about US presidential performance.

Most of the international television broadcasts we examined were produced by public broadcasters that enjoyed some measure of ongoing government support and/or protection. In other words, they operated within a very different incentive system than the dominant US media outlets, which are for-profit companies operating in public markets. And those markets are not clamoring for more international news, which can be seen to reflect geographic realities. After all, a nation nearly surrounded by oceans and political and economic allies might need far less international discussion on its evening newscasts than a nation on a continent using a vulnerable common currency and having nearly open borders with its neighbors.

These political, economic, and geographical differences explain many of the differences in news coverage between America and Europe. But what about explaining the similarities uncovered here? Given the diversity of media cultures examined here, our findings make the issue of what seems to be a growing international convergence in news reporting beyond the United States all the more interesting, a development worth examining further in the years ahead.

Implications for Future Research

The massive content analysis projects that formed the backbone of this book point to the importance of examining international news content analytically. The coverage similarities and differences revealed here offer many opportunities for future research examining the role of the US president in trying to shape international political discourse, as well as the varying perspectives on the United States offered by a range of media outlets.

The modern international television news environment is tailor-made for an American president. While a president often fails to generate coverage that the White House sees as sufficiently powerful from either domestic or international media, the fact remains that presidents have an exceedingly large capacity to shape international discourse. While America's influence may be less than it was in the heady days after the end of the Cold War, the possibility that any single nation could effectively challenge America's privileged place in global influence—not to mention global political communication—is a distant vision at best. While the world may not have a global spinner in chief, an American president remains probably the closest thing to that in the current media environment.

Personal leadership makes good television at home and abroad. Presidents weigh in on a vast range of public policy topics, and a presidential trip abroad is major news nearly everywhere. The president's ability to use public events and public statements to shape the domestic political discourse has been well studied. Our research suggests the need for far more extensive studies of how presidential agenda setting and framing efforts—a design or as a side effect of US political communication strategies—helps shape the international media landscape. While scholars have long been aware of efforts to tailor messages to appeal to audiences in the Middle East and to key allies in Europe, our research suggests the utility of considering a wider range of nations far beyond the focus of most US marketing efforts. As we saw in the television news from South Africa, a US president's efforts can be influential far from the intended domestic and international media audiences being targeted.

Our research focused on the political dimensions of international news relating to the United States. But many international news reports on America have little to do with presidents and politics. News about US culture and business are two key areas that seem particularly promising for more extensive investigation. Similarly, studies of the government, leadership, and culture of other globally influential nations—China, Germany, and the United Kingdom come to mind—would also place the discussion of international news coverage of the United States into a wider context.

Of course, we examined news about only two US presidents (and only parts of those two presidencies). Future research could determine whether our findings are unique to the years of news content we examined or whether they apply to other presidents at other times as well.

Along these same lines, we examined only television news, which tends to be more superficial than newspapers, particularly the elite newspapers commonly read by political insiders and highly educated citizens around the globe. Future research into other media outlets, from newspapers to entertainment media, and new distribution systems such as social media, may also offer insights into the linkages between international news and international public opinion regarding the United States and its presidents.

Finally, we recognize that our sample was quite limited when compared to the nearly two hundred countries that belong to the United Nations. We suggest future scholars consider whether the patterns we have discovered are replicated in the news content of the many nations we did not examine here. They range from Latin American countries and Canada, our hemispheric neighbors, to Russia, China, and India, rising nations and potential future superpower allies or rivals with the United States in the years ahead. News from Israel might also offer interesting contrasts to the Arabic-language media examined here.

A Postelection Postscript

Barack Obama's reelection in November 2012 may have been greeted with enthusiasm in many nations whose publics found Mitt Romney less appealing, but the fundamental challenges of the United States' role in the world, and the world's role with the United States in it, remain unchanged. Nor have the media's challenges gone away. Even a president like Obama, who seeks to work collaboratively on international problems, faces profound challenges in trying to explain to international reporters—and their audiences—the global utility of US policies. Convincing those skeptical reporters and publics of the wisdom of US policies poses an even greater challenge.

But if there is one thing that this study of these two presidents and their treatment in international television news reports has taught us, it is that the news does not wait. Challenges from around the world pile up for presidents in the best of times, and the past dozen years have been far from the best of times. Looking ahead provides scant justification for optimism either at home or abroad. The Euro crisis, which threatens to destabilize the world economy, is far from resolved. The long-running budgetary stalemates in Washington could do severe damage to the domestic and global economy if no agreement is reached. An assertive Russia occupies much of Georgia, and the rising power of China makes nervous a range of nations stretching from India to Japan. A new, young leader in North Korea adds to the world's anxiety.

But the list does not end there. The US-led sanctions regime does not seem to have driven Iran off course in its drive to develop nuclear weapons technology, if not such weapons themselves. A pattern of extreme weather month after month is starting to raise the specter of climate change consequences sooner than we have imagined. The chaotic political environments in Iraq, Afghanistan, Pakistan, Syria, and elsewhere do not inspire confidence in peaceful outcomes.

And the conflict between Israeli and Palestinian peoples may be the most intractable of them of all.

In short, we need healthy and effective international news outlets now more than ever. If there is any chance the nations of this world can work though the many challenges we now face (along with those increasingly visible on the horizon), it will depend in no small measure on the ability of the world's media to describe, explain, and interpret our increasingly interrelated community of nations to each other. We hope that the analysis contained here will help identify the strengths and weaknesses of US and international news coverage in recent years and help illuminate the way to even more effective global news reporting in the years ahead.

Appendix

THE MEDIA TENOR CONTENT
ANALYSIS DATA

The Data

Chapter 2: 131,086 television news stories in 2002; 278,947 television news stories in 2007; and 251,333 television news stories in 2009 for the overall calculation of domestic and international news content. The analysis of international news relating to the United States involves 52,326 international and 10,608 US stories in 2005 and 42,551 international and 6,396 US stories in 2010. In addition, 6,997 international news stories about the United States in 2002, 7,608 international stories about the United States in 2007, and 13,398 international stories about the United States in 2009 were analyzed for subject matter and tone. (Note that the different volume of stories in different years relate more to the number of media outlets examined in a given year rather than large changes in the amount of attention paid to the United States.)

Chapter 3: 29,834 statements on international television and 46,890 statements on US television newscasts relating to Barack Obama from January 1, 2009, through June 30, 2010.

Chapter 4: 43,811 statements on international television and 85,762 statements on US television newscasts relating to George W. Bush from January 1, 2005, through December 31, 2008.

Chapter 5: 172,739 statements relating to the United States on international television between January 1, 2009, and June 30, 2010, and 138,379 statements relating to the United States on international television between January 1, 2005, and June 30, 2006. The chapter also used the US and international data listed above for Bush and Obama identified in chapter 3 and chapter 4.

Chapter 6: The nomination phase discussion is based on 2,169 statements about the leading Republican presidential candidates and 5,314 statements about the leading Democratic presidential candidates on international television between December 16, 2007, and March 22, 2008. The general election discussion is based on 3,991 statements about the McCain campaign, 2,032 statements about the Palin campaign, and 5,256 statements about the Obama campaign on evening newscasts from two German television news providers and four UK television news providers between August 23 and November 3, 2008.

The News Outlets

(Note that not all news outlets are examined in all years or in all portions of the study.)

Germany: ARD Tagesthemen, ZDF heute journal, RTL Aktuell, ARD Tagesschau, ZDF Heute, SAT.1 News, ProSieben Newstime

United Kingdom: BBC1 10 O'clock News, ITV News at Ten, BBC2 Newsnight, ITN Early Evening News, BBC1 6 O'clock News, BBC World

South Africa: SABC 2 Afrikaans News, SABC 3 English News, E-TV News, SABC Zulu/Xhosa News, SABC Sotho News, SABC 3 News @ One, SABC 3 News @ Ten, SABC 3 Africa News Update, SABC SiSwati/Ndebele News, SABC Venda/Tsonga News (2009 only), Summit TV

France: TF1

Italy: RAI Uno

Switzerland: SF DRS Tagesschau, SF Rundschau, SF Eco, SF Börse

Spain: TVE1

Arabic: Al-Arabiyah, Al-Jazeera, Nile News, LBC, Al-Manar, Dubai TV

Turkey: TRT

China: CCTV

United States: ABC, CBS, NBC, Fox News

References

Abelson, Reed. 2010. "In Health Care Reform, Boons for Hospitals and Drug Makers." *New York Times*, March 21.

Aberbach, Joel D. 2012. "'Change We Can Believe In' Meets Reality." In *The Obama Presidency: Appraisals and Prospects*, eds. Bert A. Rockman, Andrew Rudalevige, and Colin Campbell. Washington, DC: Sage/CQ Press.

Abramowitz, Michael, and Peter Baker. 2007. "Embattled, Bush Held to Plan to Salvage Iraq." *Washington Post*, January 21.

Abramowitz, Michael, and Lori Montgomery. 2007. "Bush to Request Billions for Wars." *Washington Post*, February 3.

Abramson, Paul, John H. Aldrich, and David W. Rohde. 2002. *Change and Continuity in the 2000 Elections*. Washington, DC: CQ Press.

Abramson, Paul, John H. Aldrich, and David W. Rohde. 2010. *Change and Continuity in the 2008 Elections*. Washington, DC: CQ Press.

Adams, Michael. 2003. *Fire and Ice: The United States, Canada and the Myth of Converging Values*. Toronto: Penguin Canada.

Adatto, Kiku. 1990. "Sound Bite Democracy." Research paper, Kennedy School Press Politics Center, Harvard University, June.

Aday, Sean, Steven Livingston, and Maeve Hebert. 2005. "Embedding the Truth: A Cross-Cultural Analysis of Objectivity and Television Coverage of the Iraq War." *International Journal of Press/Politics* 10(1):3–21.

Alter, Jonathan. 1992. "Go Ahead, Blame the Media." *Newsweek*, November 2.

Alter, Jonathan. 2010. *The Promise: President Obama, Year One*. New York: Simon & Schuster.

Andrew, Blake, Antonia Maioni, and Stuart Soroka. 2006. "Just When You Thought It Was Out, Policy Is Pulled Back In." *Policy Options* 27(3) (March):74–79.

Andrew, Blake, Lori Young, and Stuart Soroka. 2008. "Back to the Future: Press Coverage of the 2008 Canadian Election Campaign Strikes Familiar and Unfamiliar Notes." *Policy Options* (November):79–84.

Arango, Tim, and Michael S. Schmidt. 2011. "Last Convoy of American Troops Leaves Iraq." *New York Times*, December 18.

Auletta, Ken. 2004. "Fortress Bush: How the White House Keeps the Press under Control." *New Yorker*, February 19.

Baker, Nancy V. 2002. "The Impact of Anti-terrorism Policies on Separation of Powers: Assessing John Ashcroft's Role." *Presidential Studies Quarterly* 32(4):765–78.

Baker, Peter. 2009. "White House Scraps Bush's Approach to Missile Shield." *New York Times*, September 17.

Baker, Peter. 2010. "For Obama, a Steep Learning Curve as Chief in War." *New York Times*, August 28.

Baker, Peter. 2012. "In a World of Complications, Obama Faces a Re-election Test." *New York Times*, June 17.

Baker, Peter, and Carl Hulse. 2010. "Deep Rifts Divide Obama and Republicans." *New York Times*, November 3.

Balz, Dan, and Jon Cohen. 2007. "Confidence in Bush Leadership at All-Time Low, Poll Finds." *Washington Post*, January 22.

Balz, Dan, and Jon Cohen. 2010. "Democrats Gain in Poll, But GOP Still Leads as Midterm Elections Near." *Washington Post*, October 5.

Balz, Dan, and Jon Cohen. 2012. "President Obama, Mitt Romney Deadlocked in Race, Poll Finds." *Washington Post*, July 10.

Barber, James David. 1992. *Presidential Character: Predicting Performance in the White House*. Englewood Cliffs, NJ: Prentice Hall.

Baum, Matthew A. 2003. *Soft News Goes to War: Public Opinion and American Foreign Policy in the New Media Age*. Princeton, NJ: Princeton University Press.

Baum, Matthew A., and Tim Groeling. 2010. *War Stories: The Causes and Consequences of Public Views of War*. Princeton, NJ: Princeton University Press.

Bennett, W. Lance, Regina G. Lawrence, and Steven Livingston. 2007. *When the Press Fails: Political Power and the News Media from Iraq to Katrina*. Chicago: University of Chicago Press.

Bernstein, Richard. 2003. "Europe Loses Advocate with Powell's Iraq Shift." *New York Times*, February 2.

Bessaiso, Ehab Y. 2005. "Al Jazeera and the War in Afghanistan: A Delivery System or a Mouthpiece?" In *The Al Jazeera Phenomenon: Critical Perspectives on the New Arab Media*, ed. Mohamed Zayani. Boulder, CO: Paradigm.

Bilbassy, Nadia. 2010. "America Is Seen at the Center of the Universe" [Interview]. *Media Tenor Research Report* 160:42–43.

Birnbaum, Michael. 2012. "In France, President Makes the Richest Pay." *Washington Post*, August 3.

Blood, Robert. 2010. "Trends in Global Activism Affecting the Energy Sector." *Media Tenor Research Report* 160:28–29.

Boaz, Cynthia. 2005. "War and Foreign Policy Framing in International Media." *Peace Review: A Journal of Social Justice* 17:349–56.

Bonner, Raymond. 2002. "Threats and Responses: Immigration; New Policy Delays Visas for Specified Muslim Men." *New York Times*, September 10.

Brewer, Paul R., Kimberly Gross, Sean Aday, and Lars Willnat. 2003. "International Trust and Public Opinion about World Affairs." *American Journal of Political Science* 48(1):93–109.

Broder, John M. 2006. "Democrats Take Senate: Concession in Virginia Completes Midterm Sweep." *New York Times*, November 10.

Broder, John M. 2010. "Climate Change Doubt Is Tea Party Article of Faith." *New York Times*, October 20.

Broder, John M. 2012. "After Federal Jolt, Clean Energy Seeks New Spark." *New York Times*, October 23.

Brooks, Stephen. 2006. *As Others See Us: The Causes and Consequences of Foreign Perceptions of America*. Peterborough, Ontario: Broadview.

Brown, Cynthia, ed. 2003. *Lost Liberties: Ashcroft and the Assault on Personal Freedom*. New York: New Press.

Brown, Robin. 2003. "Clausewitz in the Age of CNN: Rethinking the Military-Media Relationship." In *Framing Terrorism: The News Media, the Government and the Public*, eds. Pippa Norris, Montague Kern, and Marion Just. New York: Routledge.

Bumiller, Elisabeth. 2003. "Keepers of Bush Image Lift Stagecraft to New Heights." *New York Times*, May 16.

Burden, Barry C. 2010. "The Nomination: Rules, Strategies and Uncertainty." In *The Elections of 2008*, ed. Michael Nelson. Washington, DC: CQ Press.

Busch, Andrew E. 2008. "The Reemergence of the Iowa Caucuses: A New Trend, an Aberration, or a Useful Reminder?" In *The Making of the Presidential Candidates 2008*, ed. William G. Mayer. Lanham, MD: Rowman & Littlefield.

Calmes, Jackie. 2011a. "Debt Talk Mired, Leader for GOP Proposes Option." *New York Times*, July 12.

Calmes, Jackie. 2011b. "Success Battling Terrorists, But Scant Glory for It." *New York Times*, October 2.

Campbell, David E. 2009. "Public Opinion and the 2008 Presidential Election." In *The American Elections of 2008*, eds. Janet M. Box-Steffensmeier and Steven E. Schier. Lanham, MD: Rowman & Littlefield.

Campbell, James E. 2012. "Political Forces on the Obama Presidency: From Elections to Governing." In *The Obama Presidency: Appraisals and Prospects*, eds. Bert A. Rockman, Andrew Rudalevige, and Colin Campbell. Washington, DC: Sage/CQ Press.

Cappella, Joseph N., and Kathleen Hall Jamieson. 1997. *Spiral of Cynicism: The Press and the Public Good*. New York: Oxford University Press.

Ceaser, James, and Andrew Busch. 1993. *Upside Down and Inside Out: The 1992 Elections and American Politics*. Lanham, MD: Rowman & Littlefield.

Ceaser, James, and Andrew Busch. 2001. *The Perfect Tie: The True Story of the 2000 Presidential Election*. Lanham, MD: Rowman & Littlefield.

Ceaser, James, and Andrew Busch. 2005. *Red over Blue: The 2004 Elections and American Politics*. Lanham, MD: Rowman & Littlefield.

Ceaser, James, Andrew Busch, and John J. Pitney Jr. 2009. *Epic Journey: The 2008 Elections and American Politics*. Lanham, MD: Rowman & Littlefield.

Chait, Jonathan. 2011. "What the Left Doesn't Understand about Obama." *New York Times* [Magazine], September 2.

Clarke, Richard A. 2004. *Against All Enemies: Inside America's War on Terror.* New York: Free Press.

Clayton, Mark. 2007. "Study Finds White House Manipulation on Climate Science." *Christian Science Monitor,* December 12.

Cohen, Jeffrey E. 2008. *The Presidency in the Era of 24-Hour News.* Princeton, NJ: Princeton University Press.

Cohen, Jon, and Jennifer Agiesta. 2009. "Obama Off to Solid Start, Poll Finds; But Release of Memos on Detainee Interrogations Reveals Deep Partisan Split." *Washington Post,* April 26.

Cohen, Marty, David Karol, Hans Noel, and John Zaller. 2008. "The Invisible Primary in Presidential Nominations, 1980–2004." In *The Making of the Presidential Candidates 2008,* ed. William G. Mayer. Lanham, MD: Rowman & Littlefield.

Conley, Patricia. 2009. "A Mandate for Change? Decisive Victory in a Time of Crisis." In *Winning the Presidency, 2008,* ed. William J. Crotty. Boulder, CO: Paradigm.

Connolly, Ceci. 2009. "Ex-Foes of Health Care Reform Emerge as Supporters." *Washington Post,* March 6.

Cook, Timothy E. 1989. *Making Laws and Making News.* Washington, DC: Brookings.

Cook, Timothy E. 2005. *Governing with the News: The News Media as a Political Institution,* 2nd edition. Chicago: University of Chicago Press.

Cooper, Michael. 2010. "GOP Senate Victory Stuns Democrats." *New York Times,* January 19.

Curran, James, Shanto Iyengar, Anker Brink Lund, and Inka Salovaara-Moring. 2009. "Media System, Public Knowledge and Democracy." *European Journal of Communication* 24(1):5–26.

Dautrich, Kenneth, and Thomas H. Hartley. 1999. *How the News Media Fail American Voters: Causes, Consequences & Remedies.* New York: Columbia University Press.

Davey, Monica, and Carl Hulse. 2009. "Franken's Win Bolsters Democratic Grip on Senate." *New York Times,* June 30.

Dempsey, Judy. 2011a. "A Deepening Rift between Germany and Israel." *New York Times,* March 7.

Dempsey, Judy. 2011b. "Germany Pushes Israel on Peace." *New York Times,* April 7.

Dempsey, Judy. 2012. "Merkel Pays a Price for Her Energy Policy Shift." *New York Times,* May 28.

Denton, Robert E. 2009. "Identity Politics and the 2008 Presidential Campaign." In *The 2008 Presidential Campaign: A Communication Perspective,* ed. Robert E. Denton. Lanham, MD: Rowman & Littlefield.

Dickson, Sandra H. 1992. "Press and U.S. Policy toward Nicaragua, 1983–1987." *Journalism Quarterly* 69(3):562–71.

Diehl, Jackson. 2012. "Forgetting the War in Afghanistan." *Washington Post,* August 6.

Dimitrova, Anelia K. 2001. "Nightmares in the Nightly News: CNN Covers Atrocities in Kosovo." *East European Quarterly* 35(1):1–47.

Dimock, Michael. 2004. "Bush and Public Opinion." In *Considering the Bush Presidency,* eds. Gary Gregg II and Mark J. Rozell. New York: Oxford University Press.

Dionne, E. J. 1988. "Bush Camp Feels Galvanized after Showdown with Rather." *New York Times,* January 27.

Donadio, Rachel, and Elisabetta Povoledo. 2011. "Berlusconi, Magnetic and Divisive, Whose Politics Were Personal." *New York Times*, November 12.

Donsbach, Wolfgang, and Thomas E. Patterson. 2004. "Political News Journalists: Partisanship, Professionalism and Political Roles in Five Countries." In *Comparing Political Communication: Theories, Cases, and Challenges*, eds. Frank Esser and Barbara Pfetsch. New York: Cambridge University Press.

Dowd, Maureen. 1999. "Name That General!" *New York Times*, November 7.

Dowd, Maureen. 2005. "The United States of Shame." *New York Times*, September 3.

Edge, Thomas. 2010. "Southern Strategy 2.0: Conservatives, White Voters and the Election of Barack Obama." *Journal of Black Studies* 40(3):426–44.

Edwards, George C., III. 2003. *On Deaf Ears: The Limits of the Bully Pulpit*. New Haven, CT: Yale University Press.

Edwards, George C., III. 2004. "Riding High in the Polls: George W. Bush and Public Opinion." In *The George W. Bush Presidency: Appraisals and Prospects*, eds. Colin Campbell and Bert A. Rockman. Washington, DC: CQ Press.

Edwards, George C., III. 2006. "The Illusion of Transformational Leadership." Paper delivered at the annual meeting of the American Political Science Association, Philadelphia, September 1.

Edwards, George C., III. 2012. "Strategic Assessments: Evaluating Opportunities and Strategies in the Obama Presidency." In *The Obama Presidency: Appraisals and Prospects*, eds. Bert A. Rockman, Andrew Rudalevige, and Colin Campbell. Washington, DC: Sage/CQ Press.

Entman, Robert M. 2000. "Declarations of Independence." In *Decision-Making in a Glass House: Mass Media, Public Opinion and American and European Foreign Policy in the 21st Century*, eds. B. L. Nacos, R. Y. Shapiro, and P. Isernia. Lanham, MD: Rowman & Littlefield.

Entman, Robert M. 2004. *Projections of Power: Framing News, Public Opinion, and U.S. Foreign Policy*. Chicago: University of Chicago Press.

Esser, Frank. 2008. "Dimensions of Political News Cultures: Sound Bite and Image Bite News in France, Germany, Great Britain and the United States." *International Journal of Press/Politics* 13(4):401–28.

Farnsworth, Stephen J. 2003. *Political Support in a Frustrated America*. Westport, CT: Praeger.

Farnsworth, Stephen J. 2009. *Spinner in Chief: How Presidents Sell Their Policies and Themselves*. Boulder, CO: Paradigm.

Farnsworth, Stephen J., and S. Robert Lichter. 2003. "The 2000 New Hampshire Democratic Primary and Network News." *American Behavioral Scientist* 46(5):588–99.

Farnsworth, Stephen J., and S. Robert Lichter. 2006a. *The Mediated Presidency: Television News and Presidential Governance*. Lanham, MD: Rowman & Littlefield.

Farnsworth, Stephen J., and S. Robert Lichter. 2006b. "The 2004 New Hampshire Democratic Primary and Network News." *Harvard International Journal of Press/Politics* 11(1):53–63.

Farnsworth, Stephen J., and S. Robert Lichter. 2008. "Trends in Television News Coverage of U.S. Elections." In *The Handbook of Election Coverage around the World*, eds. Lynda Lee Kaid and Jesper Stromback. London: Routledge.

Farnsworth, Stephen J., and S. Robert Lichter. 2011a. *The Nightly News Nightmare: Media Coverage of U.S. Presidential Elections, 1988-2008*, 3rd edition. Lanham, MD: Rowman & Littlefield.

Farnsworth, Stephen J., and S. Robert Lichter. 2011b. "The Return of the Honeymoon: Television News Coverage of New Presidents, 1981–2009." *Presidential Studies Quarterly* 41(3):590–603.

Farnsworth, Stephen J., and S. Robert Lichter. 2012a. "How Television Covers the Presidential Nomination Process." In *The Making of the Presidential Candidates 2012*, ed. William G. Mayer. Lanham, MD: Rowman & Littlefield.

Farnsworth, Stephen J., and S. Robert Lichter. 2012b. "News Coverage of New Presidents in the *New York Times*, 1981–2009." *Politics & Policy* 40(1):69–91.

Farnsworth, Stephen J., and S. Robert Lichter. 2013 [forthcoming]. "An Extended Presidential Honeymoon? Coverage of Barack Obama in the *New York Times* during 2009 and 2010." Accepted for publication, *Politics & Policy*.

Farnsworth, Stephen J., S. Robert Lichter, and Roland Schatz. 2008. "Struggling to Control the Message: International News Coverage of U.S. Foreign Policy, 2005–2007." Paper delivered at American Political Science Association Pre-Conference in Political Communication, Boston.

Farnsworth, Stephen J., S. Robert Lichter, and Roland Schatz. 2009. "CBC News Coverage of Canada's 2006 Liberal Leadership Candidates." *American Review of Canadian Studies* 39:290–302.

Farnsworth, Stephen J., S. Robert Lichter, and Roland Schatz. 2010. "President Bush on the World Stage: International News Coverage of the U.S. Government, 2005–2007." Paper delivered at the Annual Meeting of the Eastern Communication Association, Baltimore.

Farnsworth, Stephen J., S. Robert Lichter, and Roland Schatz. 2011. "International News Coverage of Barack Obama as a New President." *Electronic Media and Politics* 1(2):27–45.

Farnsworth, Stephen J., S. Robert Lichter, and Roland Schatz. 2012. "The 2008 U.S. Presidential Nomination Campaigns on German and UK Television: Policy, Horserace and Character Coverage from across the Atlantic." Paper presented at the Midwest Political Science Association Annual Meeting, Chicago.

Farnsworth, Stephen J., S. Robert Lichter, and Roland Schatz. 2013. "Election News Coverage across the Atlantic: 2008 U.S. Presidential Election Campaigns on German, UK and US Television." Paper presented at the Midwest Political Science Association Annual Meeting, Chicago.

Farnsworth, Stephen J., Stuart Soroka, and Lori Young. 2010. "The International Two-Step Flow in Foreign News: Canadian and U.S. Television News Coverage of U.S. Affairs." *International Journal of Press/Politics* 15(4):401–19.

Filkins, Dexter. 2001. "The Legacy of the Taliban Is a Sad and Broken Land." *New York Times*, December 31.

Finn, Peter, and Anne E. Kornblut. 2011. "Guantanamo Bay: Why Obama Hasn't Fulfilled His Promise to Close the Facility." *Washington Post*, April 23.

Fiorina, Morris P. 2008. "A Divider, Not a Uniter—But Did It Have to Be?" In *The George W. Bush Legacy*, eds. Colin Campbell, Bert A. Rockman, and Andrew Rudalevige. Washington, DC: CQ Press.

Fisher, Ian. 2005. "Bush Phones Italy's Leader as Ire Lingers over Killing." *New York Times*, May 5.

Fisher, Louis. 2004. "The Way We Go to War: The Iraq Resolution." In *Considering the Bush Presidency*, eds. Gary Gregg II and Mark J. Rozell. New York: Oxford University Press.

Fletcher, Michael. 2009. "Obama Leaves DC to Sign Stimulus Bill." *Washington Post*, February 18.

Fraser, Graham. 2007. Interview with Former Washington Bureau Chief. (Toronto) *Globe & Mail*, March 26.

Fraser, Matthew. 2000. "The CBC's Choice: Constellations or Core Competencies?" *Policy Options* (September):43–49.

Frum, David. 2003. *The Right Man: The Surprise Presidency of George W. Bush, an Inside Account*. New York: Random House.

Gaines, Brian J. 2002. "Where's the Rally? Approval and Trust of the President, Cabinet, Congress and Government since September 11." *PS: Political Science & Politics* 35(3):531–36.

Gall, Carlotta. 2011. "Pakistani Military Investigates How bin Laden Was Able to Hide in Plain View." *New York Times*, May 4.

Gall, Carlotta, and Eric Schmitt. 2011. "Amid Skepticism, Pakistan Calculates Its Response." *New York Times*, May 2.

Gall, Carlotta, and Jeff Zeleny. 2008. "Obama's Visit Renews Focus on Afghanistan." *New York Times*, July 20.

Gawthorne, Michael. 2010. "Copenhagen or Bust: Coverage of Climate Issues in International TV News." *Media Tenor Research Report* 160:50–51.

Gidengil, Elisabeth. 2008. "Media Matter: Election Coverage in Canada." In *The Handbook of Election News Coverage around the World*, eds. Jesper Stromback and Lynda Lee Kaid. New York: Routledge.

Gidengil, Elisabeth, Andre Blais, Neil Nevitte, and Richard Nadeau. 2002. "Priming and Campaign Context: Evidence from Recent Canadian Elections." In *Do Political Campaigns Matter? Campaign Effects in Elections and Referendums*, eds. David M. Farrell and Rudiger Schmitt-Beck. London: Routledge.

Gilboa, Eytan. 2005. "Global Television News and Foreign Policy: Debating the CNN Effect." *International Studies Perspectives* 6:325–41.

Gilliam, Frank D., Jr., and Shanto Iyengar. 2011. "News Coverage Effects on Public Opinion about Crime." In *Media Power in Politics*, ed. Doris Graber. Washington, DC: CQ Press.

Goldbloom, Michael. 2007. Interview with former *Toronto Star* publisher. May 4.

Goldfarb, Zachary. 2007. "Mobilized Online, Thousands Gather to Hear Obama." *Washington Post*, February 3.

Goodman, J. David. 2012. "Arrest in Thailand after U.S. Terror Alert." *New York Times*, January 13.

Gordon, Michael R., and Eric Schmitt. 2012. "Libya Attack Shows Pentagon's Limits in Region." *New York Times*, November 3.

Graber, Doris. 1988. *Processing the News: How People Tame the Information Tide*, 2nd edition. New York: Longman.

Gregg, Gary L. 2004. "Dignified Authenticity: George W. Bush and the Symbolic Presidency." In *Considering the Bush Presidency*, eds. Gary Gregg II and Mark J. Rozell. New York: Oxford University Press.

Gronbeck, Bruce E. 2009. "The Web, Campaign 07–08 and Engaged Citizens." In *The 2008 Presidential Campaign: A Communication Perspective*, ed. Robert E. Denton Jr. Lanham, MD: Rowman & Littlefield.

Grossman, Michael B., and Martha Joynt Kumar. 1981. *Portraying the President: The White House and the News Media*. Baltimore: Johns Hopkins University Press.

Gutierrez-Villalobos, Sonia, James K. Hertog, and Ramona R. Rush. 1994. "Press Support for the U.S. Administration during the Panama Invasion: Analyses of the Strategic and Tactical Critique in the Domestic Press." *Journalism & Mass Communication Quarterly* 71(3):618–27.

Hadland, Adrian. 2012. "Africanizing Three Models of Media and Politics: The South African Experience." In *Comparing Media Systems beyond the Western World*, eds. Daniel C. Hallin and Paolo Mancini. Cambridge: Cambridge University Press.

Haglund, David G. 2006. "Quebec's 'America Problem': Differential Threat Perceptions in the North American Security Community." *American Review of Canadian Studies* 36:552–67.

Hall, Jim. 2001. *Online Journalism: A Critical Primer*. London: Pluto Press.

Hallin, Daniel. 1986. *The "Uncensored War": The Media and Vietnam*. Berkeley: University of California Press.

Hallin, Daniel C., and Paolo Mancini. 2004a. *Comparing Media Systems: Three Models of Media and Politics*. New York: Cambridge University Press.

Hallin, Daniel C., and Paolo Mancini. 2004b. "Americanization, Globalization and Secularization." In *Comparing Political Communication: Theories, Cases, and Challenges*, eds. Frank Esser and Barbara Pfetsch. New York: Cambridge University Press.

Hallin, Daniel C., and Paolo Mancini. 2012. "Introduction." In *Comparing Media Systems beyond the Western World*, eds. Daniel C. Hallin and Paolo Mancini. Cambridge: Cambridge University Press.

Hamilton, John Maxwell, and Eric Jenner. 2003. "The New Foreign Correspondence." *Foreign Affairs* 82(5) (September/October):131–38.

Han, Lori Cox. 2001. *Governing from Center Stage: White House Communication Strategies during the Television Age of Politics*. Cresskill, NJ: Hampton Press.

Hannerz, Ulf. 2004. *Foreign News: Exploring the World of Foreign Correspondents*. Chicago: University of Chicago Press.

Harris, John F., and Jonathan Martin. 2009. "The George W. Bush and Bill Clinton Legacies in the 2008 Elections." In *The American Elections of 2008*, eds. Janet M. Box-Steffensmeier and Steven E. Schier. Lanham, MD: Rowman & Littlfield.

Hatlapa, Ruth, and Andrei S. Markovits. 2010. "Obamamania and Anti-Americanism as Complementary Concepts in Contemporary German Discourse." *German Politics and Society* 28(1):69–94.

Hawkins, Virgil. 2002. "The Other Side of the CNN Factor: The Media and Conflict." *Journalism Studies* 3(2):225–40.

Healy, Jack. 2012. "Coordinated Attacks Bombard Iraq, Killing Dozens." *New York Times*, February 23.

Heilemann, John, and Mark Halperin. 2010. *Game Change: Obama and the Clintons, McCain and Palin, and the Race of a Lifetime*. New York: Harper.

Herszenhorn, David. 2009. "Recovery Bill Gets Final Approval." *New York Times*, February 13.

Herszenhorn, David, and Robert Pear. 2010. "Health Vote Is Done, But Partisan Debate Rages On." *New York Times*, March 22.

Hess, Stephen. 2005. *Through Their Eyes: Foreign Correspondents in the United States*. Washington, DC: Brookings.

Hollihan, Thomas A. 2001. *Uncivil Wars: Political Campaigns in a New Media Age*. Boston: Bedford/St. Martin's.

Holsti, Ole. 2008. *To See Ourselves as Others See Us*. Ann Arbor: University of Michigan Press.

Hughes, William J. 1995. "The 'Not-So-Genial' Conspiracy: The *New York Times* and Six Presidential 'Honeymoons,' 1953–1993." *Journalism and Mass Communication Quarterly* 72(4):841–50.

Iyengar, Shanto. 1991. *Is Anyone Responsible? How Television Frames Political Issues*. Chicago: University of Chicago Press.

Jacobs, Lawrence R. 2006. "The Presidency and the Press: The Paradox of the White House Communications War." In *The Presidency and the Political System*, 8th edition, ed. Michael Nelson. Washington, DC: CQ Press.

Jacobs, Lawrence R. 2012. "The Privileges of Access: Interest Groups and the White House." In *The Obama Presidency: Appraisals and Prospects*, eds. Bert A. Rockman, Andrew Rudalevige, and Colin Campbell. Washington, DC: Sage/CQ Press.

Jacobson, Gary C. 2008. "George W. Bush, Polarization and the War in Iraq." In *The George W. Bush Legacy*, eds. Colin Campbell, Bert A. Rockman, and Andrew Rudalevige. Washington, DC: CQ Press.

Jacobson, Gary C. 2012. "Polarization, Public Opinion and the Presidency: The Obama and Anti-Obama Coalitions." In *The Obama Presidency: Appraisals and Prospects*, eds. Bert A. Rockman, Andrew Rudalevige, and Colin Campbell. Washington, DC: Sage/CQ Press.

Jasperson, Amy, and Mansour O. El-Kikhia. 2003. "CNN and al Jazeera's Media Coverage of America's War in Afghanistan." In *Framing Terrorism: The News Media, the Government and the Public*, eds. Pippa Norris, Montague Kern, and Marion Just. New York: Routledge.

Jeffords, James M. 2003. *An Independent Man: Adventures of a Public Servant*. New York: Simon and Schuster.

Jones, Charles O. 1994. *The Presidency in a Separated System*. Washington, DC: Brookings.

Jones, Charles O. 1995. *Separate but Equal Branches: Congress and the Presidency*. Chatham, NJ: Chatham House.

Jones, Timothy M. 2006. "Framing and Social Identity: A Cross-National News Analysis of the Abu Ghraib Prison Scandal." Paper presented at the International Studies Association Annual Meeting, San Diego.

Kagan, Robert. 2003. *Of Paradise and Power: America and Europe in the New World Order*. New York: Knopf.

Kahn, Joseph. 2002. "A Nation Challenged: American Muslims; Raids, Detentions and Lists Lead Muslims to Cry Persecution." *New York Times*, March 27.

Keller, Bill. 2011. "Fill in the Blanks." *New York Times*, September 18.

Kernell, Samuel. 2007. *Going Public: New Strategies of Presidential Leadership*, 4th edition. Washington, DC: CQ Press.

Kessler, Glenn, and Robin Wright. 2007. "Hughes to Leave State Dept. after Mixed Results in Outreach Post." *Washington Post*, November 1.

Khan, Ismail. 2012. "Jail Term for Helping CIA Find bin Laden." *New York Times*, May 23.

Kinsley, Michael. 2003. "An Apology Would Help." *Washington Post*, September 12.

Knowlton, Brian. 2011. "In Libyan Conflict, European Power Was Felt." *New York Times*, October 20.

Kolmer, Christian, and Holli Semetko. 2009. "Framing the Iraq War: Perspectives from American, UK, Czech, German, South African and Al-Jazeera News." *American Behavioral Scientist* 52(5):643–56.

Kolmer, Christian, and Holli Semetko. 2010. "International Television News: Germany Compared." *Journalism Studies* 11(5):700–717.

Kornblut, Anne E. 2006. "Spotlight on Lobbying Swings to Little-Known Congressman." *New York Times*, January 17.

Kraidy, Marwan M. 2012. "The Rise of Transnational Media Systems: Implications of Pan-Arab Media for Comparative Research." In *Comparing Media Systems beyond the Western World*, eds. Daniel C. Hallin and Paolo Mancini. Cambridge: Cambridge University Press.

Kristof, Nicholas D. 2004. "Dithering as Others Die." *New York Times*, June 26.

Kristof, Nicholas D. 2012. "Why Is Europe a Dirty Word?" *New York Times*, January 14.

Krugman, Paul. 2006. "The Crony Fairy." *New York Times*, April 28.

Kull, Steven. 2004. "The Press and Public Misperception about the Iraq War." *Nieman Reports* (Summer):64–66.

Kupchan, Charles A. 2012. *No One's World: The West, the Rising Rest, and the Coming Global Turn*. Oxford: Oxford University Press.

Kurtz, Howard. 2000. "The Shot Heard Round the Media." *Washington Post*, September 6.

Kurtz, Howard. 2007a. "Campaign Allegation a Source of Vexation." *Washington Post*, January 22.

Kurtz, Howard. 2007b. "Headmaster Disputes Claim That Obama Attended Islamic School." *Washington Post*, January 23.

Landler, Mark. 2005. "Schröder Loses Confidence Vote; Early Election Is Likely." *New York Times*, July 1.

Lazarsfeld, P. F., B. Berelson, and H. Gaudet. 1944. *The People's Choice*. New York: Columbia University Press.

Leenders, Reinoud. 2007. "Regional Conflict Formations: Is the Middle East Next?" *Third World Quarterly* 28(5):959–82.

Lengle, James I. 1981. *Representation and Presidential Primaries: The Democratic Party in the Post-Reform Era*. Westport, CT: Greenwood.

Lindsay, James M. 2003. "Deference and Defiance: The Shifting Rhythms of Executive-Legislative Relations in Foreign Policy." *Presidential Studies Quarterly* 33(3):530–46.

Liptak, Adam. 2012. "Supreme Court Upholds Health Care Law, 5–4, in Victory for Obama." *New York Times*, June 28.

Lowi, Theodore J. 1985. *The Personal President: Power Invested, Promise Unfulfilled.* Ithaca, NY: Cornell University Press.

MacFarquhar, Neil. 2006. "Terror Fears Hamper US Muslims' Travel." *New York Times*, June 1.

MacFarquhar, Neil. 2007. "Abandon Stereotypes, Muslims in America Say." *New York Times*, September 4.

Maioni, Antonia. 2007. "What I Saw at the Liberal Party." *Policy Options* (February):46–49.

Maltese, Racheline. 2010. "Blown Up." *Media Tenor Research Report* 160:9–10.

Maraniss, David. 2012. "The Audacity of Doubt." *Washington Post*, July 29.

Mayer, William G. 2004. "The Basic Dynamics of the Contemporary Nomination Process: An Expanded View." In *The Making of the Presidential Candidates 2004*, ed. William G. Mayer. Lanham, MD: Rowman & Littlefield.

Mayer, William G., and Andrew E. Busch. 2004. *The Front-Loading Problem in Presidential Nominations.* Washington, DC: Brookings.

Mazur, Allan. 2009. "American Generation of Environmental Warnings: Avian Influenza and Global Warming." *Human Ecology Review* 16:17–26.

McCright, Aaron M., and Riley E. Dunlap. 2003. "Defeating Kyoto: The Conservative Movement's Impact on U.S. Climate Change Policy." *Social Problems* 50(3):348–73.

McKenna, Barrie. 2005. "Canadian Speaker." *Canada-United States Law Journal* 31:177–87. Remarks delivered by the Toronto *Globe & Mail* correspondent at the Canada–United States Law Institute Conference, Cleveland, Ohio, April.

Media Monitor. 2003. "The Media Go to War." Washington, DC: Center for Media and Public Affairs 17(2). http://www.cmpa.com/files/media_monitor/03julaug.pdf. Downloaded August 17, 2012.

Media Monitor. 2010. "White House Watch: Obama's First Year." Washington, DC: Center for Media and Public Affairs 26(1).

Menz, Jan-Oliver. 2010. "Accounting for News Reports on Inflation." *Media Tenor Research Report* 160:79–81.

Mermin, Jonathan. 1997. "Television News and the American Intervention in Somalia: The Myth of a Media-Driven Foreign Policy." *Political Science Quarterly* 112 (Fall):385–402.

Milbank, Dana. 2012. "Romney's Aid and Comfort to the Obama Nuts." *Washington Post*, July 22.

Miljan, Lydia, and Barry Cooper. 2005. "The Canadian 'Garrison Mentality' and Anti-Americanism at the CBC." *Studies in Defense and Foreign Policy.* Vancouver, BC: Fraser Institute.

Milkis, Sidney. 2006. "The Presidency and the Political Parties." In *The Presidency and the Political System*, 8th edition, ed. Michael Nelson. Washington, DC: CQ Press.

Minutaglio, Bill. 1999. *First Son: George W. Bush and the Bush Family Dynasty.* New York: Times Books.

Moore, Leonard J. 2009. "George W. Bush and the Reckoning of American Conservatism." *American Review of Politics* 29 (Winter):291–309.

Morton, Desmond. 2006/2007. "Afghanistan, Famously Inhospitable to Foreigners." *Policy Options* (December/January):17–20.

Mueller, John. 2006. *Overblown: How Politicians and the Terrorism Industry Inflate National Security and Why We Believe Them.* New York: Free Press.

Mulroney, Brian. 2003/2004. "Memo to the White House: Burden-Sharing Requires Decision Sharing." *Policy Options* (December/January):5–8.

Murphy, Emma C. 2006. "Agency and Space: The Political Impact of Information Technologies in the Gulf States." *Third World Quarterly* 27(6):1059–83.

Murray, Shailagh, and Perry Bacon Jr. 2010. "GOP Deciding Which Direction to Go with New Authority after Midterm Victory." *Washington Post*, November 5.

Nagourney, Adam. 2006. "Democrats Looking to Use Katrina Like the GOP used 9/11." *New York Times*, April 22.

Nelson, Michael. 2010. "The Setting: Diversifying the Talent Pool." In *The Elections of 2008*, ed. Michael Nelson. Washington, DC: CQ Press.

Neustadt, Richard. 1990. *Presidential Power and the Modern Presidents.* New York: Free Press.

Niebuhr, Reinhold. 2008 [originally published 1952]. *The Irony of American History.* Chicago: University of Chicago Press.

Norris, Pippa, Montague Kern, and Marion Just. 2003. "Framing Terrorism." In *Framing Terrorism: The News Media, the Government and the Public*, eds. Pippa Norris, Montague Kern, and Marion Just. New York: Routledge.

Okrent, Daniel. 2004. "Weapons of Mass Destruction? Or Mass Distraction?" *New York Times*, May 30.

Oldfield, Duane, and Aaron Wildavsky. 1989. "Reconsidering the Two Presidencies." *Society* 26 (July/August):54–59.

Oppel, Richard A., Jr. 2012. "A Romney Attack on Spending." *New York Times*, July 18.

Owen, Diana. 2009. "The Campaign and the Media." In *The American Elections of 2008*, eds. Janet M. Box-Steffensmeier and Steven E. Schier. Lanham, MD: Rowman & Littlefield.

Page, Benjamin, with Marshall M. Bouton. 2006. *The Foreign Policy Disconnect: What Americans Want from Our Leaders and Don't Get.* Chicago: University of Chicago Press.

Paletz, David. 2002. *The News Media in American Politics: Contents and Consequences*, 2nd edition. New York: Longman.

Parker, Ashley. 2012. "Critics from Base See Romney Pulling Punches on 'Nice Guy' Obama." *New York Times*, June 1.

Patterson, Thomas E. 1994. *Out of Order.* New York: Vintage.

Pear, Robert. 2011. "Obama's Job Plan Is Again Blocked by Senate Republicans." *New York Times*, October 20.

Pew Forum on Religion and Public Life. 2012. "Little Voter Discomfort with Romney's Religion." Release dated July 26.

Pew Global Attitudes Project. 2006. "America's Image Slips, But Allies Share Concerns over Iran, Hamas." Released June 13. http://pewglobal.org/reports/pdf/252.pdf. Downloaded August 17, 2008.

Pew Global Attitudes Project. 2010a. "Obama More Popular Abroad Than at Home, Global Image of the U.S. Continues to Benefit." Released June 17. http://www.pew global.org/2010/06/17/obama-more-popular-abroad-than-at-home/. Downloaded April 28, 2013.

Pew Global Attitudes Project. 2010b. "Global Publics Embrace Social Networking." Released June 17. http://www.pewglobal.org/2010/12/15/global-publics-embrace -social-networking/. Downloaded August 4, 2011.

Pew Global Attitudes Project. 2012. "Global Opinion of Obama Slips, International Policies Faulted." Released June 13. http://www.pewglobal.org/2012/06/13/global -opinion-of-obama-slips-international-policies-faulted/. Downloaded July 15, 2012.

Pew Research Center for the People and the Press. 2008. "High Marks for the Campaign, a High Bar for Obama." Released November 13. http://www.people-press .org/2008/11/13/high-marks-for-the-campaign-a-high-bar-for-obama/. Downloaded April 28, 2013.

Pew Research Center for the People and the Press. 2009a. "Independents Take Center Stage in Obama Era: Trends in Political Values and Core Attitudes, 1987–2009." Released May 21. http://www.people-press.org/2009/05/21/independents-take-center -stage-in-obama-era/. Downloaded April 28, 2013.

Pew Research Center for the People and the Press. 2009b. "Confidence in Obama Lifts U.S. Image around the World." http://www.pewglobal.org/reports/pdf/264.pdf. Downloaded August 18, 2009.

Pew Research Center for the People and the Press. 2009c. "Mixed Views of Economic Policies and Health Care Reform Persist." Released October 8. http://www.people -press.org/2009/10/08/mixed-views-of-economic-policies-and-health-care-reform -persist/. Downloaded April 28, 2013.

Pew Research Center for the People and the Press. 2010a. "Public's Priorities for 2010: Economy, Jobs, Terrorism." Released January 25. http://www.people-press .org/2010/01/25/publics-priorities-for-2010-economy-jobs-terrorism/. Downloaded April 28, 2013.

Pew Research Center for the People and the Press. 2010b. "Growing Number of Americans Say Obama Is a Muslim." Released August 19. http://www.pewforum.org/Poli tics-and-Elections/Growing-Number-of-Americans-Say-Obama-is-a-Muslim.aspx.

Pew Research Center for the People and the Press. 2011. "Economy Dominates Public Agenda, Dims Hopes for the Future." Released January 20. http://www.people-press .org/2011/01/20/economy-dominates-publics-agenda-dims-hopes-for-the-future/. Downloaded April 28, 2013.

Pfetsch, Barbara. 2004. "From Political Culture to Political Communications Culture: A Theoretical Approach to Comparative Analysis." In *Comparing Political Communication: Theories, Cases, and Challenges*, eds. Frank Esser and Barbara Pfetsch. New York: Cambridge University Press.

Pfiffner, James P. 2004a. *The Character Factor: How We Judge America's Presidents*. College Station: Texas A&M Press.

Pfiffner, James P. 2004b. "Introductions: Assessing the Bush Presidency." In *Considering the Bush Presidency*, eds. Gary Gregg II and Mark J. Rozell. New York: Oxford University Press.

Polsby, Nelson. 1983. *Consequences of Party Reform*. Oxford: Oxford University Press.

Porter, Eduardo. 2012. "Stimulus Is Maligned, but Options Were Few." *New York Times*, February 28.

Power, Samantha. 2002. *"A Problem from Hell": America and the Age of Genocide*. New York: Basic Books.

Project for Excellence in Journalism. 2012. "The State of the News Media, 2012." Amy Mitchell and Tom Rosenstiel. Released March 19. http://stateofthemedia.org/2012/overview-4/. Downloaded April 28, 2013.

Quirk, Paul J., and Sean C. Matheson. 2001. "The Presidency: The Election and Prospects for Leadership." In *The Elections of 2000*, ed. Michael Nelson. Washington, DC: CQ Press.

Raboy, Mark. 1996. "Canada: The Hybridization of Public Broadcasting." In *Public Broadcasting for the 21st Century*, ed. Mark Raboy. Luton, UK: University of Luton Press.

Reiter, Howard L. 2009. "The Nominating Process." In *Winning the Presidency 2008*, ed. William J. Crotty. Boulder, CO: Paradigm.

Revkin, Andrew. 2005. "Bush Aide Edited Climate Reports." *New York Times*, June 8.

Revkin, Andrew. 2006. "Climate Expert Said NASA Tried to Silence Him." *New York Times*, January 29.

Rich, Robert F., and Kelly R. Merrick. 2007. "Use and Misuse of Science: Global Climate Change and the Bush Administration." *Virginia Journal of Social Policy and the Law* 14 (Spring):223–52.

Richter, Paul. 2010. "Obama's Ratings Ebb in Muslim World." *Los Angeles Times*, June 18.

Robinson, Michael J., and Margaret A. Sheehan. 1983. *Over the Wire and on TV*. New York: Russell Sage Foundation.

Robinson, Piers. 2002. *The CNN Effect: The Myth of News, Foreign Policy and Intervention*. London: Routledge.

Rockman, Bert A., and Andrew Rudalevige. 2012. "Introduction: A Counterfactual Presidency." In *The Obama Presidency: Appraisals and Prospects*, eds. Bert A. Rockman, Andrew Rudalevige, and Colin Campbell. Washington, DC: Sage/CQ Press.

Rudalevige, Andrew. 2008. "'The Decider': Issue Management and the Bush White House." In *The George W. Bush Legacy*, eds. Colin Campbell, Bert A. Rockman, and Andrew Rudalevige. Washington, DC: CQ Press.

Rutenberg, Jim. 2008. "The Man behind the Whispers about Obama." *New York Times*, October 12.

Rutenberg, Jim, and Jackie Calmes. 2009. "False Death Panel Rumor Has Some Familiar Roots." *New York Times*, August 13.

Rutenberg, Jim, and Bill Carter. 2001. "Network Coverage a Target of Fire from Conservatives." *New York Times*, November 7.

Rutenberg, Jim, and Sarah Lyall. 2007. "British Prime Minister Holds Talks with Bush." *New York Times*, July 30.

Sanger, David E. 2001. "Bush Tells Blair He Doesn't Oppose New Europe Force." *New York Times*, February 23.

Sanger, David E. 2007. "Bush Adds Troops in Bid to Secure Iraq." *New York Times*, January 11.

Sanger, David E. 2010a. *The Inheritance: The World Obama Confronts and the Challenges to America's Power*. New York: Broadway.

Sanger, David E. 2010b. "Deficits May Alter U.S. Politics and Global Power." *New York Times*, February 2.

Sanger, David E. 2012. *Confront and Conceal: Obama's Secret Wars and Surprising Use of American Power*. New York: Crown.

Schaefer, Todd M. 2003. "Framing the U.S. Embassy Bombings and September 11 Attacks in African and U.S. Newspapers." In *Framing Terrorism: The News Media, the Government and the Public*, eds. Pippa Norris, Montague Kern, and Marion Just. New York: Routledge.

Schatz, Roland. 2009. "2008 Was a Year When Everyone Everywhere Seemed to Lose Trust in Almost Everybody." In *Annual Dialogue Report on Religion and Values*, eds. Alistair Macdonald-Radcliff and Roland Schatz. Zurich: Innovatio.

Schatz, Roland. 2010a. "Only a Few Options Left for the Banking Industry to Regain Trust." In *Trust Meltdown: The Financial Industry Needs a Fundamental Restart*, eds. Roland Schatz and Matthias Vollbracht. Zurich: Innovatio.

Schatz, Roland. 2010b. "It's the Reputation Stupid: Media Coverage of BP and the Energy Sector." *Media Tenor Research Report* 160:75–76.

Schmitt, Eric, Thom Shanker, and David E. Sanger. 2011. "U.S. Was Braced for Fight with Pakistanis in bin Laden Raid." *New York Times*, May 9.

Schmitt, Richard B. 2007. "Congress, Bush Poised for First Friction." *Los Angeles Times*, January 3.

Sciolino, Elaine. 2004. "Spain Struggles to Absorb the Worst Terrorist Attack in Its History." *New York Times*, March 11.

Scott, Ian. 2000. *American Politics in Hollywood Film*. Chicago, IL: Fitzroy Dearborn.

Seib, Philip. 2004. *Beyond the Front Lines: How the News Media Cover a World Shaped by War*. New York: Palgrave Macmillan.

Seib, Philip. 2005. "Hegemonic No More: Western Media, the Rise of Al-Jazeera, and the Influence of Diverse Voices." *International Studies Review* 7:601–15.

Semple, Kirk. 2010. "At Last Allowed, a Muslim Scholar Visits." *New York Times*, April 7.

Shane, Scott. 2009. "Waterboarding Used 266 Times on Two Subjects." *New York Times*, April 19.

Shane, Scott, and Eric Lipton. 2005. "Storm and Crisis: Federal Response; Government Saw Flood Risk but Not Levee Failure." *New York Times*, September 2.

Shanor, Donald R. 2003. *News from Abroad*. New York: Columbia University Press.

Shear, Michael. 2010. "Obama Seeks New Approach on Gaza; He Calls for Israeli Blockade to Consider Aide as Well as Security." *Washington Post*, June 10.

Shear, Michael. 2011. "With Document, Obama Seeks to End 'Birther' Issue." *New York Times*, April 27.

Shear, Michael, and Kevin Sullivan. 2009. "Obama Portrays Another Side of U.S.; President Wraps up Overseas Tour in Which Humility, Partnership Were Key Themes." *Washington Post*, April 7.

Shenon, Philip. 2007. "Ney Is Sentenced to 2.5 Years in Abramoff Case." *New York Times*, January 20.

Sinclair, Barbara. 2008. "Living (and Dying) by the Sword: George W. Bush as a Legislative Leader." In *The George W. Bush Legacy*, eds. Colin Campbell, Bert A. Rockman, and Andrew Rudalevige. Washington, DC: Sage/CQ Press.

Sinclair, Barbara. 2012. "Doing Big Things: Obama and the 111th Congress." In *The Obama Presidency: Appraisals and Prospects*, eds. Bert A. Rockman, Andrew Rudalevige, and Colin Campbell. Washington, DC: Sage/CQ Press.

Singh, Robert S. 2012. "Continuity and Change in Obama's Foreign Policy." In *The Obama Presidency: Appraisals and Prospects*, eds. Bert A. Rockman, Andrew Rudalevige, and Colin Campbell. Washington, DC: Sage/CQ Press.

Smith, Andrew E. 2004. "The Perils of Polling in New Hampshire." In *The Making of the Presidential Candidates 2004*, ed. William G. Mayer. Lanham, MD: Rowman & Littlefield.

Smith, Rogers M., and Desmond S. King. 2009. "Barack Obama and the Future of American Racial Politics." *Du Bois Review* 6(1):25–35.

Soderlund, Walter, Ronald H. Wagenberg, and Ian C. Pemberton. 1994. "Cheerleader or Critic? Television News Coverage in Canada and the United States of the U.S. Invasion of Panama." *Canadian Journal of Political Science* 27(3):581–604.

Soroka, Stuart. 2002a. *Agenda-Setting Dynamics in Canada*. Vancouver: University of British Columbia Press.

Soroka, Stuart. 2002b. "Issue Attributes and Agenda-Setting by Media, the Public and Policymakers in Canada." *International Journal of Public Opinion Research* 14:264–85.

Soroka, Stuart, Stephen J. Farnsworth, Andrea Lawlor, and Lori Young. 2012. "Event-Driven Environmental News in the U.S. and Canada." *Electronic Media and Politics* 1(10):143–57.

Soroka, Stuart, Andrea Lawlor, Stephen J. Farnsworth, and Lori Young. 2013. "Mass Media and Policymaking." In *Routledge Handbook of Public Policy*, eds. Eduardo Araral, Scott Fritzen, Michael Howlett, M. Ramesh, and Xun Wu. London: Routledge.

Stacks, John F. 2003/2004. "Hard Times for Hard News: A Clinical Look at U.S. Foreign Coverage." *World Policy Journal* (Winter):12–21.

Steinberg, Jacques. 2008. "Rather's Lawsuit Shows Role of GOP in Inquiry." *New York Times*, November 17.

Stolberg, Sheryl Gay. 2006. "Buzzwords: The Decider." *New York Times*, December 24.

Stolberg, Sheryl Gay. 2010. "Obama and the Republicans Clash over Stimulus Bill, One Year Later." *New York Times*, February 17.

Stolberg, Sheryl Gay, and Robert Pear. 2010. "Obama Signs Health Care Overhaul Bill, with a Flourish." *New York Times*, March 23.

Stromback, Jesper. 2007. "Four Phases of Mediatization: An Analysis of the Mediatization of Politics." Paper presented at the International Communication Association. San Francisco, May.

Stromback, Jesper, and Daniela V. Dimitrova. 2006. "Political and Media Systems Matter: A Comparison of Election News Coverage in Sweden and the United States." *International Journal of Press/Politics* 11(4):131–47.

Stromback, Jesper, and Lynda Lee Kaid. 2008. "A Framework for Comparing Election News Coverage around the World." In *The Handbook of Election News Coverage around the World*, eds. Jesper Stromback and Linda Lee Kaid. New York: Routledge.

Sullivan, Terry. 2001. "A Matter of Fact: The Two Presidencies Thesis Revisited." In *The Two Presidencies: A Quarter Century Assessment*, ed. Steven Shull. Chicago: Nelson-Hall.

Suskind, Ron. 2004. *The Price of Loyalty: George W. Bush, the White House and the Education of Paul O'Neill*. New York: Simon & Schuster.

Sussman, Gerald, and Lawrence Galizio. 2003. "The Global Reproduction of American Politics." *Political Communication* 20:309–28.

Swarns, Rachel. 2003. "Muslims Protest Month-Long Detention without a Charge." *New York Times*, April 20.

Tanter, Raymond, and Stephen Kersting. 2008. "Grand Strategy as National Security Policy: Politics, Rhetoric and the Bush Legacy." In *The George W. Bush Legacy*, eds. Colin Campbell, Bert A. Rockman, and Andrew Rudalevige. Washington, DC: CQ Press.

Tenpas, Kathryn Dunn, and Stephen Hess. 2002. "The Contemporary Presidency: The Bush White House: First Appraisals." *Presidential Studies Quarterly* 32(3):577–85.

Turner, Leigh. 2003/2004. "Americans Are from Mars, Europeans Are from Venus." *Policy Options* (December/January):114–15.

Van Natta, Don, Jr. 2008. "They Got Game, It May Just Be the Wrong Game." *New York Times*, April 6.

Voltmer, Katrin. 2012. "How Far Can Media Systems Travel? Applying Hallin and Mancini's Comparative Framework outside the Western World." In *Comparing Media Systems beyond the Western World*, eds. Daniel C. Hallin and Paolo Mancini. Cambridge: Cambridge University Press.

Walsh, Declan. 2012. "Pakistani Parliament Demands an End to U.S. Drone Strikes." *New York Times*, March 20.

Ward, John. 2007. "Tories, Liberals in Political Dead Heat, New Poll Suggests." *The Gazette* (Montreal) (January 4):A9.

Waterman, Richard W., Robert Wright, and Gilbert St. Clair. 1999. *The Image-Is-Everything Presidency: Dilemmas in American Politics*. Boulder, CO: Westview.

Weatherford, M. Stephen. 2012. "Economic Crisis and Political Change: A New New Deal?" In *The Obama Presidency: Appraisals and Prospects*, eds. Bert A. Rockman, Andrew Rudalevige, and Colin Campbell. Washington, DC: Sage/CQ Press.

Weisman, Jonathan. 2012. "In Senate, Republicans Block Debate on 'Buffet Rule.'" *New York Times*, April 16.

Wells, Paul. 2006. *Right Side Up: The Fall of Paul Martin and the Rise of Stephen Harper's New Conservatism*. Toronto: McClelland & Stewart.

Werdigier, Julia. 2011. "Its Growth Slowing, Britain Extends Austerity Measures." *New York Times*, November 29.

Werdigier, Julia. 2012a. "Britain Defends Its Austerity Measures." *New York Times*, February 14.

Werdigier, Julia. 2012b. "British Economy Slips Back into Recession." *New York Times*, April 25.

Westen, Drew. 2012. "If He Loses, Here's Why." *Washington Post*, July 29.

Wildavsky, Aaron. 1966. "The Two Presidencies." *Transaction* 4 (December):7–14.

Wilson, Scott. 2010. "New U.S. Envoy Tries to Bridge Two Worlds." *Washington Post*, March 1.

Wilson, Scott. 2012. "Where Obama Failed on the Middle East." *Washington Post*, July 15.

Wirth, Werner, and Steffen Kolb. 2004. "Designs and Methods of Comparative Political Communication Research." In *Comparing Political Communication: Theories, Cases, and Challenges*, eds. Frank Esser and Barbara Pfetsch. New York: Cambridge University Press.

Wittebols, James H. 1992. "Media and the Institutional Perspective: U.S. and Canadian Coverage of Terrorism." *Political Communication* 9:267–78.

Wittebols, James H. 1996. "News from the Noninstitutional World: U.S. and Canadian Television News Coverage of Social Protest." *Political Communication* 13:345–61.

Wolffe, Richard. 2009. *Renegade: The Making of Barack Obama*. New York: Crown.

Woodward, Bob. 2006. *State of Denial*. New York: Simon & Schuster.

Woodward, Bob. 2010. *Obama's Wars*. New York: Simon & Schuster.

Wright, Robin. 2005a. "President Hails Election as a Success and a Signal." *Washington Post*, January 31.

Wright, Robin. 2005b. "European Bitterness over Iraq Dissipates." *Washington Post*, February 5.

Youssef, Mervat. 2009. "Their Word against Ours: News Discourse of the 2003 Gulf War and Civilian Casualties in CNN and Al-Jazeera." *Global Media Journal* 4(2):13–24.

Zaharna, R. S. 2005. "Al Jazeera and American Public Diplomacy: A Dance of Intercultural (Mis-) Communication." In *The Al Jazeera Phenomenon: Critical Perspectives on New Arab Media*, ed. Mohamed Zayani. Boulder, CO: Paradigm.

Zakaria, Fareed. 2008. *The Post-American World*. New York: Norton.

Zeleny, Jeff. 2010. "To Help Democrats in the Fall, Obama May Stay Away." *New York Times*, July 31.

Zeleny, Jeff, and Alan Cowell. 2009. "Addressing Muslims, a Blunt Obama Takes on Mideast Issues." *New York Times*, June 5.

Zeleny, Jeff, and Steven Erlanger. 2008. "Three Hours in Paris, and Smiles All Around." *New York Times*, July 26.

Zeleny, Jeff, and Nicholas Kulish. 2008. "Obama, in Berlin, Calls for a Renewal of Ties with Allies." *New York Times*, July 25.

Index